IMAGES
of America

ALONG THE APPALACHIAN TRAIL
NEW JERSEY, NEW YORK, AND CONNECTICUT

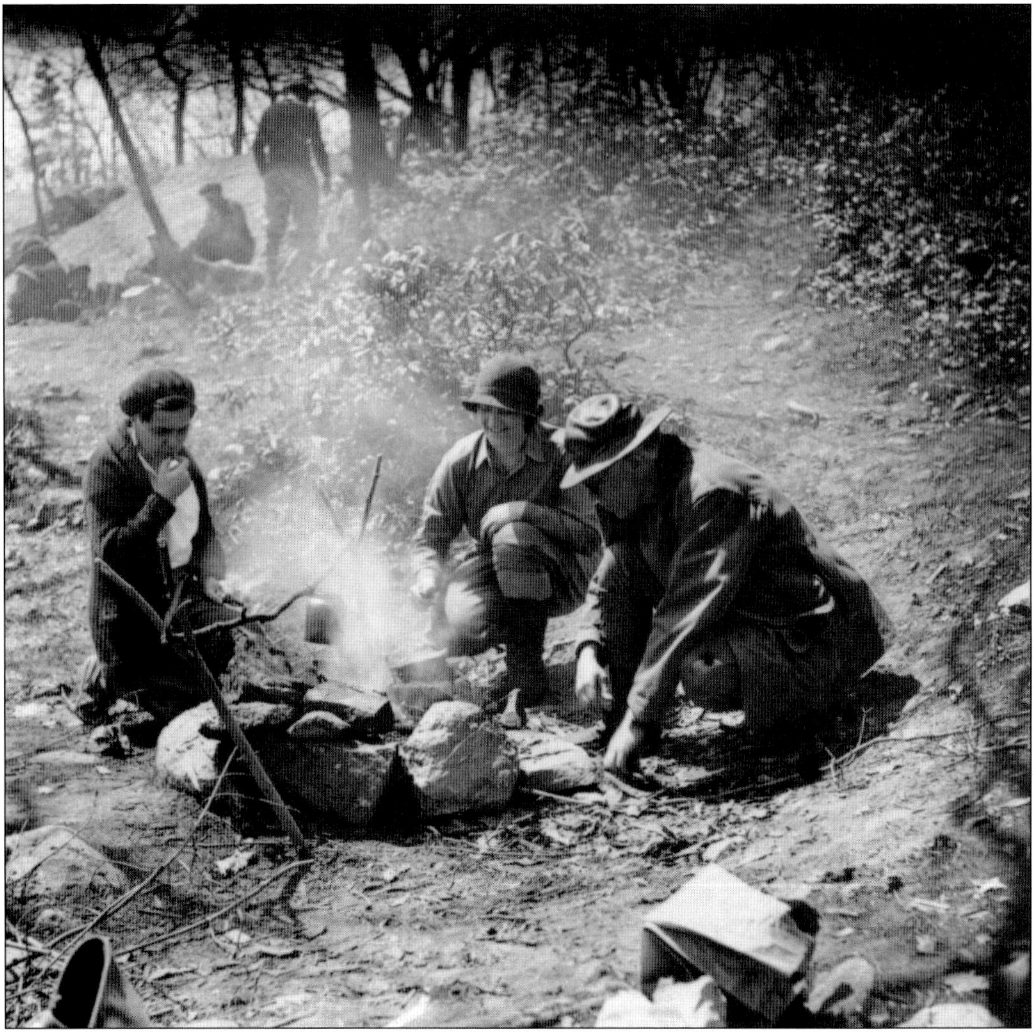

In the 1920s and 1930s, James P. Tate (right) was a leader in organizing one of the Appalachian Trail's earliest local maintaining clubs, the Warwick Appalachian Trail Club. The club was active in hiking and maintaining the trail in both New York and New Jersey. Tate's daughter Florence is on the left; the other person in unidentified. (Courtesy of Warwick Historical Society.)

On the Cover: A stand of red pines, planted in the 1930s along the western side of the Housatonic River, was once one of the most photographed scenes on the Appalachian Trail in Connecticut. By the late 1980s, age and a blight had brought down many of the trees, some of which were harvested to build a number of lean-tos in the state. (Courtesy of Appalachian Trail Conservancy.)

IMAGES
of America

Along the Appalachian Trail
New Jersey, New York, and Connecticut

Leonard M. Adkins and the
Appalachian Trail Conservancy

ARCADIA
PUBLISHING

ISBN 978-1-4671-2151-4

Published by Arcadia Publishing
Charleston, South Carolina

Printed in the United States of America

Library of Congress Control Number: 2013950188

For all general information, please contact Arcadia Publishing:
Telephone 843-853-2070
Fax 843-853-0044
E-mail sales@arcadiapublishing.com
For customer service and orders:
Toll-Free 1-888-313-2665

Visit us on the Internet at www.arcadiapublishing.com

I had written a dedication thanking Appalachian Trail volunteers for all of the hard, backbreaking, tedious, and laborious work they do on behalf of the Appalachian Trail, but then I came across this phrase in the Appalachian Trail Conservancy member handbook that beautifully describes their efforts: "And what is the Trail . . . It always was a place for people. People who care for land and tend a simple footpath as if it were their garden."

Contents

Acknowledgments

A tremendous thank-you goes to the following people. They not only spent hours searching for and providing photographs, but they also patiently answered questions about the smallest of details to help make this book as accurate and thorough as possible.

Thanks to Brian King, Appalachian Trail Conservancy; Pieter Van Why, Appalachian Long Distance Hikers Association; Tim Messerich and Bill and Amy Bancroft, Ralphs Peak Hikers Cabin Volunteer Club; Allen Ramsey, Connecticut State Library; David Boone and Norman Sills, Connecticut Chapter of the Appalachian Mountain Club; Dr. Warren Doyle, Appalachian Trail Institute; John Donahue and Michelle Jacques, Delaware Water Gap National Recreation Area; Gloria Thorne, Sherman Historical Society; Jules Orkin, New York-New Jersey Trail Conference; Christine Woodside, Connecticut Forest and Park Association; Cathryn Anders, Warwick Historical Society; and Peter Olivia, Palisades Interstate Park Commission.

To Laurie—so many splendid AT memories; thanks for a wonderful life.

Key to Abbreviations Used Throughout the Text

AT—Appalachian Trail
ATC—Appalachian Trail Conference (Appalachian Trail Conservancy)
CT-AMC—Connecticut Chapter of the Appalachian Mountain Club
CSL—Connecticut State Library
DWGNRA—Delaware Water Gap National Recreation Area
NYNJTC—New York-New Jersey Trail Conference
PIPC—Palisades Interstate Park Commission
RPHCVC—Ralphs Peak Hikers Cabin Volunteer Club
SHS—Sherman Historical Society
WHS—Warwick Historical Society

A portion of the author's royalties from Images of America: *Along the Appalachian Trail: New Jersey, New York, and Connecticut* will be donated to the Appalachian Trail Conservancy.

Introduction

The establishment, construction, maintenance, and protection of the Appalachian Trail in New Jersey, New York, and Connecticut is one of those chapters in history that involves an extraordinary convergence of ideas, people, and cultural and political environments.

Books such as Emerson's *Nature*, Thoreau's *Walden* and *Civil Disobedience*, and George Perkin Marsh's *Man and Nature* produced a deeper appreciation of nature, as well as a conservation movement that felt it could obtain its objectives, in part, though political action. The Chautauqua movement, started in western New York, helped give rise to populist thinking and the Progressive movement. In addition, the construction, begun in 1912, of Vermont's Long Trail showed what the organized labor of dedicated volunteers could accomplish on the ground.

These ideas also spurred the creation of many local walking and hiking clubs in New Jersey, New York, and Connecticut. Among them were the Fresh Air Club, in 1877; the Connecticut Forest and Park Association, in 1895; the Paterson Rambling Club, in 1904; the New York Chapter of the Appalachian Mountain Club, in 1914; and the New York Chapter of the Green Mountain Club, in 1915.

So it was that when Benton MacKaye's article putting forth the idea of a long-distance pathway, "An Appalachian Trail, a Project in Regional Planning," was published in the *Journal of the American Institute of Architects* in 1921, the movement to hike, conserve land, and build trails was so strong that volunteers of the Palisades Interstate Park Trail Conference (renamed the New York-New Jersey Trail Conference in 1922) were already constructing pathways on lands administered by the Palisades Interstate Park Commission. The commission was established around 1900 in response to public protests over the destruction of the palisades and mountains overlooking the Hudson River by quarrying operations. Citizens' objections to a proposed prison on Bear Mountain also helped create Harriman and Bear Mountain State Parks, both part of the Palisades Interstate Park system.

Barely a year after MacKaye's article was published, volunteers, inspired by the idea of the Appalachian Trail, began working on the first section of trail built specifically for the AT, and, by the end of 1922, a pathway was marked from Arden to close to Tiorati Lake. Another year brought the trail through both state parks to the Hudson River.

Acting upon a request by MacKaye and others, the Federal Societies on Planning and Parks met in Washington, DC, in 1925 to further action on the AT. A constitution establishing the Appalachian Trail Conference (renamed the Appalachian Trail Conservancy in 2005) was adopted, and Maj. William A. Welch—already the general manager and chief engineer of PIPC, the chairman of NYNJTC, and a proponent of state and national parks—was named its chairman. During the meeting, it was decided that the AT would run 1,700 miles, from Mount Washington in New Hampshire to Cohutta Mountain in Georgia. A northern extension was to stretch to Mount Katahdin in Maine, while a southern addition would reach Birmingham, Alabama. Among various proposed branch routes, one was to follow the Long Trail in Vermont, another would extend into the Catskills, and another into Kentucky. All positions within the conference, and all work on the trails, would be done on a volunteer basis. The ATC did not have its first paid employee until the late 1960s.

In 1928, retired Connecticut judge Arthur Perkins, who had been active in trail work and president of the Connecticut Chapter of the Appalachian Mountain Club, was appointed ATC chairman. Perkins was instrumental in bringing two other men important to the AT into the fold: Ned Anderson and Myron Avery.

When he met Perkins, Nestell Kip "Ned" Anderson, a farmer and avid outdoorsman, was walking in the late 1920s on one of the newer blue-blazed hiking trails—a system that now includes close to 800 miles of trails—that had been constructed under the auspices of the Connecticut Forest and Park Association. During their conversation, Perkins told Anderson about the AT and soon introduced him to Myron Avery, who was then living in Hartford. Motivated by Avery's enthusiasm and his own knowledge of the area, Anderson began planning, mapping, and building Connecticut's section of the AT, going so far as meeting with public officials and private landowners to reach agreements to let the trail pass through their property.

Although those who knew Anderson said he did much of the work himself, he was aided by Boy Scout Troop No. 47 of Sherman, Connecticut, of which he became Scoutmaster in 1931, and members of the Housatonic Trail Club, which he founded in 1932. Due to failing health, he relinquished a portion of the trail east of the Housatonic River to Seymour Smith in 1945. Smith became president of the Connecticut Chapter of the Appalachian Mountain Club and maintained all 23 miles of the AT east of the Housatonic River from 1949 to 1979.

Benton MacKay was a proponent and vocal promoter of the Appalachian Trail, but, although he did scouting trips, he did very little, if any, actual building of the trail. On the other hand, Myron Avery not only recruited volunteers and spread the word about the AT, but, more importantly, he also went into the field scouting routes for the trail and building and blazing multiple miles of the pathway. By doing so, he became the first person to walk its full length. Avery assumed ATC chairmanship in 1931, after which construction of the trail accelerated, with more than 1,900 miles completed by 1934.

Murray Stevens, another active member of NYNJTC, is credited with building the more than 50 miles of trail in the 1930s that were needed to connect the AT from the Bear Mountain Bridge to the pathway Ned Anderson was building northward from the New York-Connecticut border. This accomplishment is more remarkable because of the fact that much of the land where Stevens built the trail was privately owned, meaning he had to negotiate with scores of people before he could begin work on the ground. He and Avery became friends, and the two often took hikes together to inspect and maintain Stevens's trail section. In fact, it was Stevens who took over the ATC chairmanship when Avery stepped down in 1952.

In the northwestern part of New Jersey, Stokes State Forest was established in 1907 and High Point State Park was dedicated in 1923, providing trailblazers public lands on which to build the pathway. However, most of the rest of the land where the trail needed to be routed in that state and west of Harriman State Park in New York was in private hands, so rights-of-way had to be negotiated. Yet, thanks to the dedication of small local clubs, almost the entire trail to the Pennsylvania border had been marked by 1930. Two of these clubs were the Wanderlusters, which built the trail from Arden, New York, to Mombasha High Point in New Jersey, and the Catskill Mountain Club, which constructed the pathway from the Wallkill River to High Point State Park.

The difficulty and delicate nature of procuring and keeping landowners' permissions was expounded upon by Raymond Torrey (second NYNJTC chairman, journalist, and influential New York-New Jersey trails promoter), who, around 1930, published the first AT guide to New York and New Jersey. In it, he wrote, "The owners of this land . . . are hesitant about permitting the trail to be marked, for fear of fires, poachers and other abuses. They are very decent about it and say they have no objection to members of walking clubs going through . . . but they object to the placing of the Appalachian Trail markers." Published shortly after this, an official ATC guidebook stated, "The owners and their representatives have been subjected to thoughtless and deliberate misuses on the property to the point where patrolling has become necessary . . . The opening of the Appalachian Trail . . . only signifies that the owner is willing that hikers cross his property."

The passage of the AT through private lands permitted trail construction to proceed at such a rapid pace that its full length was completed by 1937. Despite some problems, this arrangement worked well until mid-century. It was at about that time that America entered its modern age of rapid development. Older landowners died or sold their property for housing developments or modern highway construction, forcing volunteers to create emergency relocations, most often on roads, to keep the AT a continuous footpath.

In response to this and other threats, trail volunteers persuaded Sen. Gaylord Nelson to introduce a bill in 1964 to protect the AT. The bill, of course, went through several revisions, and its original scope expanded, but Nelson's intentions became reality when the National Trails System Act was passed and signed by Pres. Lyndon Johnson in 1968. The AT and the Pacific Crest Trail, which runs from Mexico to Canada through California, Oregon, and Washington, were designated as America's first two national scenic trails. The act gave the National Park Service the primary responsibility for administering the AT and authorized the agency to protect it through easements, agreements, land exchanges, donations or purchases, and, as a final resort, eminent domain. A total of $5 million in public funds was appropriated for the purchases.

An AT project office was opened by the National Park Service in 1976, but disappointment and apprehension about the federal government's lack of progress on procuring lands remained high. Eventually, trail supporters influenced Congress to pass the Appalachian Trail Act, signed in 1978 by Pres. Jimmy Carter. At that time, less than 1,250 miles of the trail were in the public trust. The act appropriated $90 million to purchase, over the next several years, the needed acreage to remove the remaining miles from roadways and private property. This land acquisition has been so successful that, in 2014, less than five miles of trail remained to be brought under public protection.

There are now dozens of Appalachian Trail Conservancy and National Park Service employees who are paid to work on behalf of the AT, but the trail's true strength always was—and is—the volunteer. The volunteer who tramps across the difficult topography of pathless mountain ranges in search of the optimum terrain on which to locate the AT. The volunteer that devotes the little leisure time in his or her busy life to do the arduous and exhausting work of digging sidehill trail, moving tons of boulders to build rock-step staircases, or standing knee-deep in cold, swirling waters to create bridges across streams. The volunteer who carries hundreds of pounds of lumber, roofing shingles, and concrete mix miles into the woods to construct a backcountry shelter for hikers he or she will never meet. The volunteer who works behind the scenes on a local maintaining club's board of directors or sits through hours of bureaucratic meetings to lobby for the trail. The volunteer who is willing to write letters, physically protest the undertakings of outside forces, or walk miles of the rough, rugged, and sometimes dangerous AT boundary so as to insure that there is no harm done to the trail's integrity, environmentally or otherwise.

It is the hard work of these past and present people that has enabled the establishment and continued existence of the AT. So, why not become a member of the Appalachian Trail Conservancy and join one of the clubs in their efforts to build, maintain, and protect this world-famous, successful venture in outdoor recreation and environmental protection?

Appalachian Trail Conservancy
P.O. Box 807
Harpers Ferry, WV 25425-0807
304-535-6331
www.appalachiantrail.org

The New York-New Jersey Trail Conference maintains the AT from the Pennsylvania-New Jersey border to the New York-Connecticut line, a distance of more than 160 trail miles:

New York-New Jersey Trail Conference
156 Ramapo Valley Road
Mahwah, NJ 07430
(*Note: This address is subject to change*)
201-512-9348
www.nynjtc.org

The Connecticut Chapter of the Appalachian Mountain Club maintains more than 50 miles of the AT from the New York-Connecticut line to the Connecticut-Massachusetts line:

Connecticut Chapter-Appalachian Mountain Club
5 Joy Street
Boston, MA 02108
617-523-0655
www.ct-amc.org

Note: When putting this book together, it became obvious that with the many route changes the AT has experienced, it would be impossible to arrange the photographs in a merely chronological or geographical order. Therefore, I have used a combination of the two, with older routes coming before newer ones and photographs arranged in a chronological order along each route.

One

New Jersey

Coming northward from Pennsylvania, the Appalachian Trail descends more than 1,000 feet into the Delaware Water Gap to enter New Jersey. Most of the land was in private hands when the trail was first scouted and built in the 1920s and 1930s. Because it took time to obtain permission to cross these lands, there were certain places, especially near the water gap, where there were multiple alternate routes. With the state's purchase of vast acreages for Worthington State Forest in the 1950s and the federal government's acquisition of land for the Tocks Island Dam project in the 1960s, the AT had a protected corridor from the water gap to High Point. Public opposition defeated the dam project, leading to the establishment of the Delaware Water Gap National Recreation Area in 1965.

The trail currently rises from the water gap to Sunfish Pond, which sits in an idyllic hollow created as glaciers slid along Kittatinny Mountain. Continuing northward, the mountain's eastern escarpment makes it possible to watch children swimming in backyard pools as parents mow the lawn, and the Catfish and Culver fire towers provide 360-degree views. The vistas from the observation platform in High Point State Park are even more impressive, taking in Lake Marcia directly below, the Catskill and Pocono Mountains in Pennsylvania, the Kittatinny ridgeline sloping into the Delaware Water Gap, and the Wawayanda and Pochuck Mountains to the east. A side path leads to a monument to "New Jersey's heroes by land, sea, and air in all wars in our country," which sits atop the state's highest point.

Descending to meander through the Wallkill and Vernon Valleys, relocations off paved roadways in the 1980s and 1990s now permit northbound hikers to encounter the boggy wetlands that become more prevalent as the trail works its way into New England. Although the route has changed through the years, it has always been in a corridor parallel to and within a short distance of the New Jersey-New York border.

After crossing the Pochuck and Wawayanda Mountains, the AT rises to Bearfort Mountain, overlooking Greenwood Lake, where it enters New York.

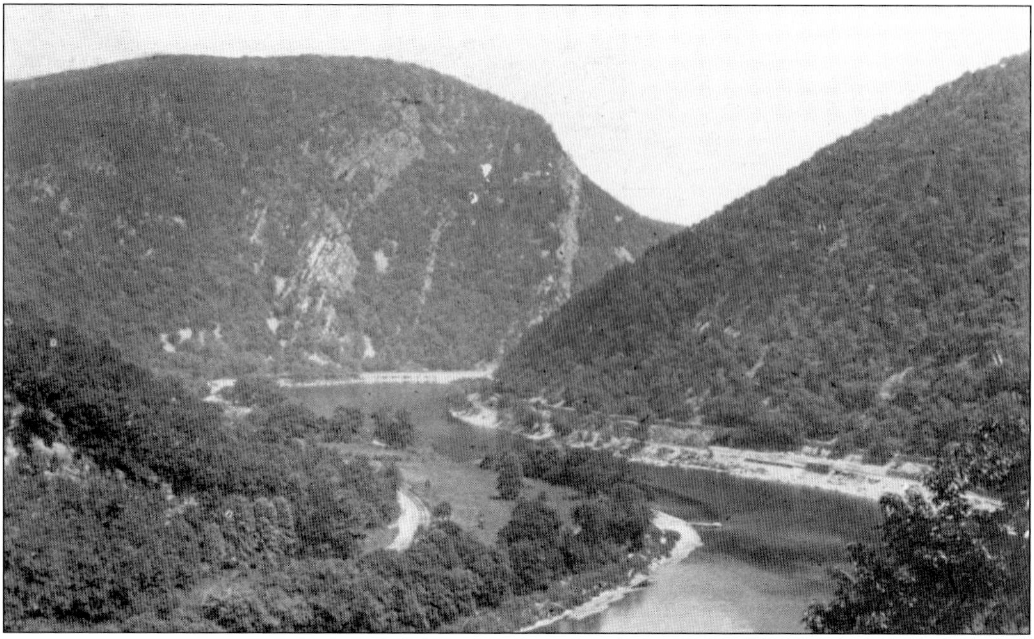

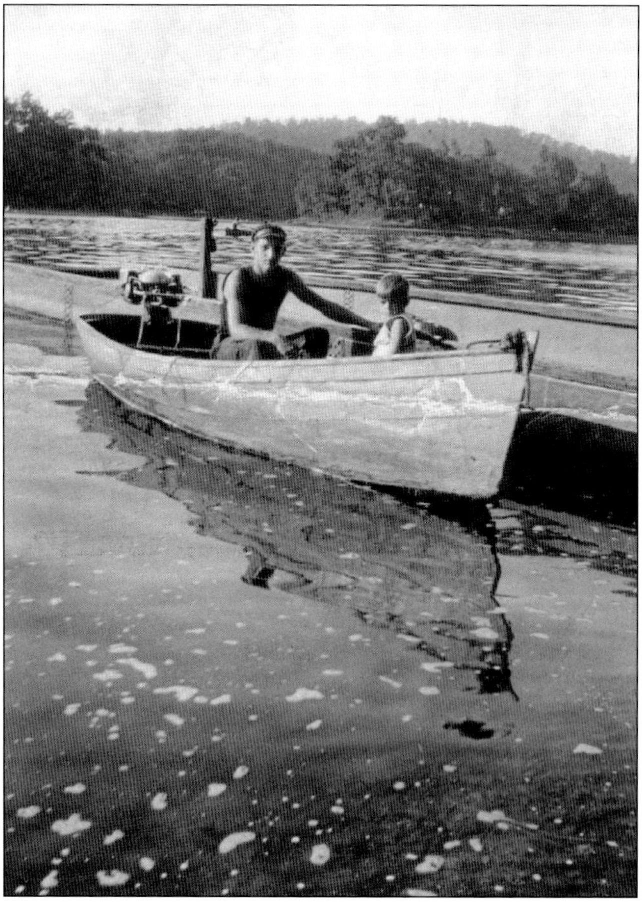

Looking across the Delaware Water Gap, northbound hikers first see New Jersey from Winona Cliff on Mount Minsi in Pennsylvania, as seen in this postcard postmarked August 2, 1906. There were several suggested routes hikers could take when the AT was first described in this area, including one over Mount Tammany, on the far side of the river. (Courtesy of Leonard M. Adkins; publisher unidentified.)

Just as there was no definite route north of the Delaware Water Gap in the AT's early days, there were only suggested ways to get across the river. One of the options was for hikers to make arrangements with Ernest Olschewsky, who lived at the mouth of Dunnfield Creek in New Jersey, to carry them over in his boat. (Courtesy of DWGNRA.)

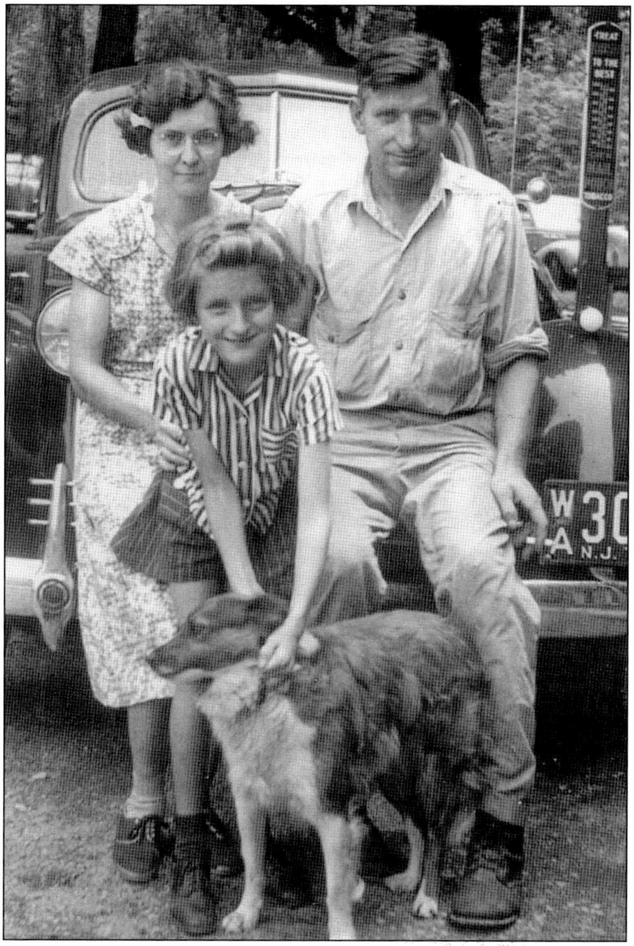

After several years of informally providing hikers passage across the Delaware River, Ernest Olschewsky, photographed at right with his wife, Edna, and daughter Ruth, purchased Kittatinny Beach and Inn. He established Kittatinny Canoes in 1941 to rent rowboats and canoes to anglers fishing the river's pool below Mount Tammany. Not long after that, a customer asked Olschewsky to drive him and his canoe upstream so that he could easily paddle back to the starting point. Olschewsky loaded the canoe in the back of his pickup truck—and the shuttle part of the business (below) began. (Both, courtesy of DWGNRA.)

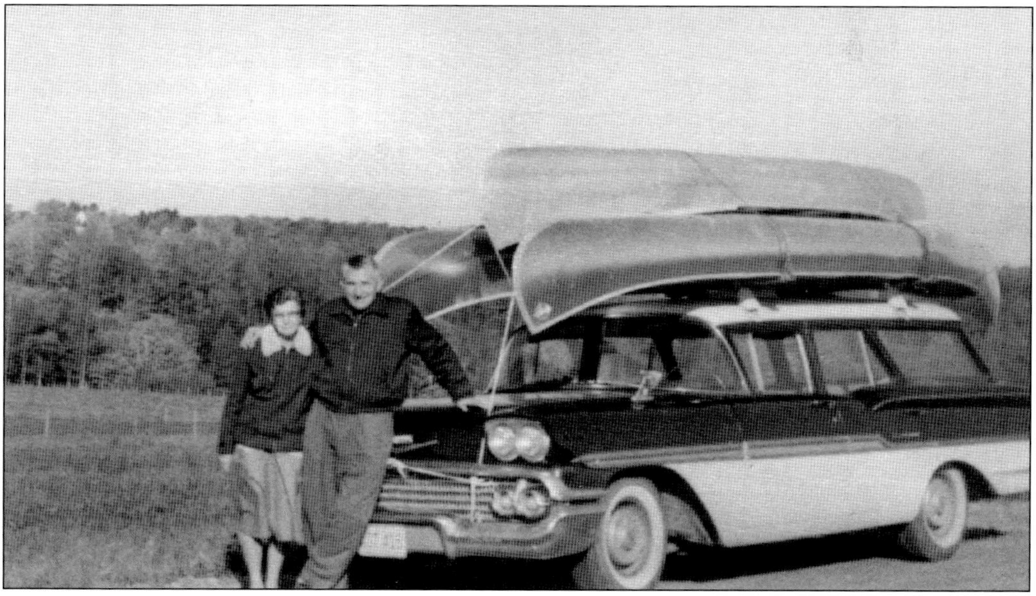

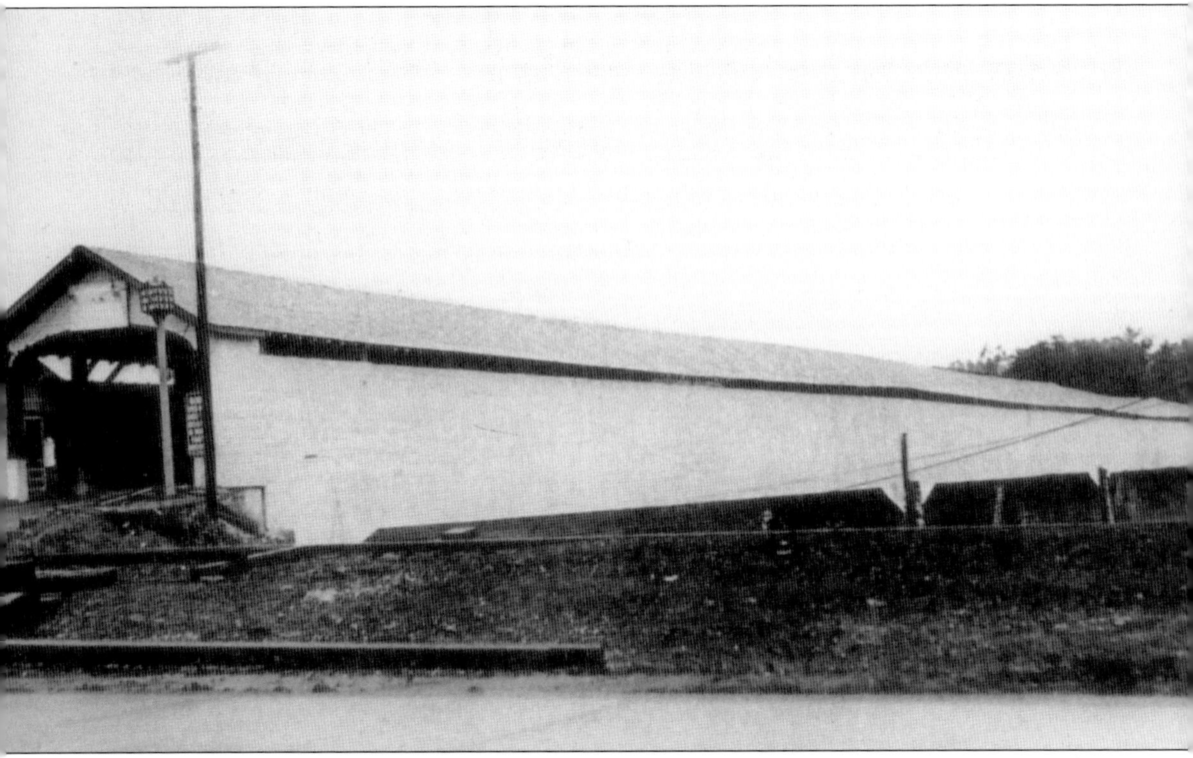

Another suggested route across the Delaware River included road walking four miles in Pennsylvania to the Portland-Columbia Covered Bridge and then hiking roads for another four miles to return to suggested AT routes ascending the Kittatinny ridgeline. The bridge was constructed in 1869 and destroyed by floods in 1955. In directions that would never be given today, the 1934 AT guidebook suggested that, close to the covered bridge, hikers could also choose to "descend right to the tracks of the Susquehanna division of the Erie Railroad . . . Caution should be used on this trestle, although there are not more than four or five trains, mostly slow freights, per day . . . Ties are fairly close together, the footing good and, at each of three piers there are walk outs to water barrels which can be reached if a train crosses the bridge. It should be borne in mind that the New York-New Jersey Trail Conference and the Appalachian Trail Conference assume no liability for walkers crossing the bridge, and they are technically trespassers on the railroad property." (Courtesy of Artvue Post Card Company.)

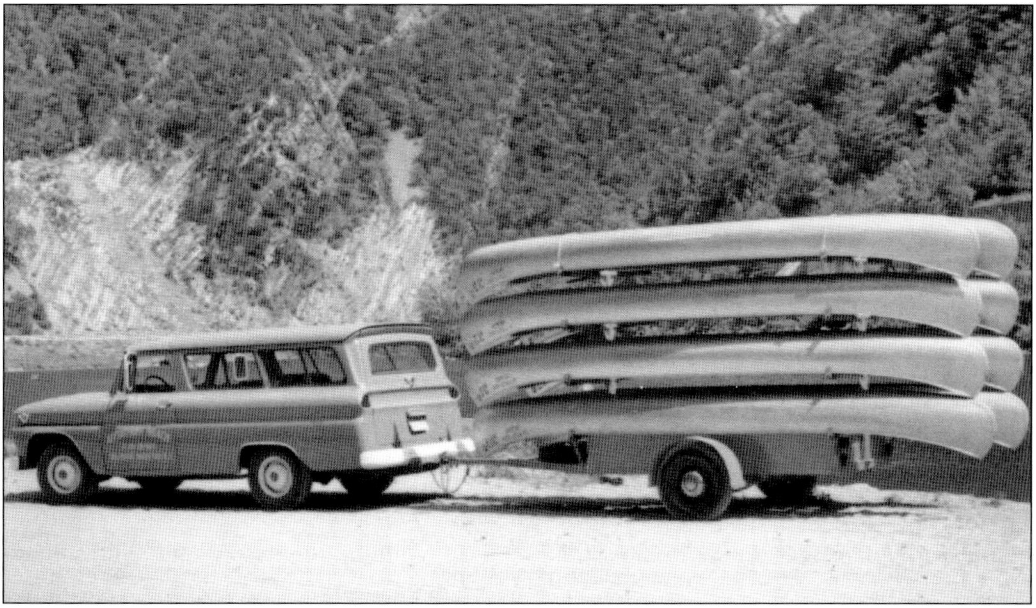

The shuttle business proved so successful for Ernest and Edna Olschewsky that, by the 1950s, the family had multiple canoes and trailers. Today, the company claims to have one of the world's largest fleets of canoes, kayaks, rafts, and tubes and services more than 120 miles of the river through Pennsylvania, New Jersey, and New York. It also provides financial support for an annual river cleanup event. (Courtesy of DWGNRA.)

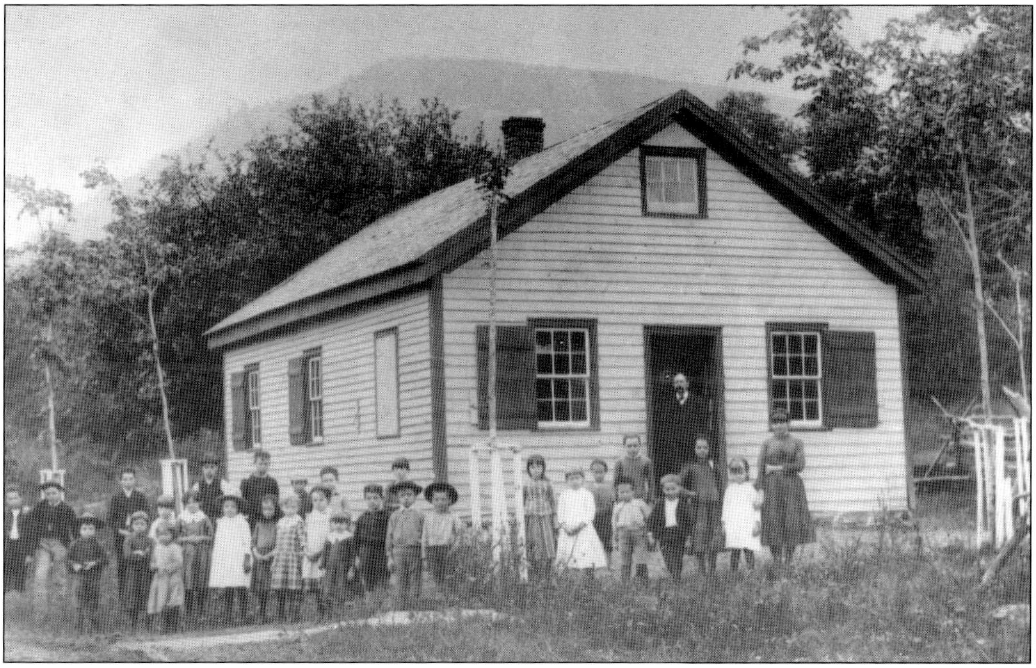

The walk along the road on the north bank of the river passed by the village of Browntown and its one-room schoolhouse, seen here in 1890. In the doorway is the teacher, James Evans. Standing in front of him is Elizabeth Vliet, and the boy in the back row to the left wearing a hat and vest is Joseph Vliet. (Courtesy of DWGNRA.)

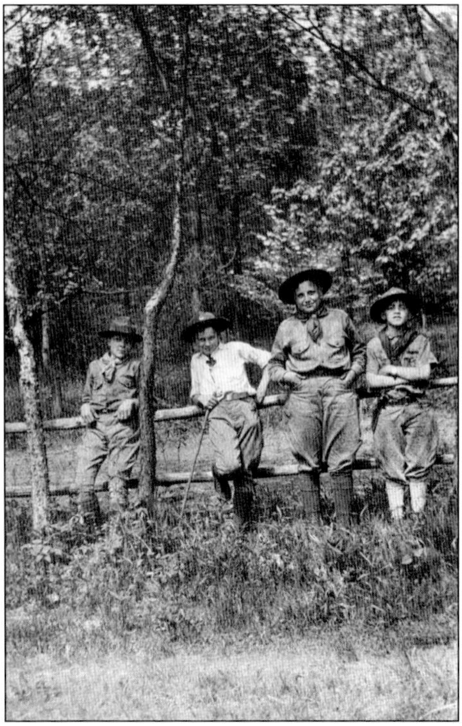

Hikers could make camping arrangements at Camp Weygadt, a Boy Scout facility established in 1930 that was also located on the road above the Delaware River. Garbed in the uniforms of the day and wearing the park ranger–type hats that were part of the uniform, these four Scouts were photographed along the road soon after the camp opened. (Courtesy of DWGNRA.)

This aerial photograph from around 1970 shows Arrow Island, Boy Scout Camp Weygadt on the southern slope of Mount Tammany, and trucks speeding along Interstate 80 almost two decades after the Delaware Water Gap Toll Bridge opened in 1953. The construction of the bridge finally provided the AT with an easy way across the river. (Courtesy of DWGNRA.)

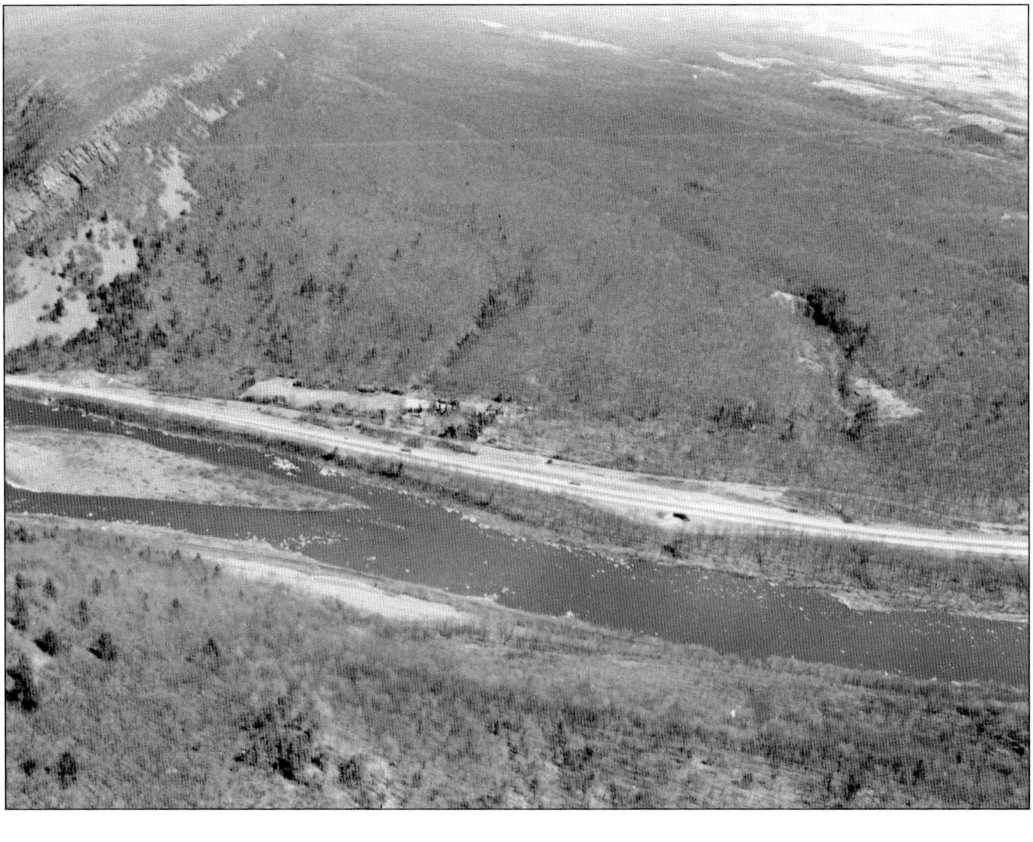

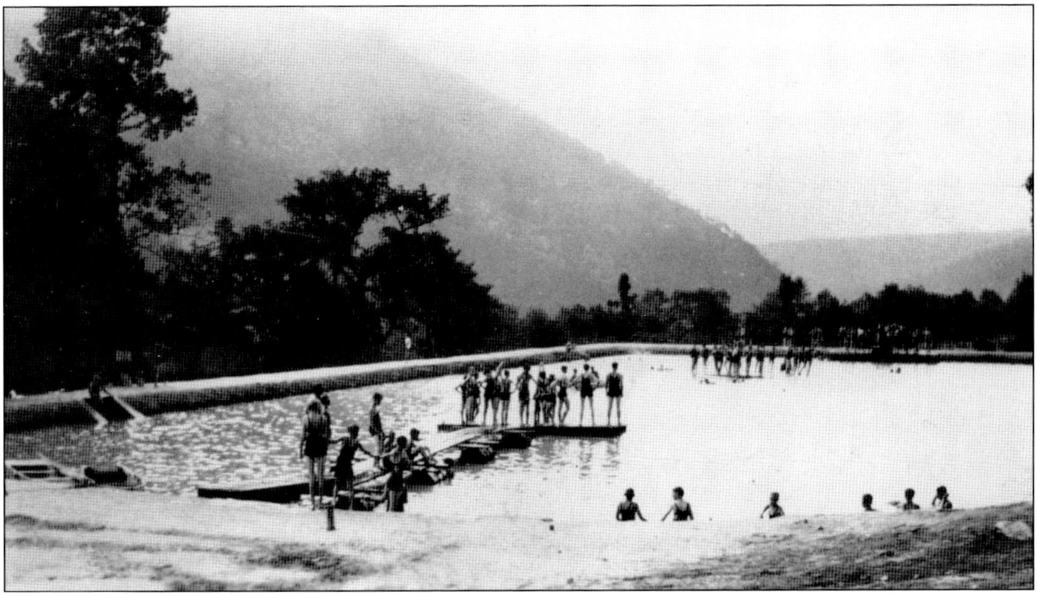

The swimming pool at Camp Weygadt, built in 1932, was filled by the waters of a stream flowing down the side of Mount Tammany, ensuring that it was a cold swim even during the warmest summer temperatures. The camp had hosted thousands of boys by the time it ceased operating in 1968. (Courtesy of DWGNRA.)

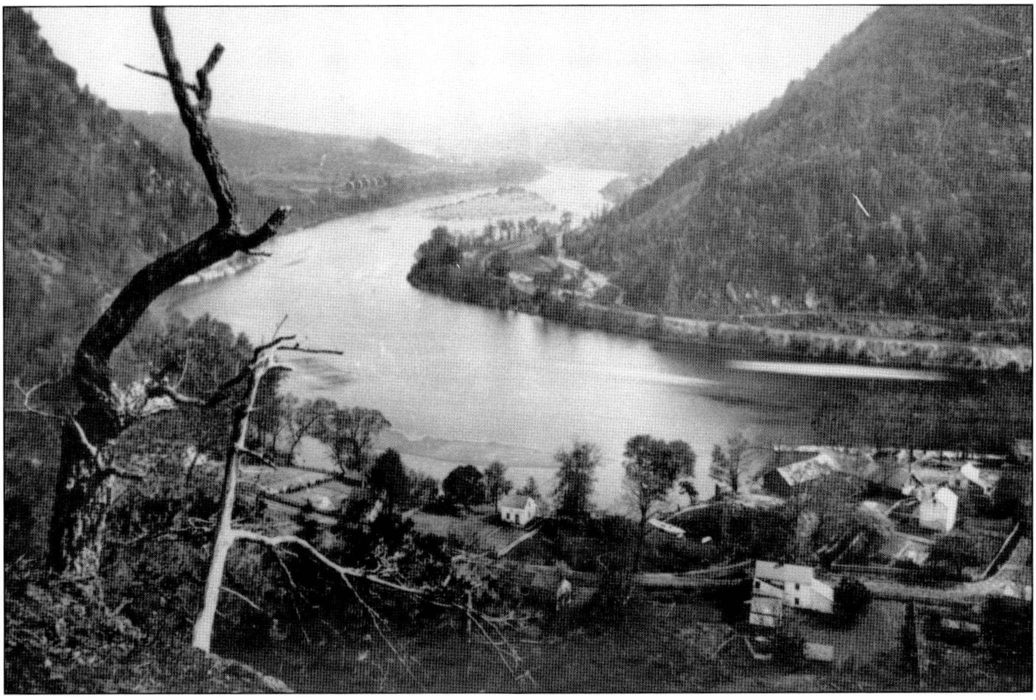

Established in the 1800s, the small town of Dunnfield was located at what is now DWGNRA's Kittatinny Point Visitor Center and the AT parking lot off Interstate 80. Many of the residents worked at nearby mines, including the Delaware Water Gap Slate Company. These companies began to cease operations in the early to mid-1900s, leading to the town's demise. (Courtesy of DWGNRA.)

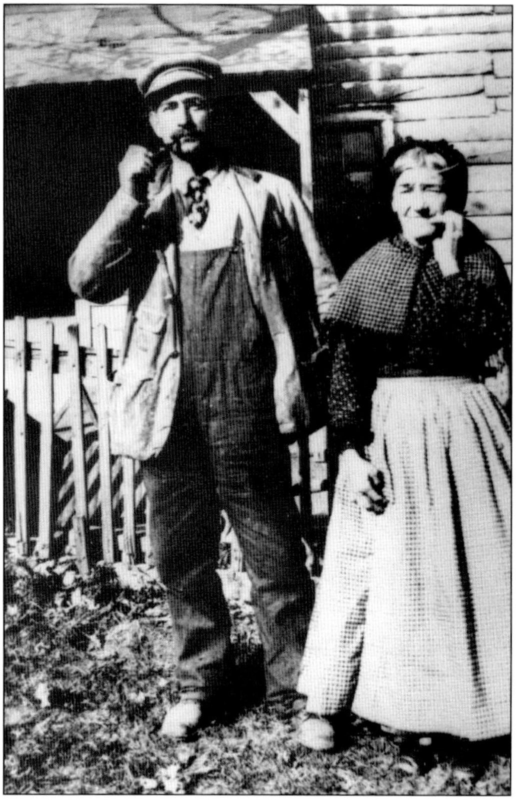

In the late 1800s, Ed Messick and Maria Vliet (some sources say "Mariah") were residents of Dunnfield, where Vliet took care of the town's bathhouse. Looking more like a shed than the town's railroad station, a one-story metal building served as a depot and freight house for the New York, Susquehanna & Western Railroad from 1882 to 1940. (Courtesy of DWGNRA.)

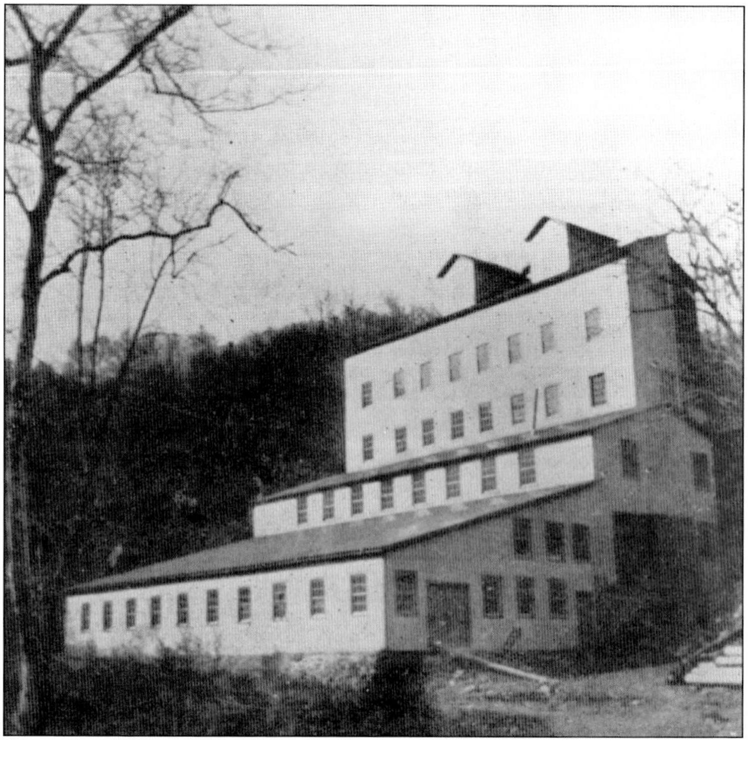

Copper mining in the Delaware River area might have begun in the early 1600s when Dutch settlers began looking for the mineral. The first known operations started in 1750 and continued for more than 150 years. The Pahaquarry mill and smelter factory, photographed in 1917, was built to process the mineral, but the area's copper was of such low quality that the last mine closed in 1918. (Courtesy of DWGNRA.)

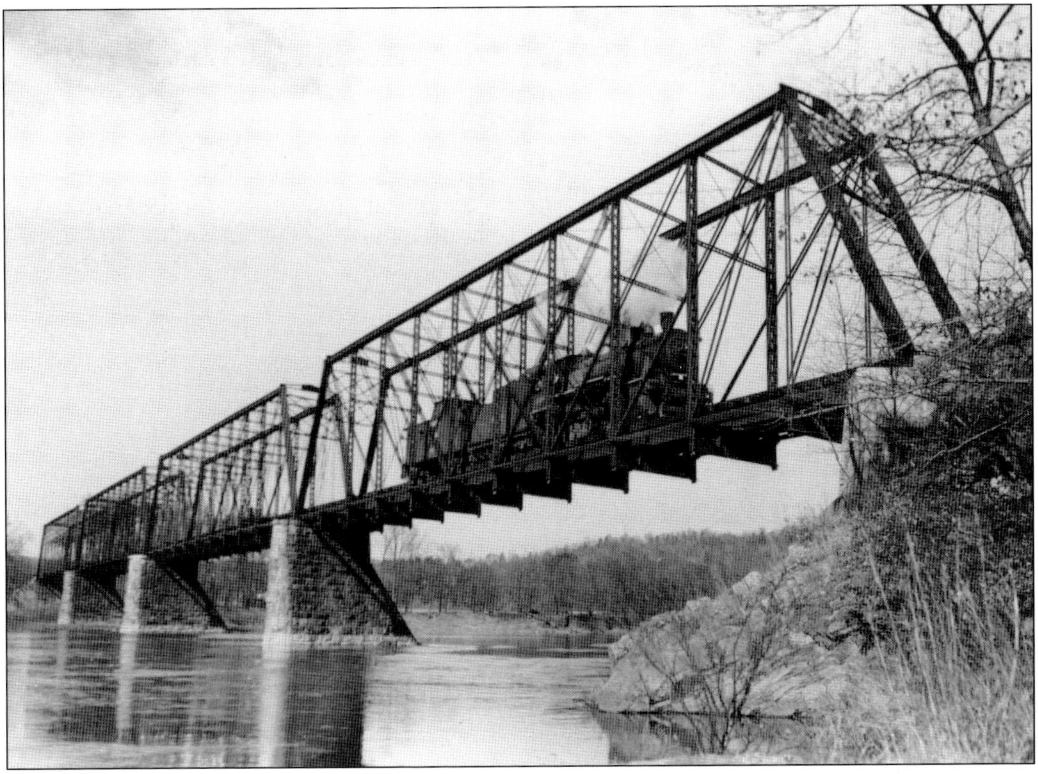

The New York, Susquehanna & Western Railroad, which operated from the Hudson River to Stroudsburg, Pennsylvania, crossed the Delaware River on a truss bridge that was built around 1882. In addition to scheduled stops in small communities, the railroad made flag stops near the water gap, enabling those who wished to hike the AT in this area to use rail transit to get close to the trail. (Courtesy of DWGNRA.)

Mining may have been the major industry around the Delaware River, but farmers also took advantage of the valley's fertile soil. Sherman Van Campen (left) and Edward Lamb (right) harvested hay near Old Mine Road in Calno. Van Campen lived until the 1930s, so this photograph is believed to have been taken in the early 1900s. (Courtesy of DWGNRA.)

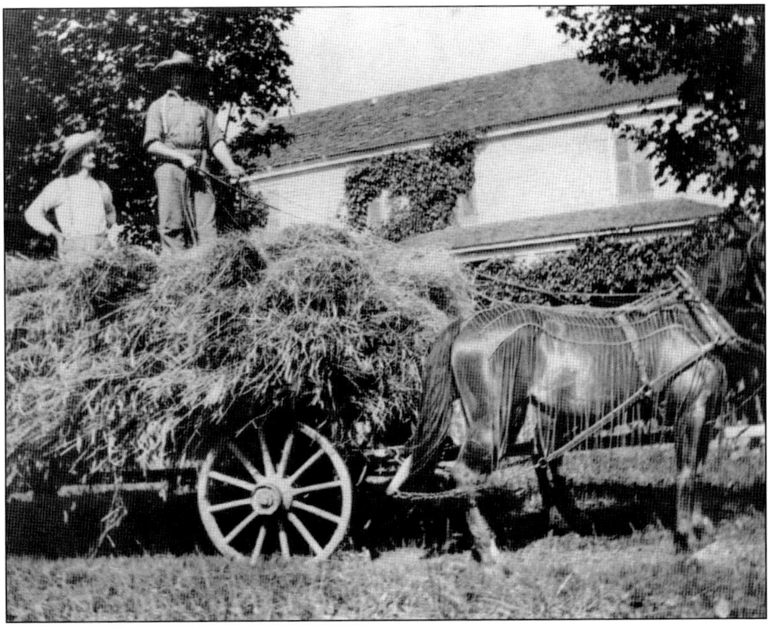

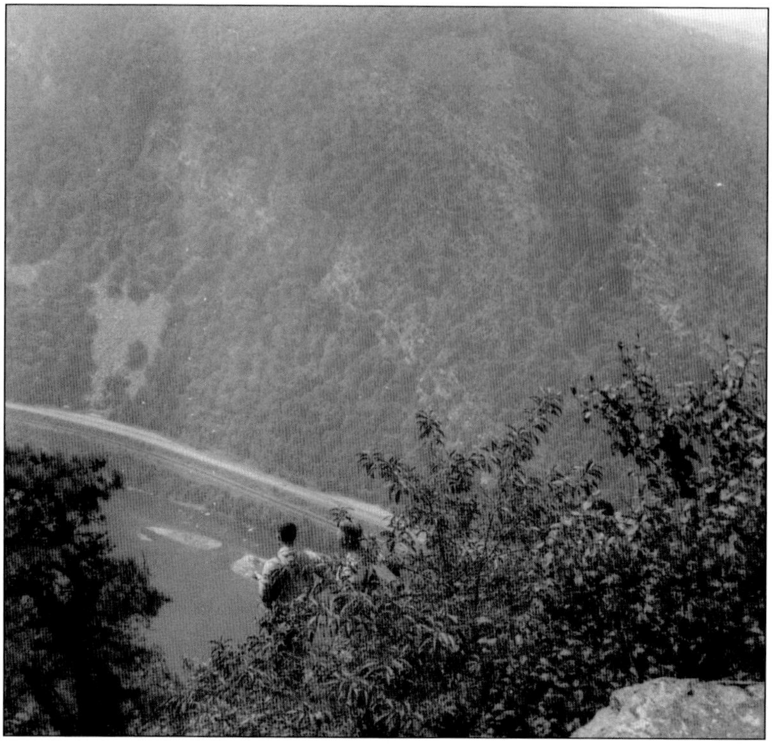

A suggested AT route from the Delaware River into what would become Worthington State Forest was a rugged trail over Mount Tammany. According to the 1934 AT guidebook, "This is an all year route and the view from a side trail on Mount Tammany is one of the finest on the entire Trail . . . climbing over ledges should be attempted with great attention when the footway may be icy." (Courtesy of DWGNRA.)

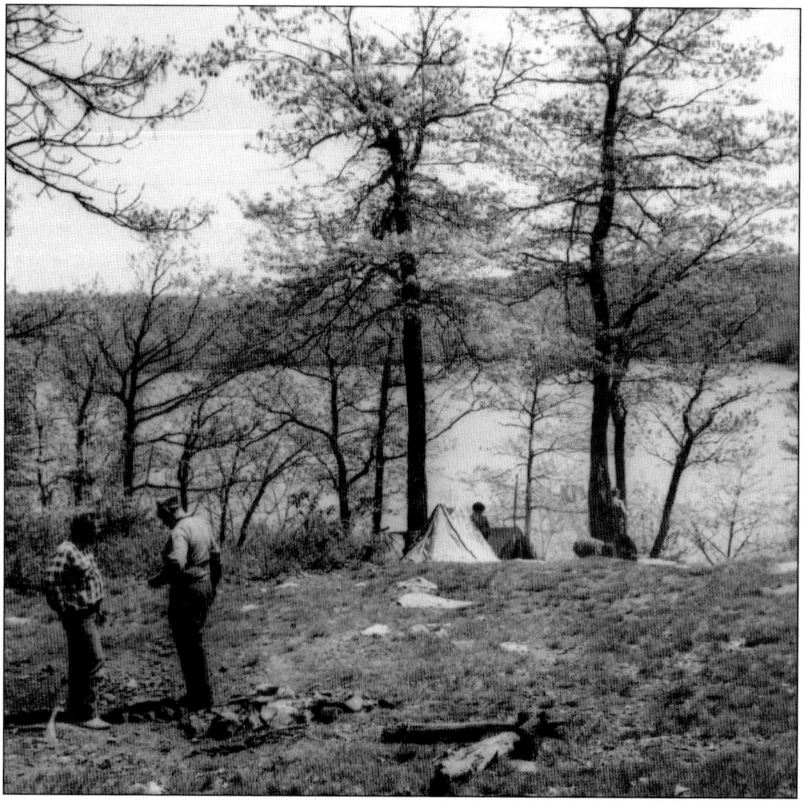

A group of hikers makes camp near Sunfish Pond in the early 1960s, something that is now prohibited in order to protect the integrity of the water, the fragile environment of the shoreline, and the thousands upon thousands of blueberries that surround it during the summer. (Courtesy of DWGNRA.)

In 1965, letter-writing campaigns by two local residents, Casey Kayes (some sources say "Kays") and Glenn Fisher, alerted the public of a proposal to turn the pristine Sunfish Pond into a reservoir for electric power companies. Fisher formed the Leni Lappe League, named for the Native Americans that once inhabited the area, and sponsored hikes to the pond to help publicize the fight against the proposal. (Courtesy of DWGNRA.)

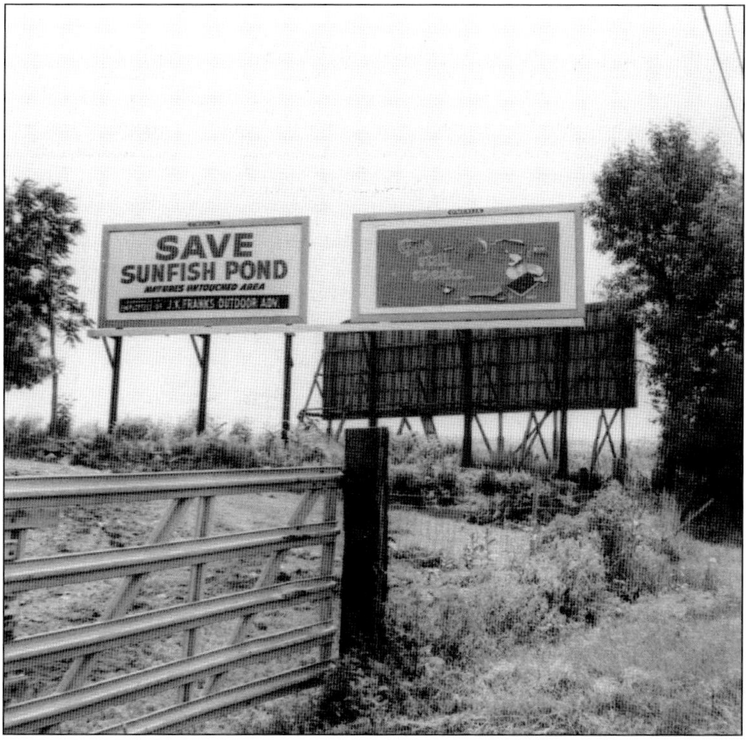

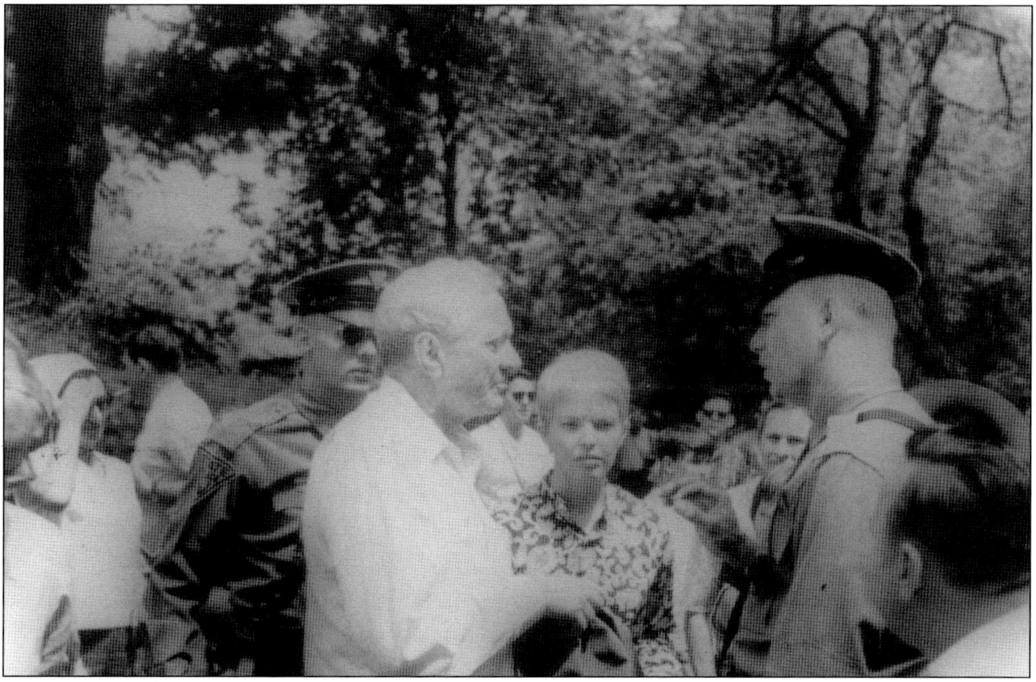

The campaign to save Sunfish Pond attracted the attention of US Supreme Court justice William O. Douglas. He and his wife, Joan, who was in her mid-20s, joined a hike to the pond. Newspaper reporters of the day seemed to be more taken with the fact that Joan did the hike in a miniskirt than with the stamina of her husband, who was in his late 60s. (Courtesy of DWGNRA.)

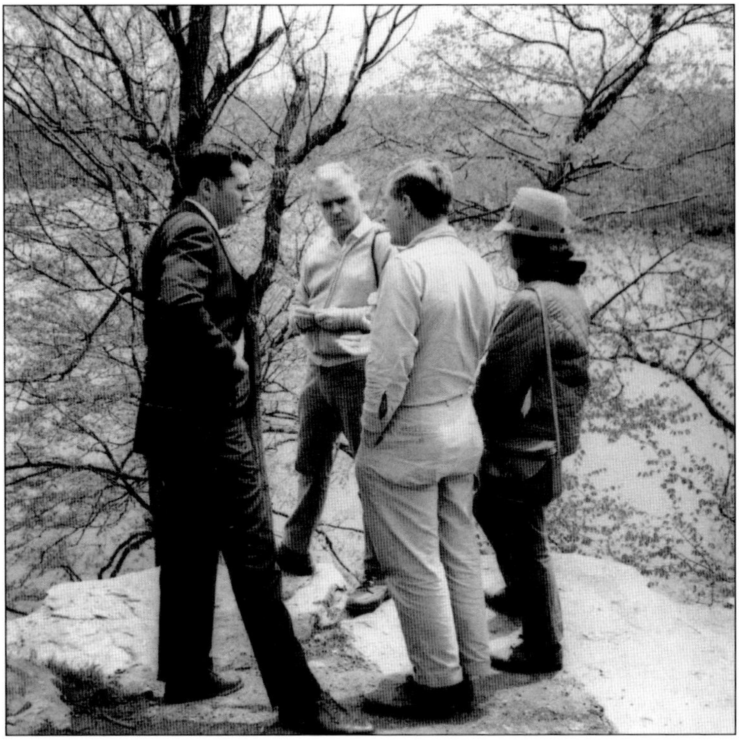

From left to right, New Jersey state senator James Howard Wallwork, Casey Kayes, Tom Ritter, and Enid Smith hike to Sunfish Pond during Kayes's campaign to save the pond. Wallwork, who served in both houses of the New Jersey Legislature, sponsored a bill that would have authorized the state to purchase the pond. (Courtesy of DWGNRA.)

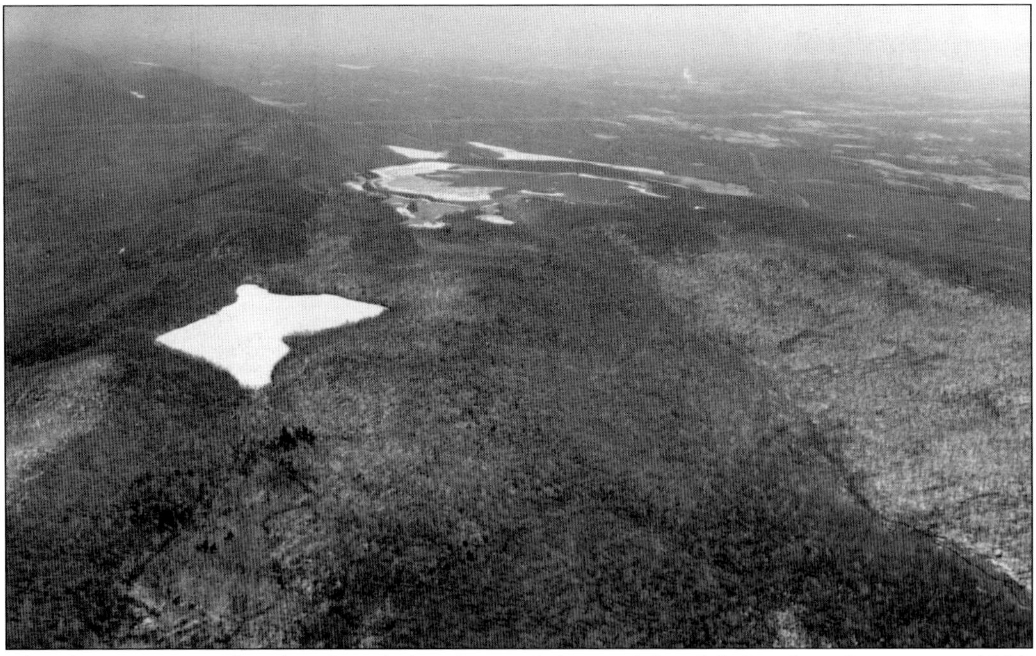

The electric companies abandoned the plan and donated Sunfish Pond to the state in 1966. This aerial view shows the pond's distinctive shape, which provided its name. The companies eventually established the Upper and Lower Yards Creek Reservoirs, seen in the background. The Sunfish Pond victory encouraged people to protest the Tocks Island Dam project, which would have flooded vast amounts of land along the Delaware River. (Courtesy of DWGNRA.)

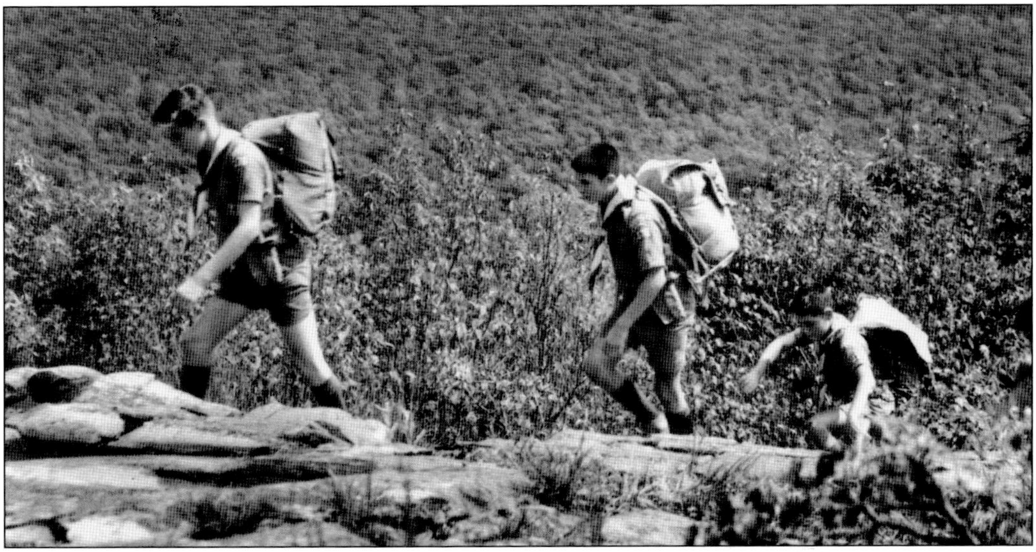

Boy Scout camps were numerous along the Delaware River and the crest of Kittatinny Mountain. This undated photograph, probably taken in the mid-1900s, shows Scouts rising onto Raccoon Ridge, having come from the nearby Mohican Boy Scout Camp, in operation from 1925 to 1978. The camp is now managed by the Appalachian Mountain Club (AMC) and is popular with thru-hikers. (Courtesy of DWGNRA.)

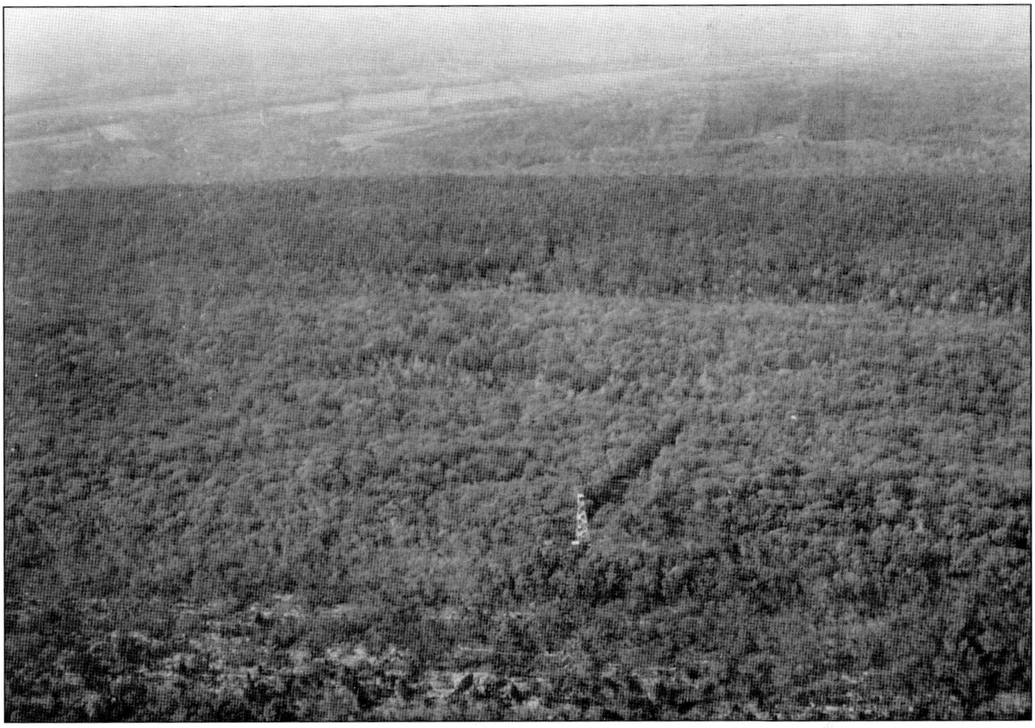

The original Catfish fire tower was made of wood, but it was replaced with a metal one in 1922. A few miles north, the Culver fire tower is also located next to the AT. Its original tower, built in 1905, was replaced with a steel one in 1918. Even though many fire towers have been abandoned across America, New Jersey still maintains close to two dozen. (Courtesy of DWGNRA.)

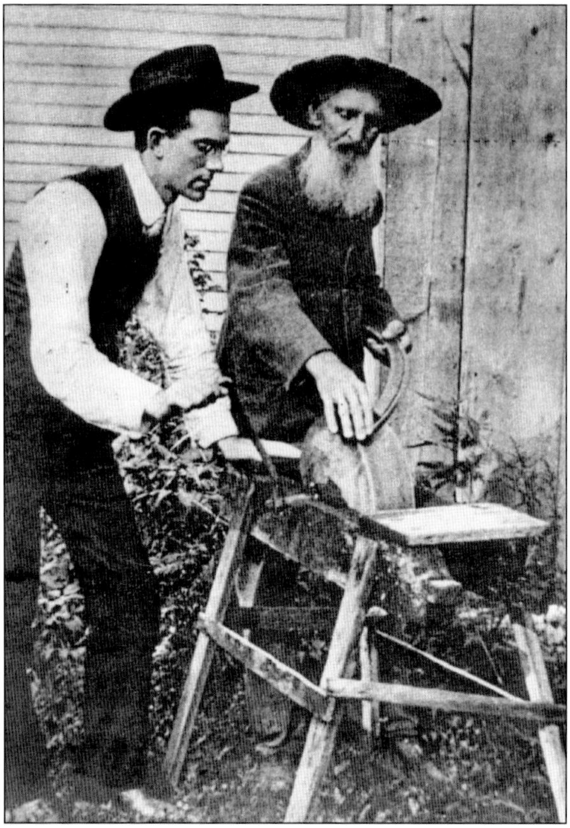

Farmer Abram Gris (right) opened a gristmill in 1832 next to Van Campens Mill Brook, a short distance from the present-day AT. This developed into the village of Millbrook, which had 75 residents in 1875. Gris's son Philip (left) operated a store in the village. Currently, during summer weekends, living history demonstrations are presented within the largely reconstructed village. (Courtesy of DWGNRA.)

When much of the land was in danger of being inundated by the Tocks Island Dam project, the National Park Service began moving historic structures to Millbrook in order to preserve them. One of those buildings was the small, simple home of a shoemaker with its stone fireplace. (Courtesy of DWGNRA.)

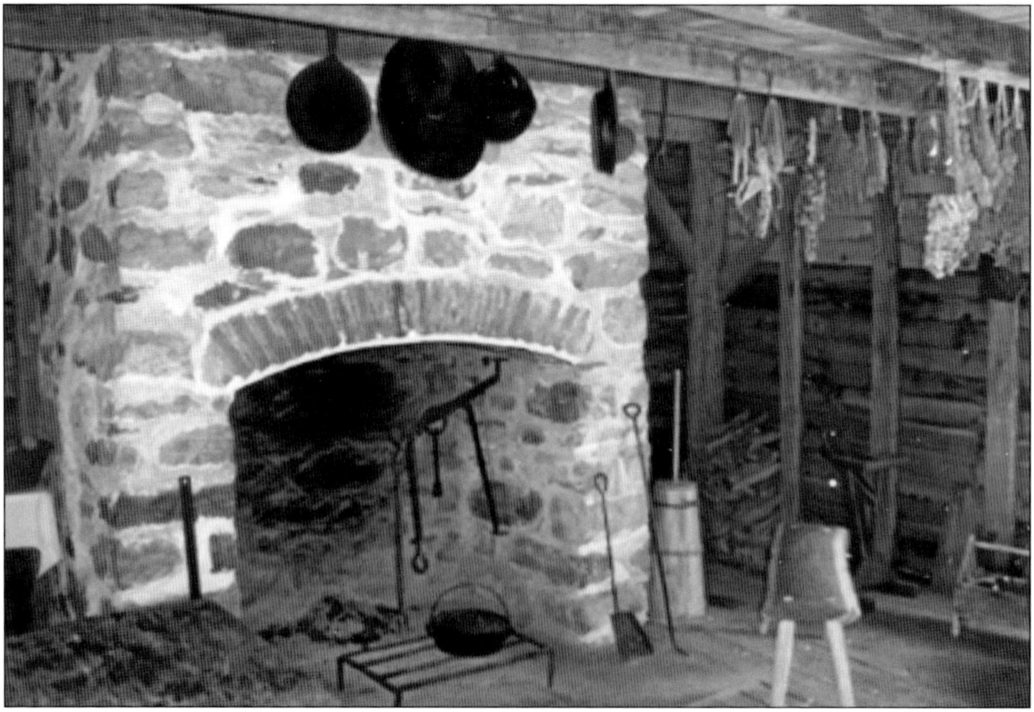

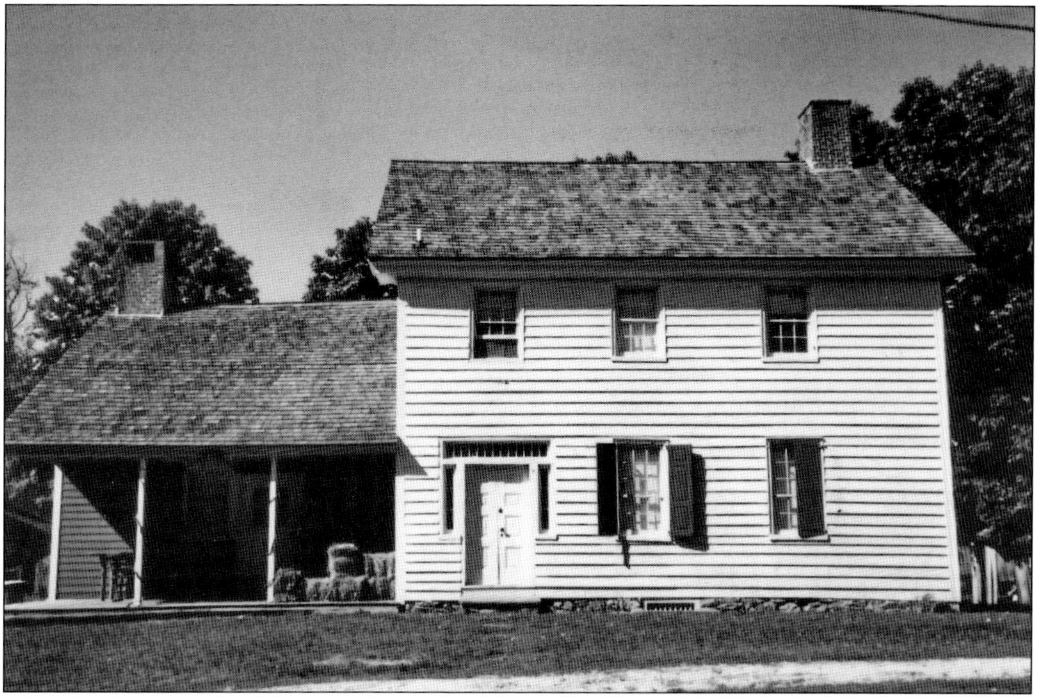

The Abraham Van Campen house, built around 1800 and moved to Millbrook in 1978, was originally located two miles south. Van Campen operated a water-powered mill and other enterprises so successfully that he eventually accumulated more than 10,000 acres of property. (Courtesy of DWGNRA.)

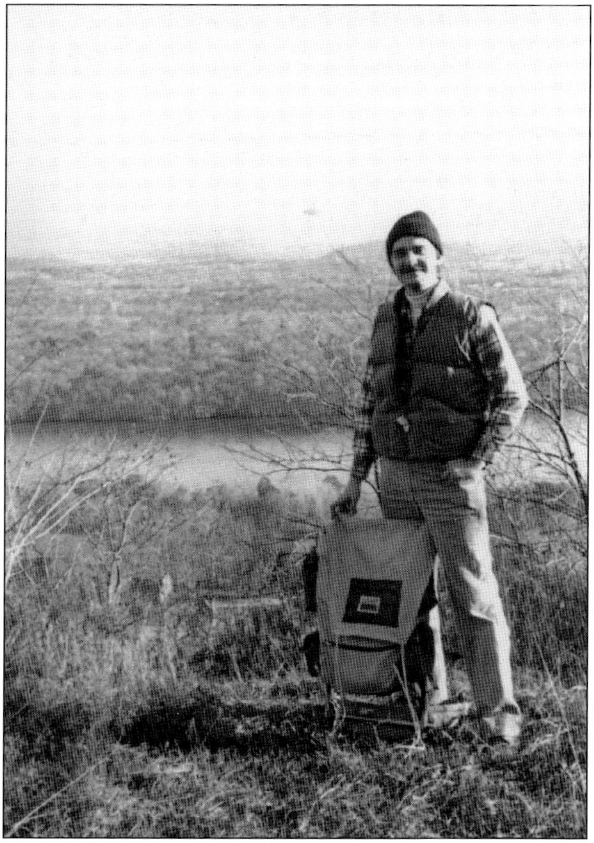

An unidentified hiker poses on the AT above Fairview Lake with his external frame backpack in the 1970s. When the trail's pioneers went for overnight hikes in the woods, they used frameless rucksacks similar to those carried by American soldiers. Manufactured metal external frame packs began to be sold in the 1950s and enabled hikers to carry heavier loads, which may or may not have been an improvement. (Courtesy of ATC.)

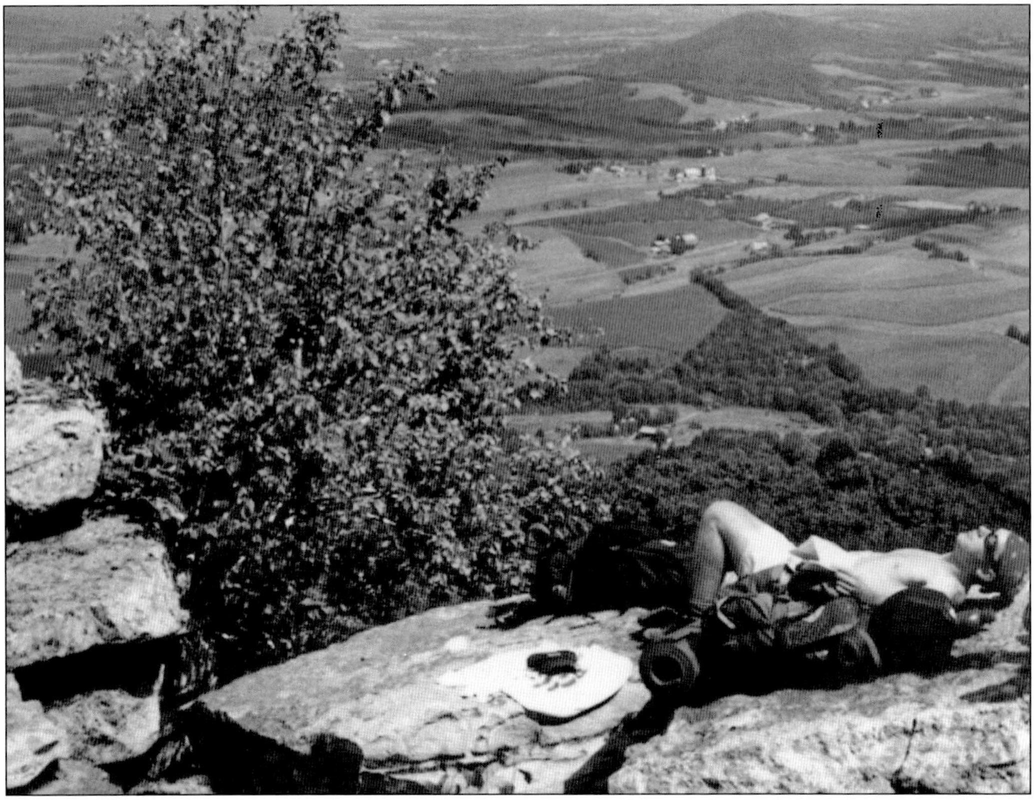

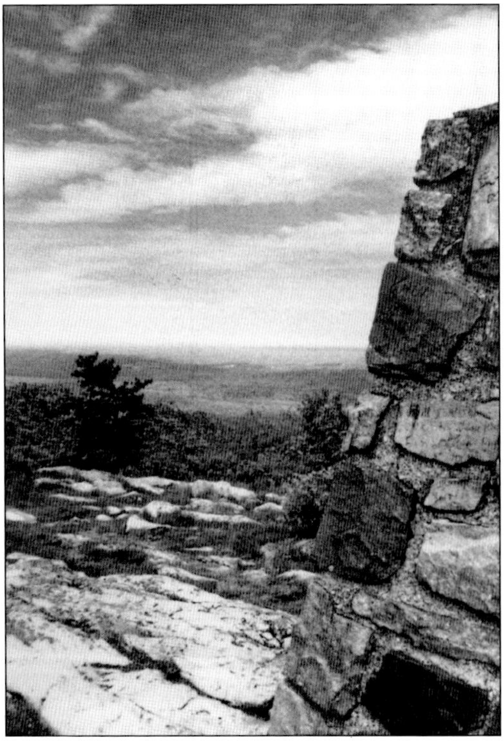

The AT leaves the Delaware Water Gap National Recreation Area about five miles south of Culvers Gap and enters Stokes State Forest. This 1970s photograph shows a hiker taking a rest on the ridgeline above the gap that provides northbound hikers with a view of Wallkill Valley, where they will be hiking once the trail drops off Kittatinny Ridge near High Point. (Courtesy of ATC.)

The view from Sunrise Mountain also takes in the Wallkill Valley. Members of the Civilian Conservation Corps (CCC), a federal government program designed to provide jobs and income for young men during the Great Depression, only worked on a few places near the trail in New Jersey, but they did construct the pavilion on Sunrise Mountain. (Photograph by Theodore Viars; courtesy of ATC.)

For close to 40 miles, the AT runs along Kittatinny Ridge, whose Native American name means "endless hills." The mountain formed 500 million years ago from the uplift that resulted from the collision of continents during the Paleozoic era. It has been eroding ever since, exposing the more erosion-resistant Silurian sandstone, composed of quartzite, sandstone, and conglomerate. (Courtesy of ATC.)

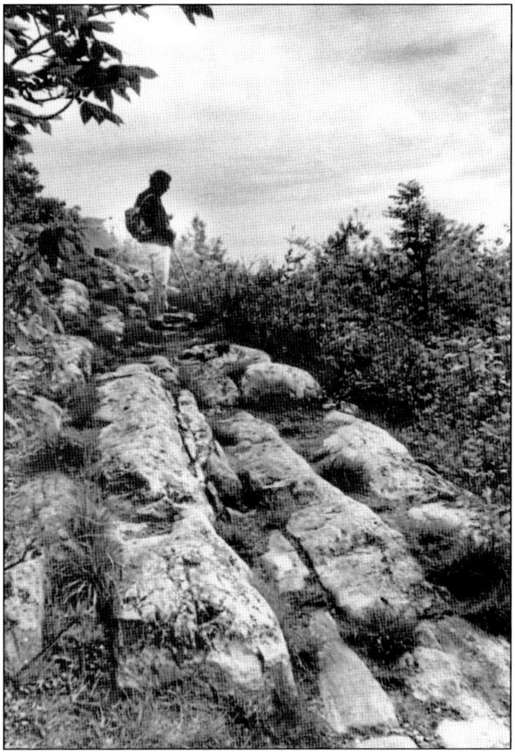

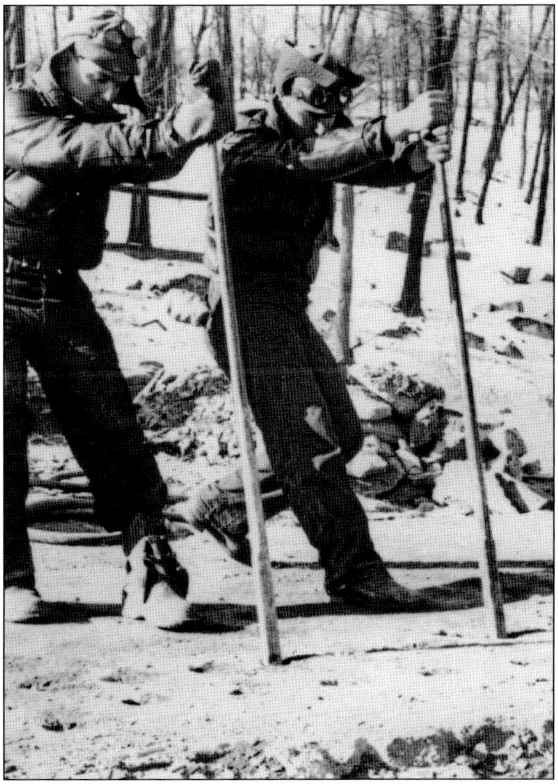

Two CCC camps were created within High Point State Park almost as soon as the corps was established in 1933. One was near where the present-day Mashipacong Shelter is located, and the other, known as Camp Kuser, was situated at the base of the mountain where the High Point Monument is located. (Courtesy of DWGNRA.)

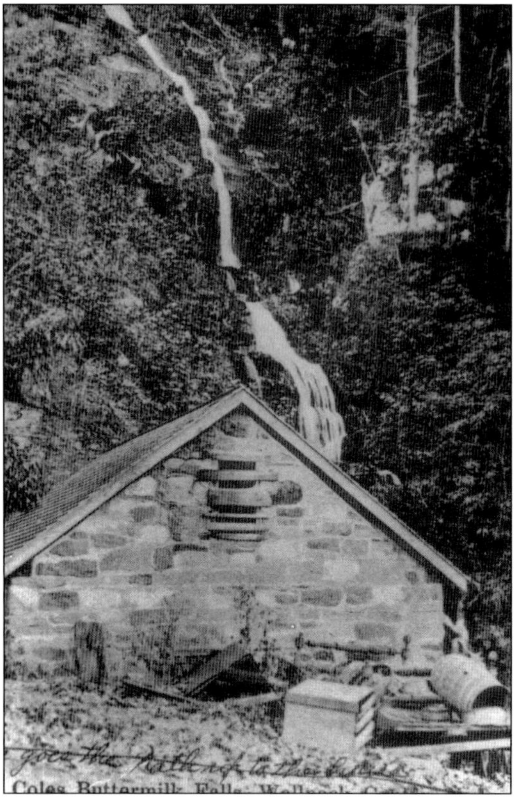

Some sources say that Buttermilk Falls (left), accessed by a 1.5-mile side trail that descends close to 1,000 feet from the AT, is New Jersey's highest cascade. However, various references provide widely ranging heights. One says the falls tumble a mere 75 feet, another states 90 feet, a third claims close to 200 feet, and another says the falls are "cascading several times over 200 feet." The springhouse in the photograph at left, taken in the early 1900s, was fed by an overshot waterwheel (below) located at the base of the falls. Neither structure is standing today, but the park service has constructed a steep staircase that enables visitors arriving from Wallpack Center on Old Mine Road to ascend to the top of the falls. (Both, courtesy of DWGNRA.)

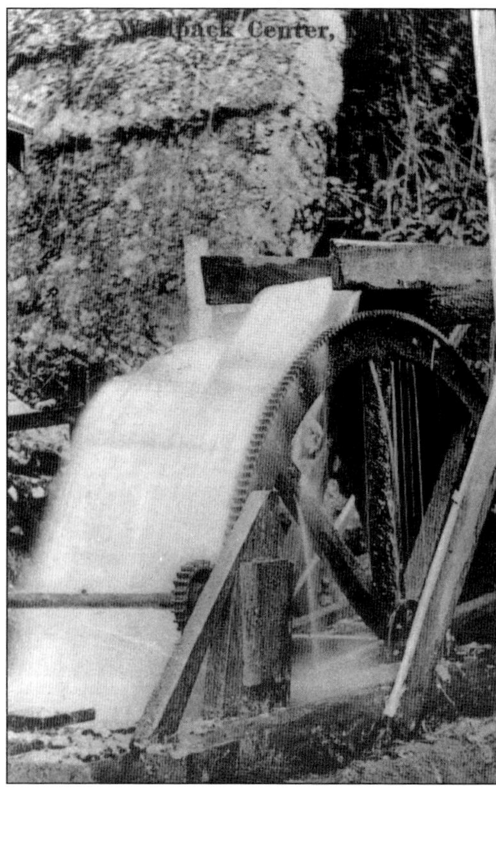

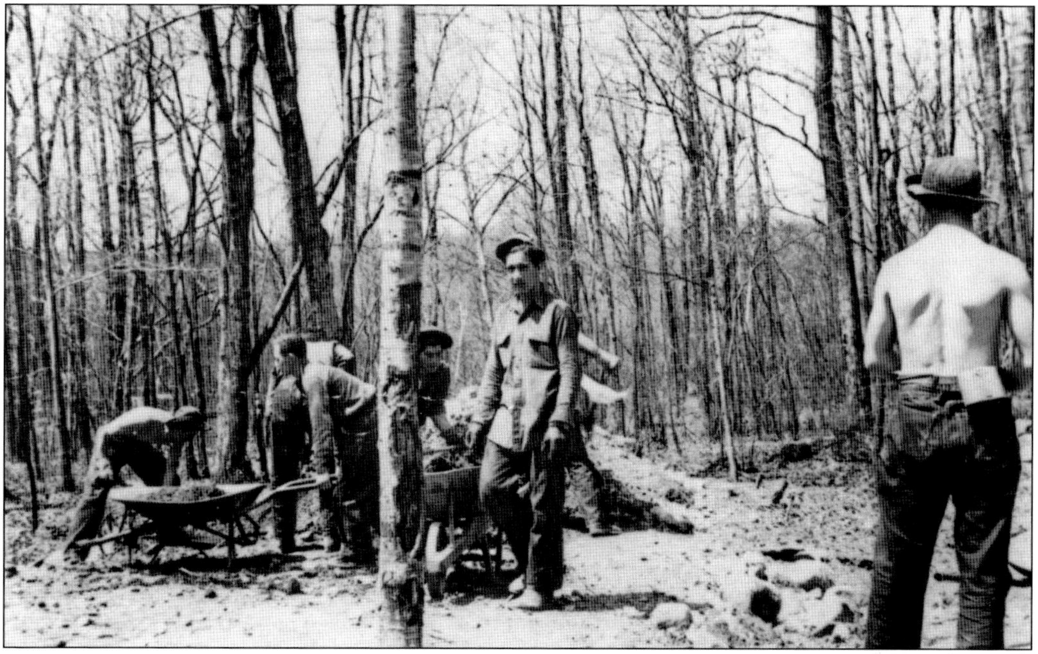

During its time in the park, the CCC built two lakes, more than two dozen miles of roads, campgrounds, shelters, multiple miles of trail, and the quarter-mile High Point Monument stone staircase. They restored the health of forests damaged by unsound management, fought fires, and planted trees to help prevent erosion. (Courtesy of DWGNRA.)

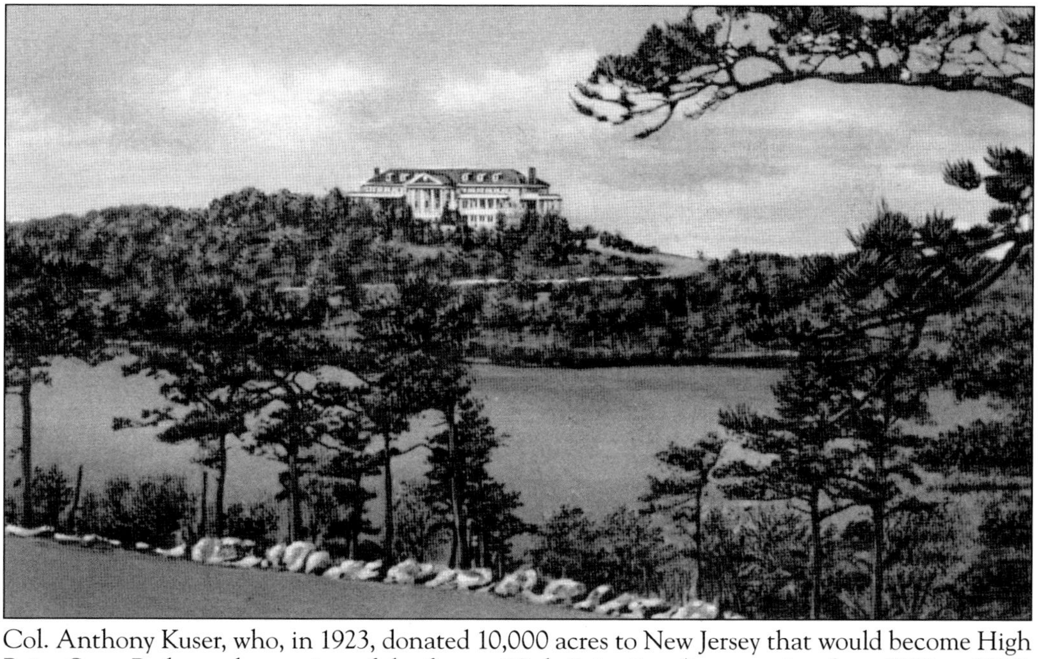

Col. Anthony Kuser, who, in 1923, donated 10,000 acres to New Jersey that would become High Point State Park, used a portion of the former High Point Inn (in operation from 1890 to 1908) to create a new lodge overlooking Lake Marcia. The lodge opened as a hotel in 1937 and was later known as the State or Administration Building after it became state park offices. (Courtesy of Imperial Press.)

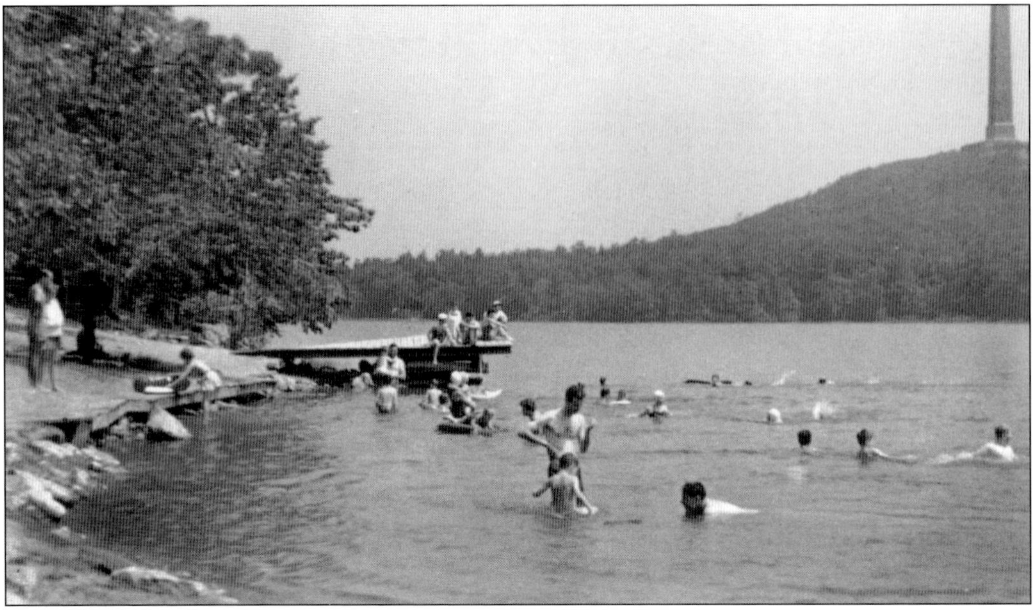

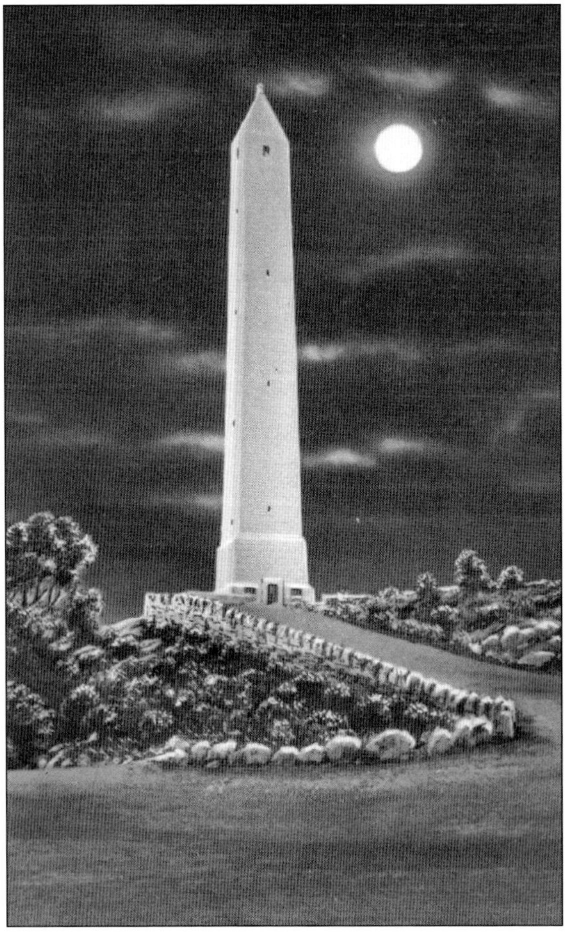

Lake Marcia, located at the base of High Point and easily accessed from the monument, had become so popular by the early 1930s that a National Park Service employee opined that the crowds were beginning to resemble those at Coney Island. In addition, there was a Boy Scout Camp on the lake's southeastern shore and Girl Scouts used a beach on the western shoreline. (Courtesy of Kingston Candy Company.)

Col. Anthony Kuser offered to erect a monument to New Jersey's veterans of all wars in 1927, and the 220-foot-tall monument was completed in 1930. The large blocks of stone were hauled from the bottom of the mountain to the summit in carrier cars running on tracks resembling those of a railroad. (Courtesy of Ruben Publishing Company.)

In 1948, Earl Shaffer (left) became the AT's first thru-hiker (although the phrase did not exist at the time) by hiking from Georgia to Maine from April 4 to August 5. He knew he might be the first person to accomplish the feat, but he said he also did it to, "Walk the army out of my system." Murray Stevens, who was chairman of both NYNJTC and ATC, is on the right. (Courtesy of ATC.)

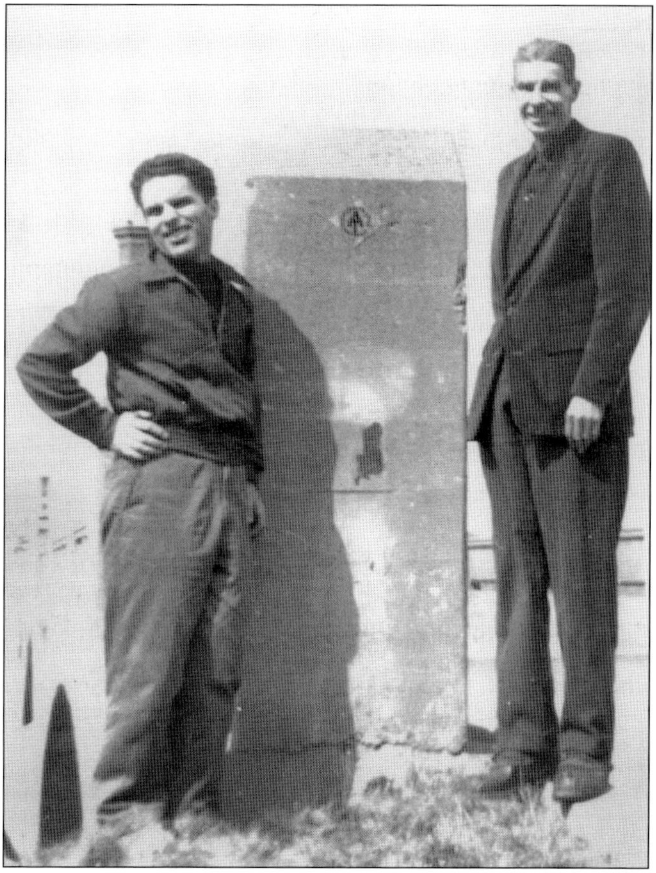

After dropping off Kittatinny Ridge, the AT closely parallels the New Jersey-New York border. Despite relocations that took the trail out of Unionville, New York, the town has remained a popular resupply point because it has always been within relatively easy walking distance. A number of buildings shown in this postcard, mailed from Unionville in 1909, are still on Main Street today. (Courtesy of Leonard M. Adkins; publisher unidentified.)

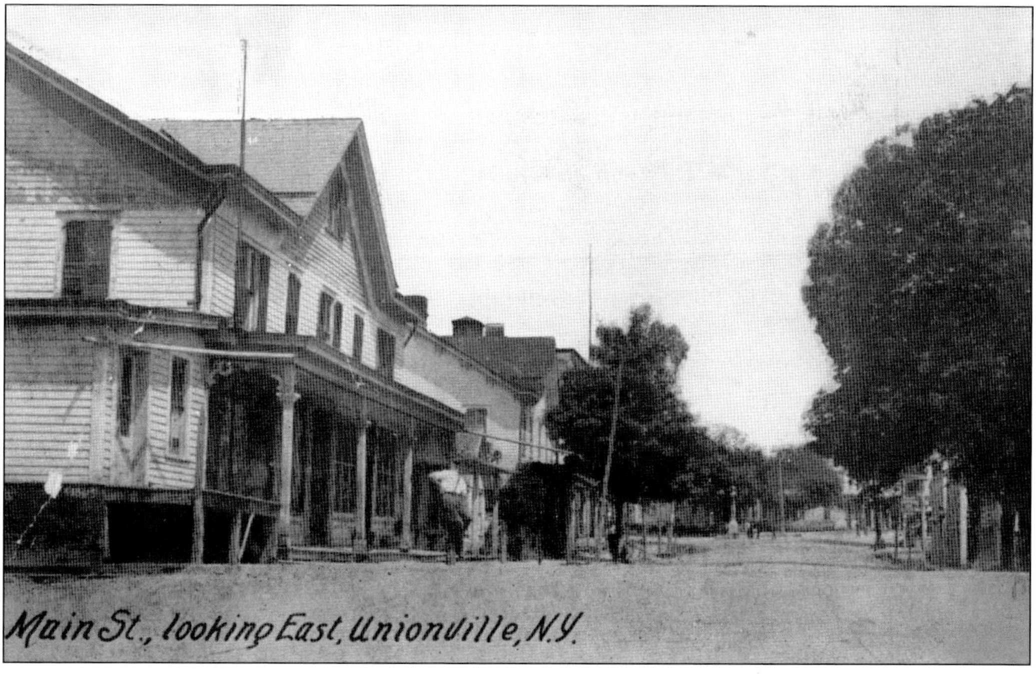

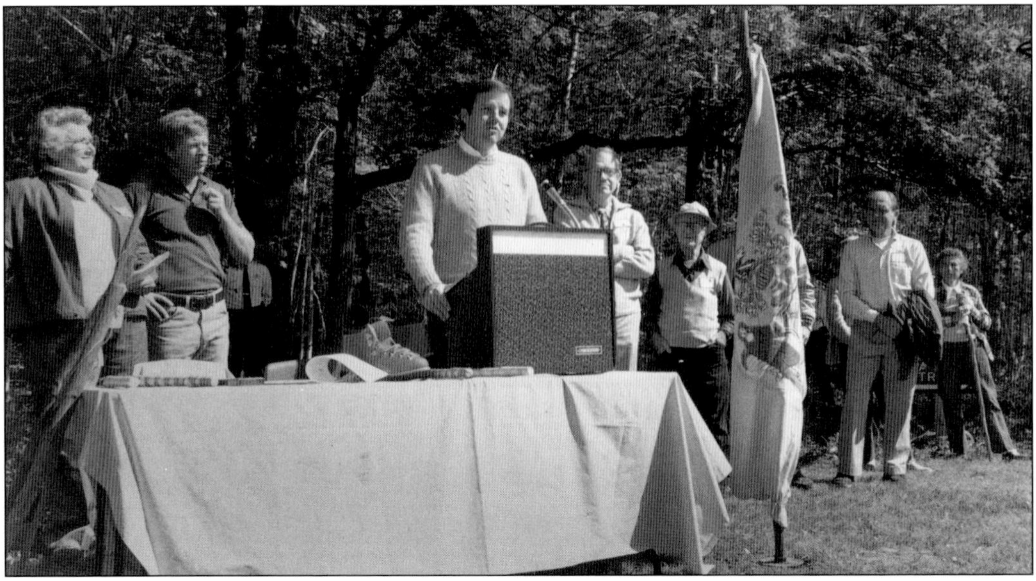

New Jersey governor Thomas Kean addressed a crowd of approximately 200 people that attended the ceremony opening a section of the AT that had recently received permanent protection in 1982. From left to right are Helen Fenske, assistant environmental commissioner; Robert Hughey, environmental commissioner; Governor Kean; Don Derr, NTNJTC president; unidentified; David Ritchie, AT project office manager; and Elizabeth Levers, a member of the ATC board of managers. (Courtesy of ATC.)

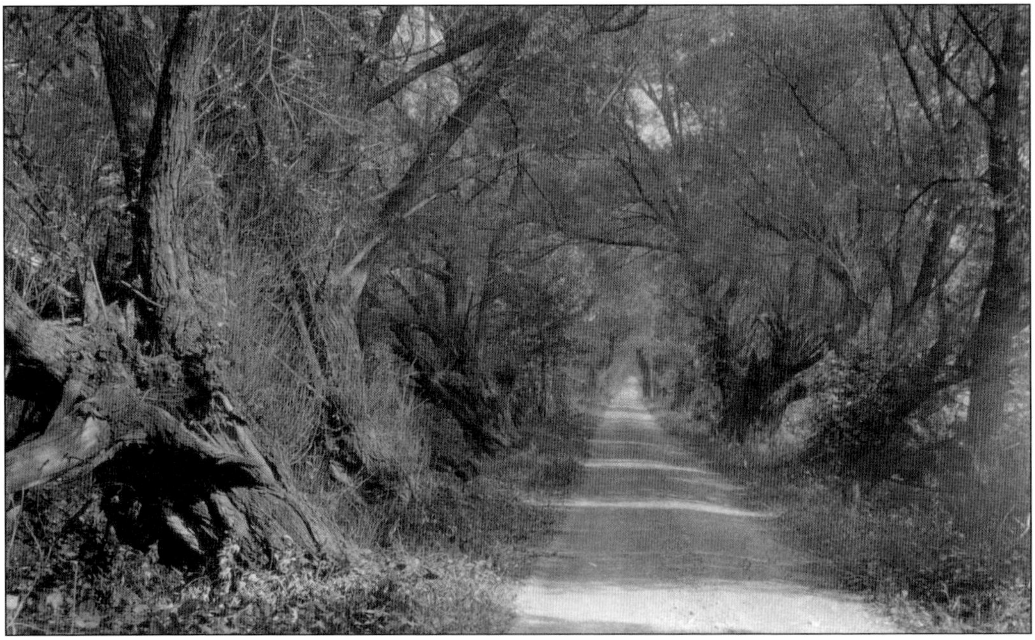

For decades, the trail followed quiet, bucolic dirt roads in the Wallkill Valley, such as this one photographed near Unionville in 1941. However, pavement and increasing traffic made hiking on them progressively less pleasant and more dangerous. Thanks to land purchases, primarily by New Jersey in the late 1900s, the trail currently travels off roads through a protected corridor. (Courtesy of ATC.)

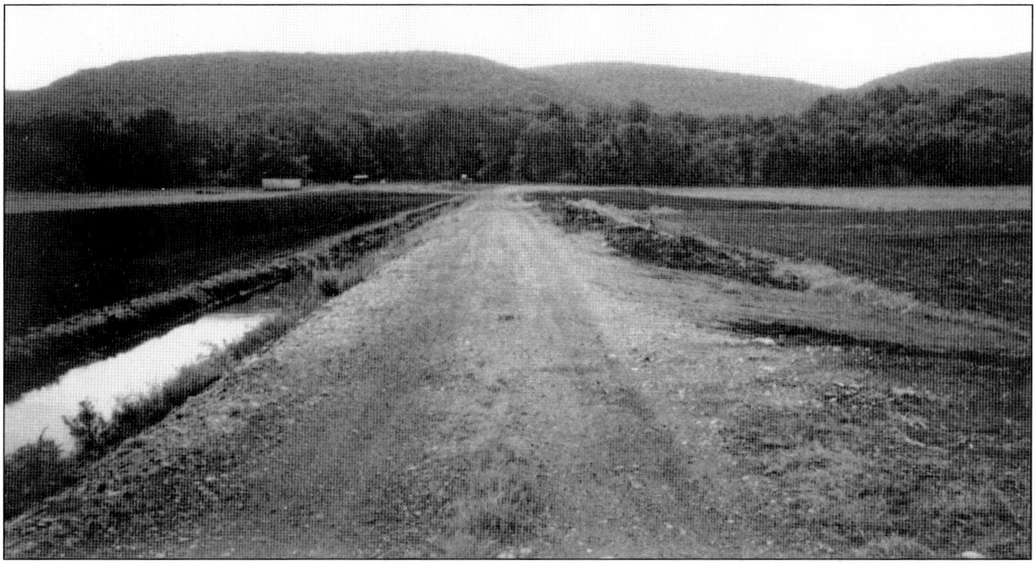

Although it seemed like a detour off a more direct route, hikers enjoyed the flat miles of walking on the bed of an ancient glacial lake through the Liberty Sod Farm up until 1990. The trail still follows the route, but this is now part of the Wallkill River National Wildlife Refuge, established to preserve the diversity of fish, migratory birds, wildlife, and plants. (Courtesy of ATC.)

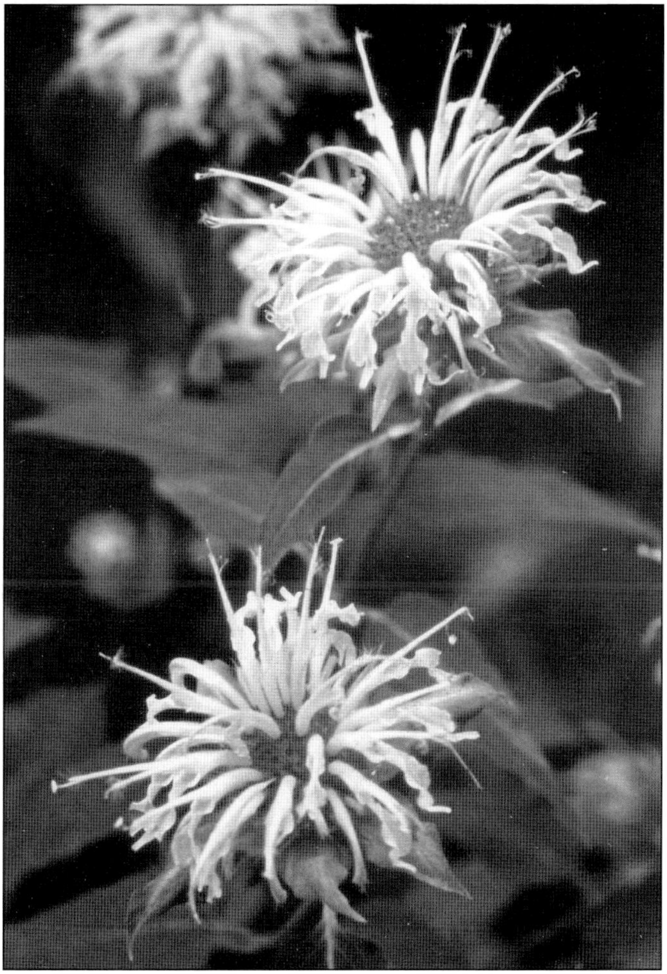

One of the aspects that has attracted people to the AT from its inception is the vast array of wildflowers found along its full length. Wild bergamot, photographed by Joe Cook, is just one of the scores of flowers that can be seen by hikers in the Wallkill River National Wildlife Refuge from late spring to early fall. Others include impatiens, sorrel, cinquefoil, and aster. (Courtesy of Joe Cook.)

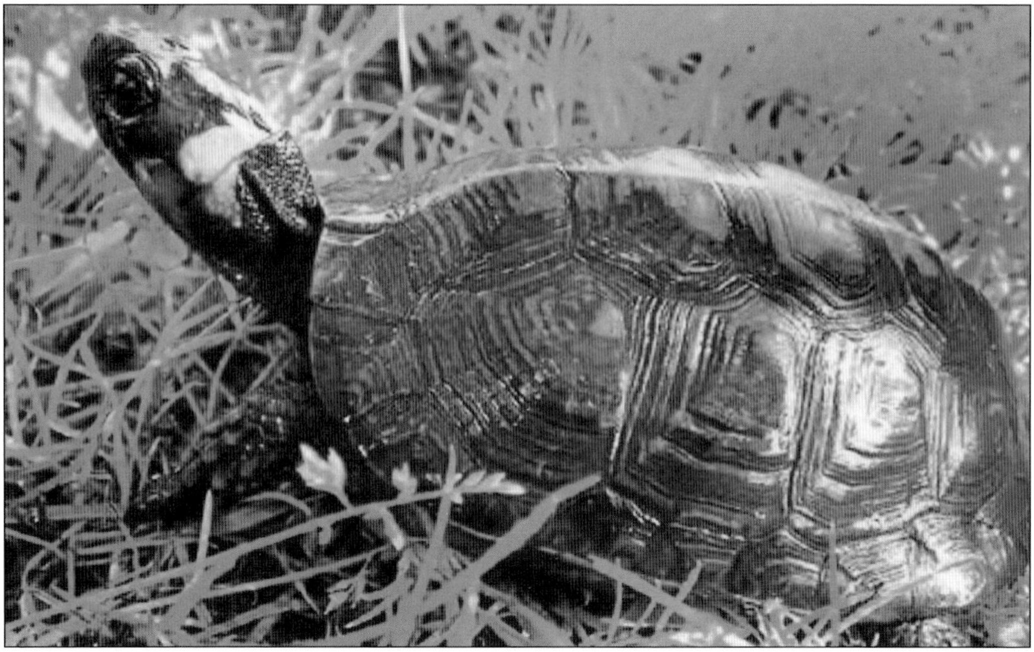

Possibly more important than the recreational opportunities the AT provides is its preservation of the natural world from the encroachments of the modern world. Because of the AT, here in the Wallkill River National Wildlife Refuge, endangered and/or rare amphibians, such as the bog turtle (above), may continue to exist and have been given the protection they need so that one day they may no longer be endangered or threatened. Large mammals such as bears and moose have the extensive tracts of land needed to insure their survival, and migratory birds like the bald eagle (below) are still able to use an unbroken forest from Georgia to Maine in which to rest during migrations. (Above, courtesy of US Fish and Wildlife Service; below, photograph by and courtesy of Ann B. Messick.)

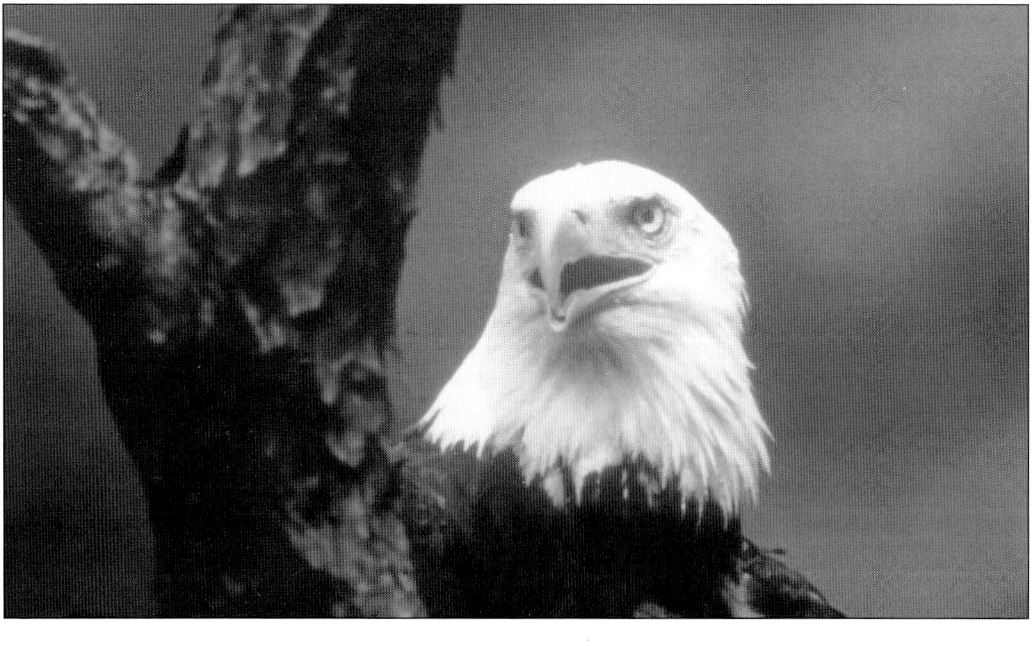

In the 1990s, a 110-foot-long, 14-foot-high suspension bridge (right) and a nearly mile-long boardwalk (below) were built across Pochuck Swamp, the result of an amazing effort by the combined forces of the ATC and its volunteers; the National Park Service; NYNJTC members; local community members, students, engineers, and bankers; an electric power company; several corporations; the US Forest Service; and the State of New Jersey. An engineering feat that had to be built not on bedrock or solid soil, but on a base of organic muck, the structures not only enable hikers to get across without getting wet feet, but they also protect the fragile environment. In addition, the bridge's foundation essentially floats, in order to withstand fluctuating water levels. (Both, photograph by and courtesy of Leonard M. Adkins.)

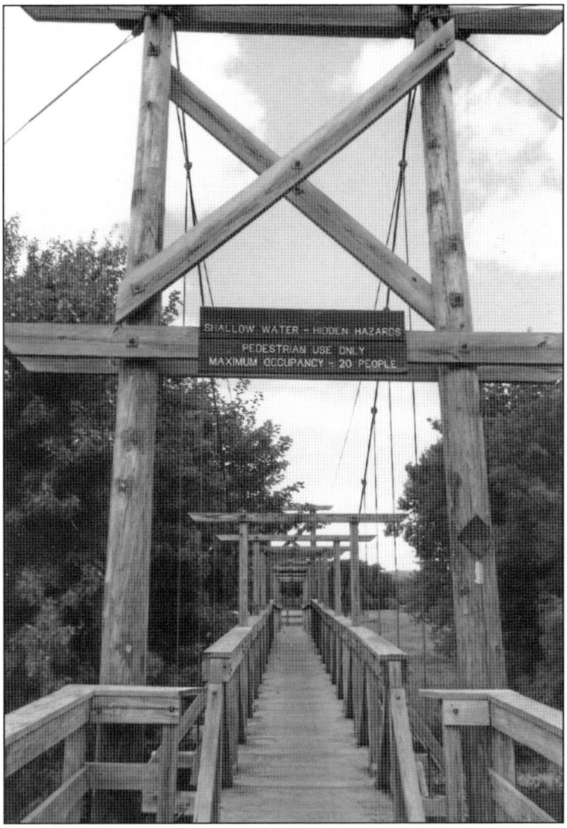

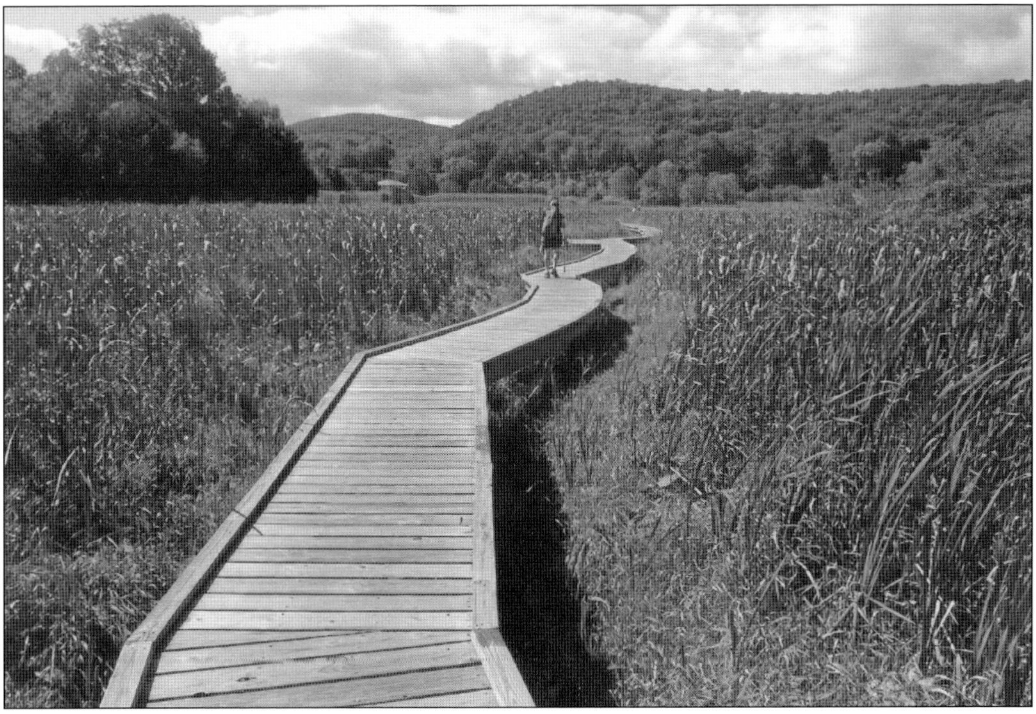

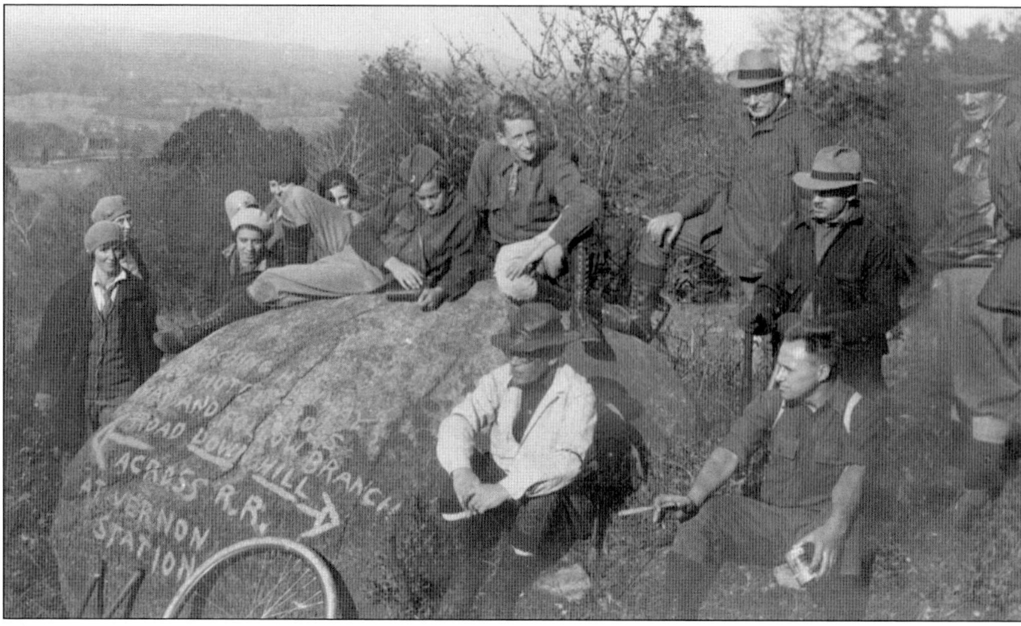

The Warwick Appalachian Trail Club (WATC) posed for this photograph on a hike in the early 1930s, when the AT was located closed to Vernon. Debra Houston is on the far left. Florence Tate is hidden by James. P. Tate Jr.'s knee. Seated next to him is J. Stanley Gorham. James P. Tate Sr. is in the foreground near the wheel, and seated to the right of him is George Hansen. All others are unidentified. (Courtesy of WHS.)

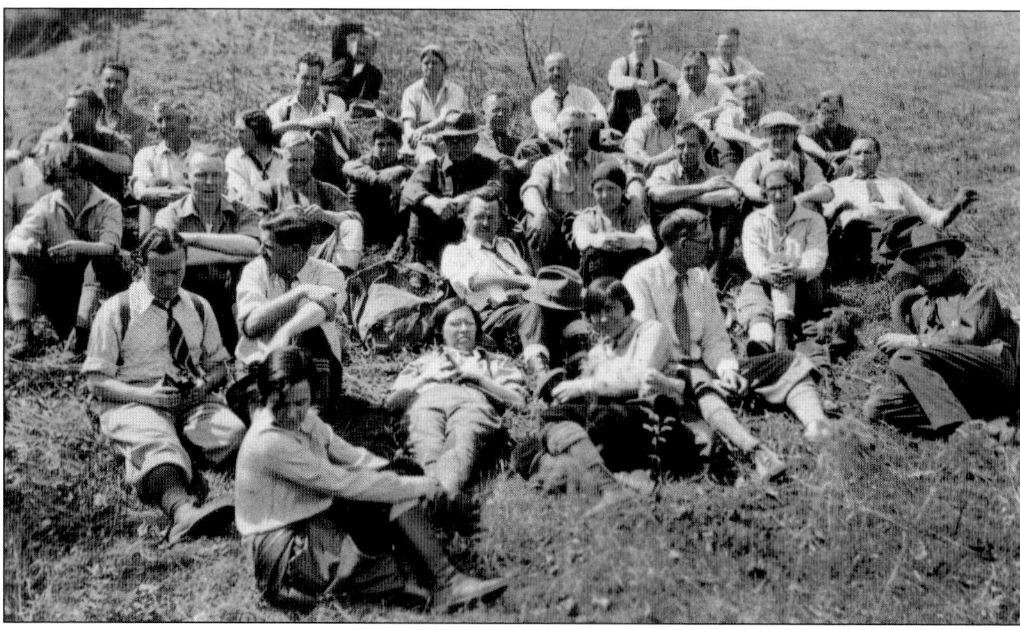

Members of the New York Chapter of the Green Mountain Club also took a hike to the Vernon High Point in the 1930s. According to Raymond H. Torrey, president of the NYNJTC from 1931 to 1938, members of this club "did most of the work of the first portion on [the AT], made in 1922 across the Bear Mountain-Harriman sections of the Palisades Interstate Park." (Courtesy of WHS.)

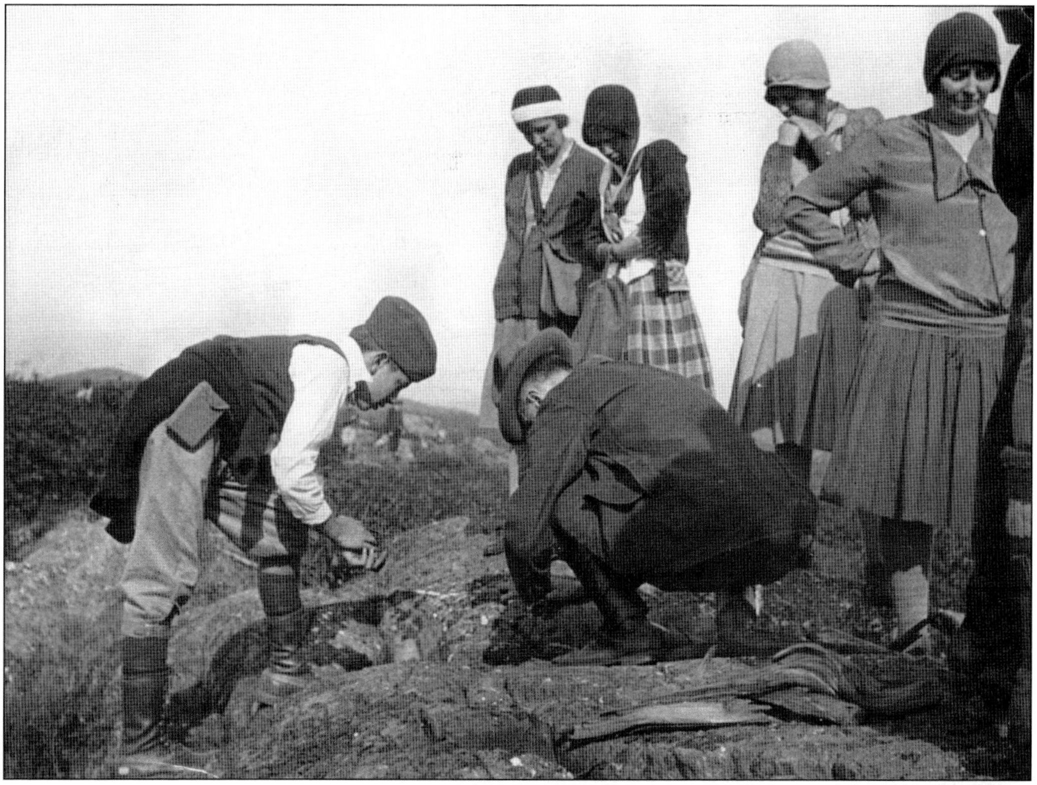

Although WATC was based in Warwick, New York, members were active in working on the trail from Fitzgerald Falls in New York to High Point, New Jersey. James P. Tate Jr. (left) and James P. Tate Sr. (squatting, center) led this group on a combination scouting and social hike in October 1930. (Courtesy of WHS.)

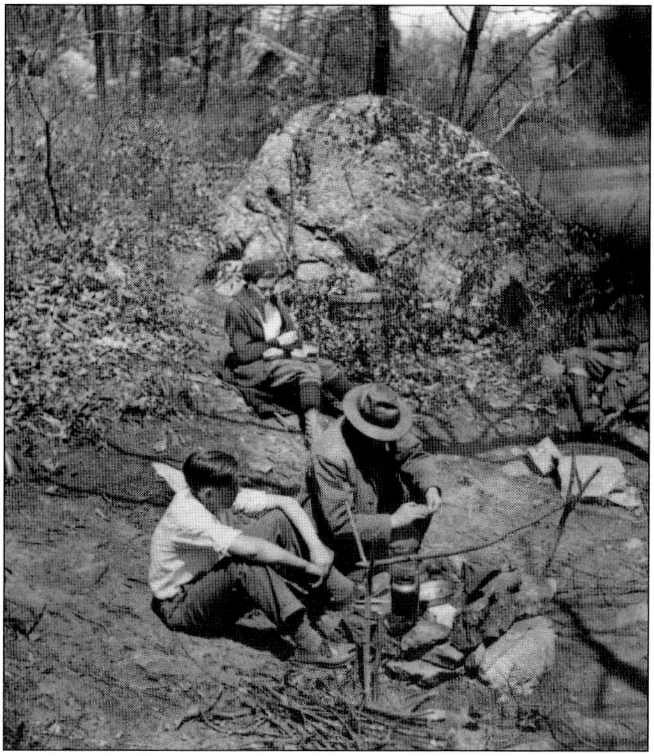

Tate family members, who often joined or led hikes with WATC, could frequently be found in the woods along the New Jersey portion of the trail throughout much of the 1930s. Here, daughter Florence Tate is in the background, father James P. Tate Sr. is in the center, and son James P. Tate Jr. is in the foreground. The person on the right is unidentified. (Courtesy of WHS.)

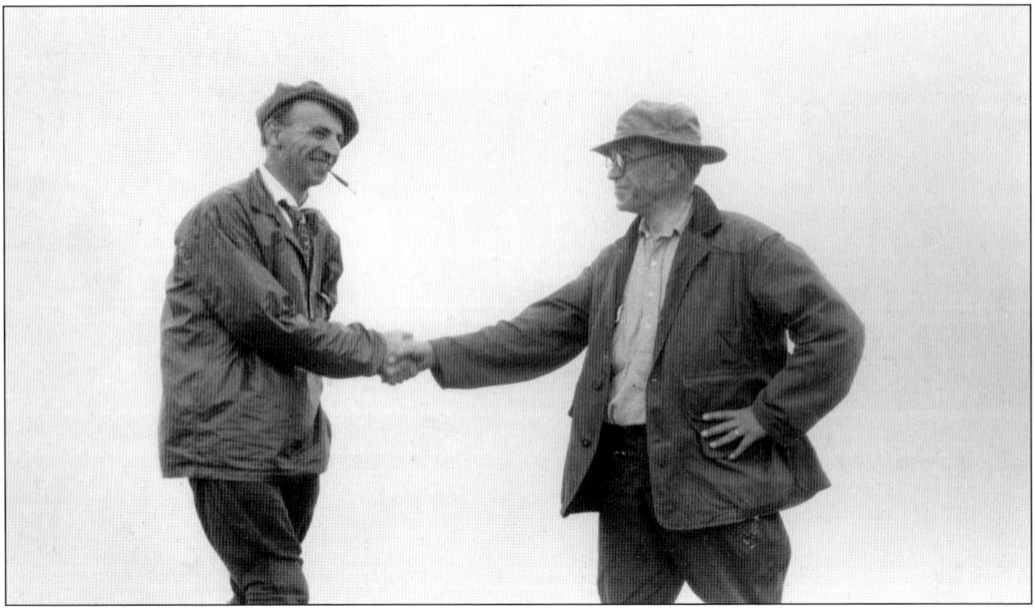

On June 7, 1931, James P. Tate Sr. (right) of WATC congratulates an unidentified member of the Interstate Hiking Club on the completion of that club's first hike. There were so many hiking clubs in New York and New Jersey that they began having trail wars, with members of some clubs putting their own blazes overtop others' blazes and otherwise trying to obliterate "opponents" trails. (Courtesy of WHS.)

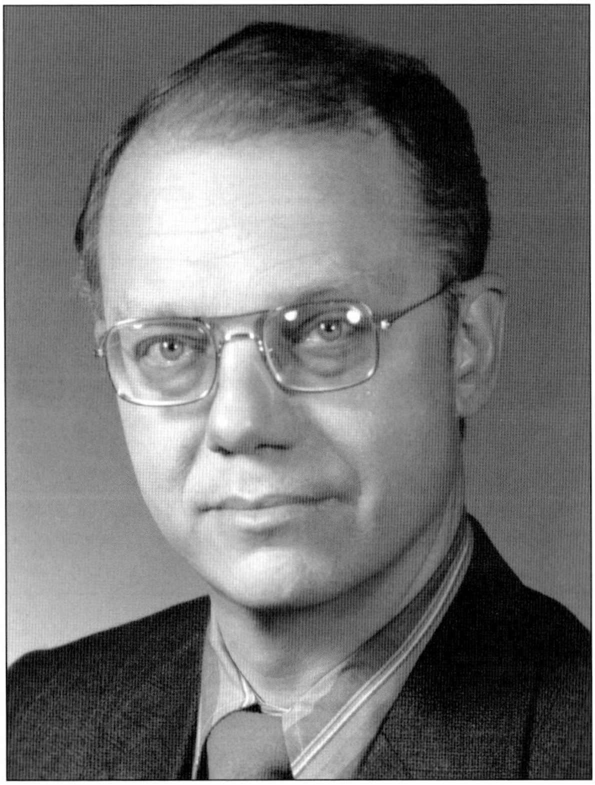

Don Derr was president of NYNJTC when ATC signed an historic 1984 cooperative agreement with the National Park Service. In the agreement, the park service turned over management of AT lands to ATC, which in turn made agreements with the local clubs for the maintenance of the trail. At the time, Derr said, "We welcome the challenge." (Courtesy of ATC.)

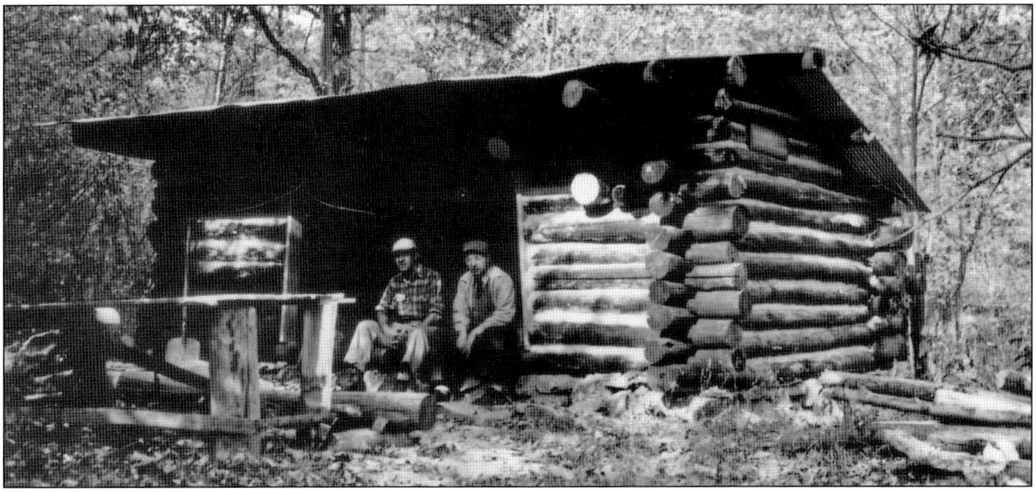

Volunteers not only have to carry in, sometimes for miles, all the materials needed to build a shelter, they often have to do so a number of times, as materials deteriorate and need to be replaced. This shelter on Wawayanda Mountain, photographed in 1952, was replaced by a new one constructed by Wawayanda State Park employees and volunteers from the town of Vernon in 1990. (Courtesy of PIPC.)

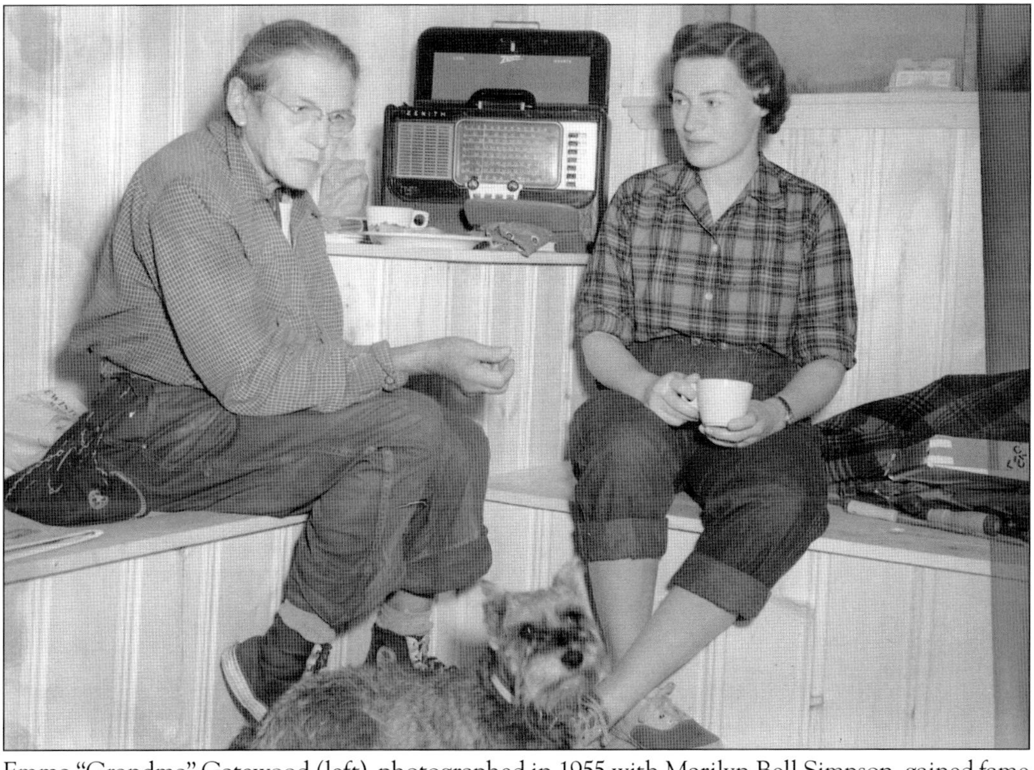

Emma "Grandma" Gatewood (left), photographed in 1955 with Marilyn Bell Simpson, gained fame that year by being the first woman to hike the AT alone. She was 67 then, and she completed two more hikes, in 1960 and 1965, making her the first person to walk the trail's full length three times. Her exploits received much publicity, with newspapers and even *Sports Illustrated* writing about her. (Courtesy of ATC.)

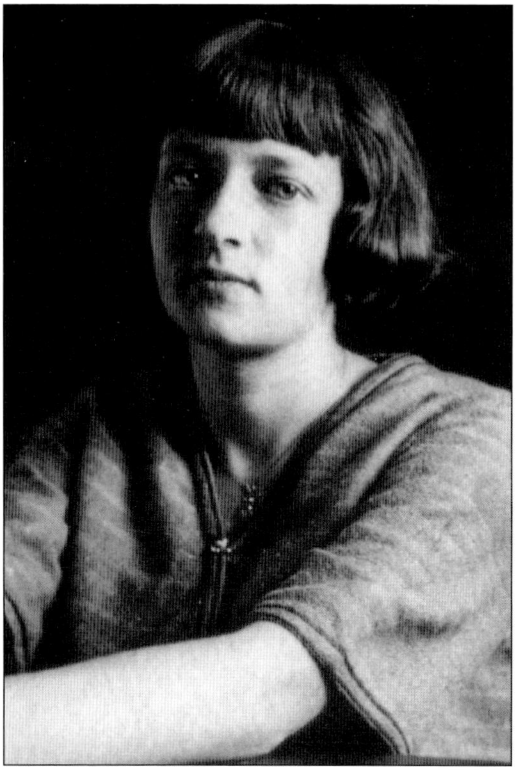

Emma "Grandma" Gatewood garnered publicity as the first female to hike the trail alone, but the first woman to thru-hike was Mildred Norman Ryder (left), born in Egg Harbor City, New Jersey. In 1952, Richard Lamb and Ryder (she was often mistakenly called Mildred Lamb) hiked northward to Pennsylvania, took a bus to Mount Katahdin, and walked back to Pennsylvania. From the trek, Ryder gained the courage to embark upon a mission. In 1953, she started a journey that lasted 28 years, walking more than 25,000 miles for peace. Known as Peace Pilgrim (below), she touched thousands of lives. She said, "This is the way of peace: overcome evil with good, and falsehood with truth, and hatred with love." (Below, photograph by James B. Burton; both, courtesy of Friends of Peace Pilgrim.)

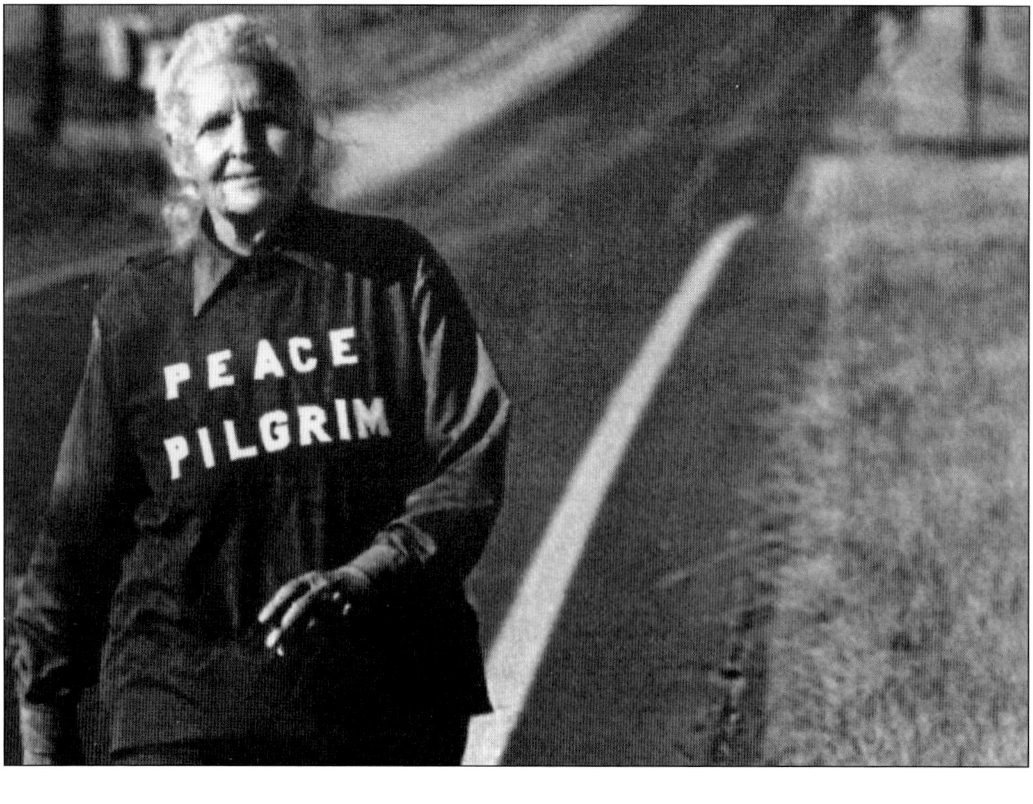

Two

New York

Atop Bearfort Mountain, overlooking Greenwood Lake, the Appalachian Trail enters New York. It soon turns eastward to cross Bellvale Mountain, Mombasha High Point, and Buchanan and Arden Mountains on a narrow strip of public land obtained by the National Park Service in the 1970s. In the 1800s, this area, named Sterling Forest after Revolutionary War general Lord Stirling (yes, different spellings), was denuded to supply charcoal to the iron industry, and hikers can still see depressions in the forest floor that are the remains of charcoal pits.

From Sterling Forest, the trail passes through Harriman and Bear Mountain State Parks, where the first miles of pathway built specifically for the AT were opened in the early 1920s. With a series of more ups and downs than the trail has seen since entering Maryland, the AT reaches the 1,305-foot summit of Bear Mountain, which offers superb views of the Hudson Highlands and the New York City skyline.

The Hudson River at Bear Mountain is actually a fjord, created by the carving actions of glaciers. It is also the only place to find saltwater on the AT; the river experiences the tides, as they bring water from the Atlantic Ocean to mix with the freshwater flowing from the mountains.

Crossing the Hudson River on the Bear Mountain Bridge a scant 44 miles from New York City, the trail climbs steeply near Anthony's Nose. It rarely tops 1,000 feet in elevation as it twists eastward over a series of low ridges, sometimes making use of old railroad grades and sometimes just a few yards above the Taconic State Parkway. Although much of the trail here is on narrow strips of public land, it must be remembered that those who hiked prior to the late 1980s and early 1990s did so on miles of paved roadway. Entering Connecticut to cross Ten Mile River, the trail deviates back into New York only long enough to traverse Schaghticoke Mountain before returning to Connecticut.

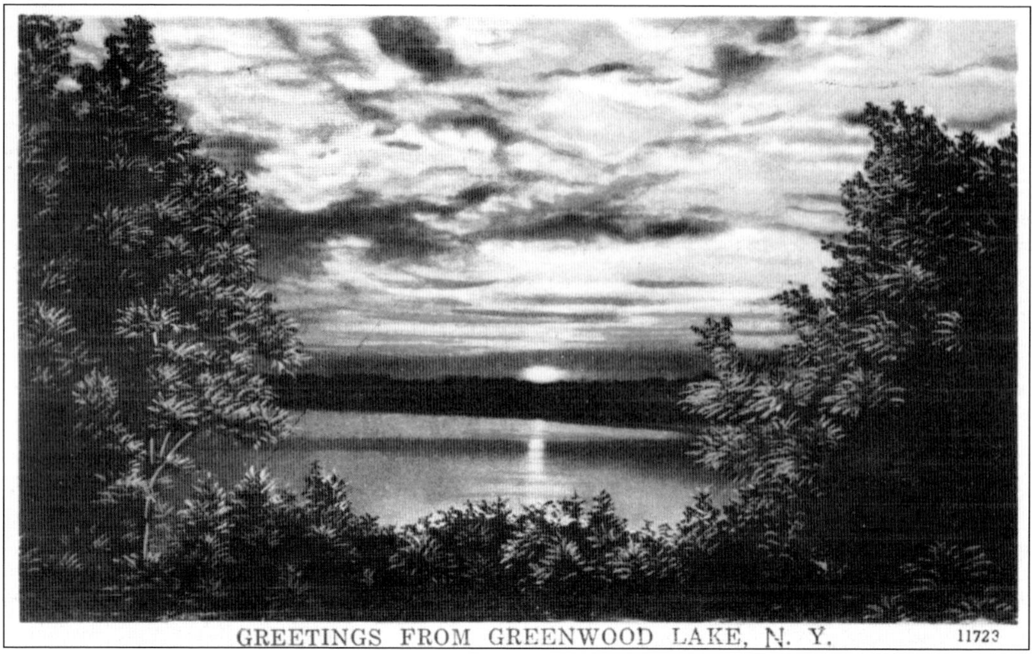

Just before entering New York, the AT turns northward and passes by the State Line Trail, a pathway that leads to Greenwood Lake, seen in these two linen postcards from the 1930s. The AT continues along Bellvale Mountain, which it has followed (with minor relocations along the ridgeline) since it was established in the 1920s and 1930s. Several rock outcroppings provide wide views of the lake just a few hundred feet below. Originally known as Long Pond, it has been enlarged substantially by two dams, one constructed in 1765 and the other in 1836. Roger Brickner, a 2,000-miler and one of the AT's original "trail angels," invited hikers in the 1970s and 1980s to stay at his Appalachia Cottage, above the lake. He continued the practice after moving to New Hampshire. (Above, courtesy of Colourpicture Publication; below, courtesy of Tichnor Bros., Inc.)

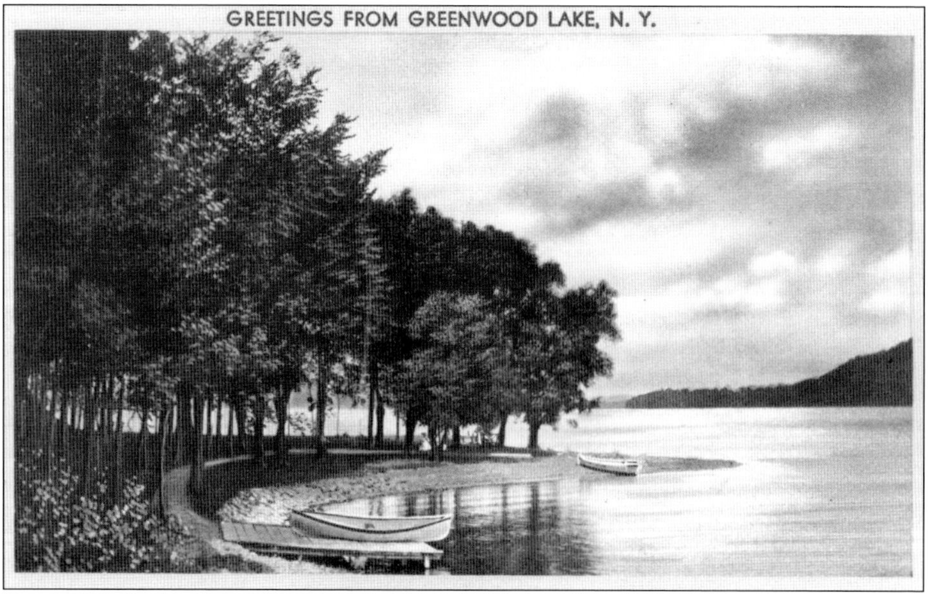

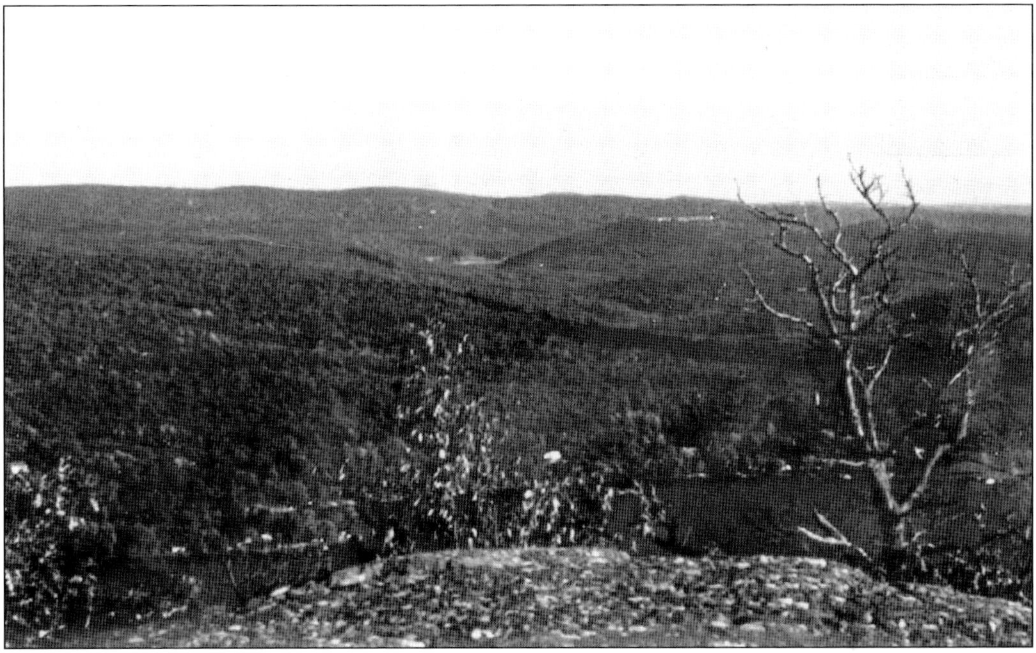

Most of the time, hikers on Bellvale Mountain photograph the beauty of Greenwood Lake directly below them. However, on September 11, 2001, Michael Rea, standing atop Prospect Rock, photographed the clouds of smoke rising above New York City after the attacks on the World Trade Center in Manhattan. (Courtesy of ATC.)

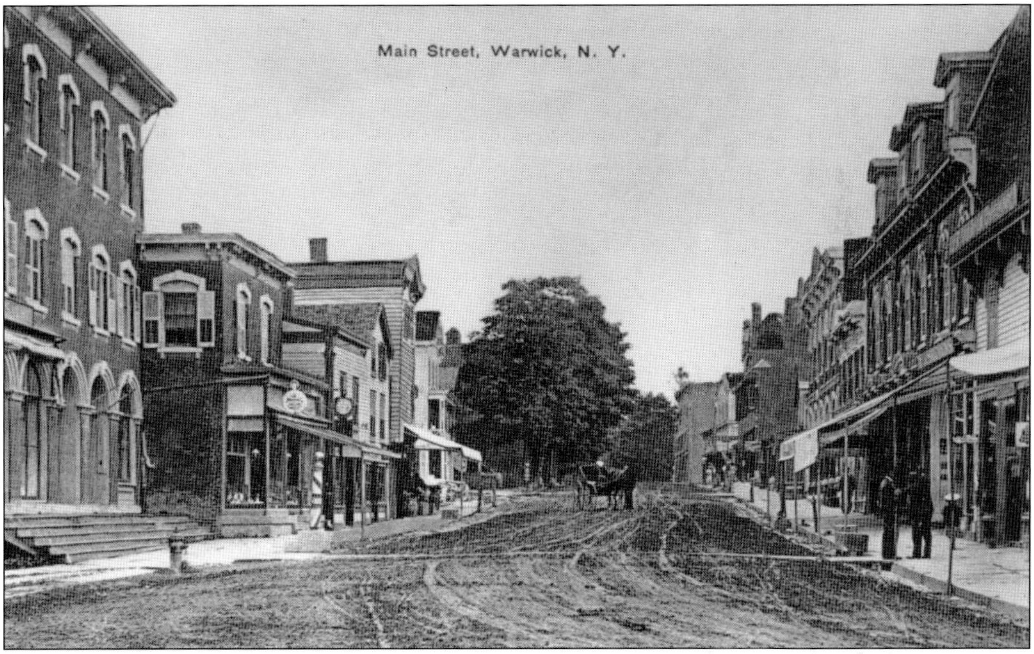

The Town of Warwick was officially established in 1788 and, as this postcard shows, its streets were still unpaved prior to the 1920s. Within a few years after the photograph was taken, a group of citizens established WATC, which took on the responsibility of constructing the AT in both New York and New Jersey. (Courtesy of WHS.)

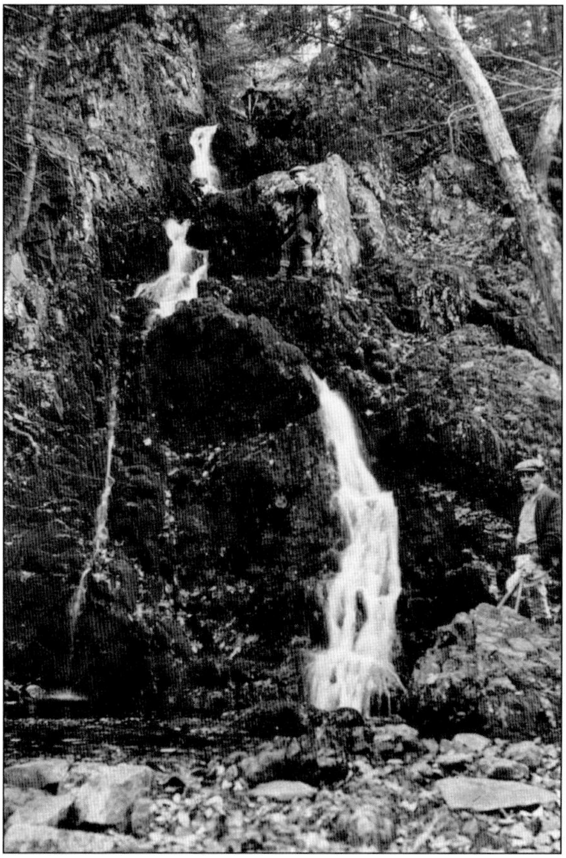

Fitzgerald Falls, photographed in the 1930s, was a popular destination long before the AT was routed next to it. V. Collins Chew, the author of *Underfoot: A Geologic Guide to the Appalachian Trail*, says Trout Creek tumbles 25 feet over slabs of gneiss with large coarse crystals in it. Hikers often fail to search out the rock walls above the falls that indicate former farms in the area. (Courtesy of WHS.)

Scenic Fitzgerald Falls is reached by a very easy walk of only 0.3 miles from Lakes Road, which enables large crowds of people to visit, especially on the weekends. Unfortunately, some of those visitors, either unthinkingly or uncaringly, leave behind so much trash that trail maintainers have filled large dump trucks with it. (Courtesy of ATC.)

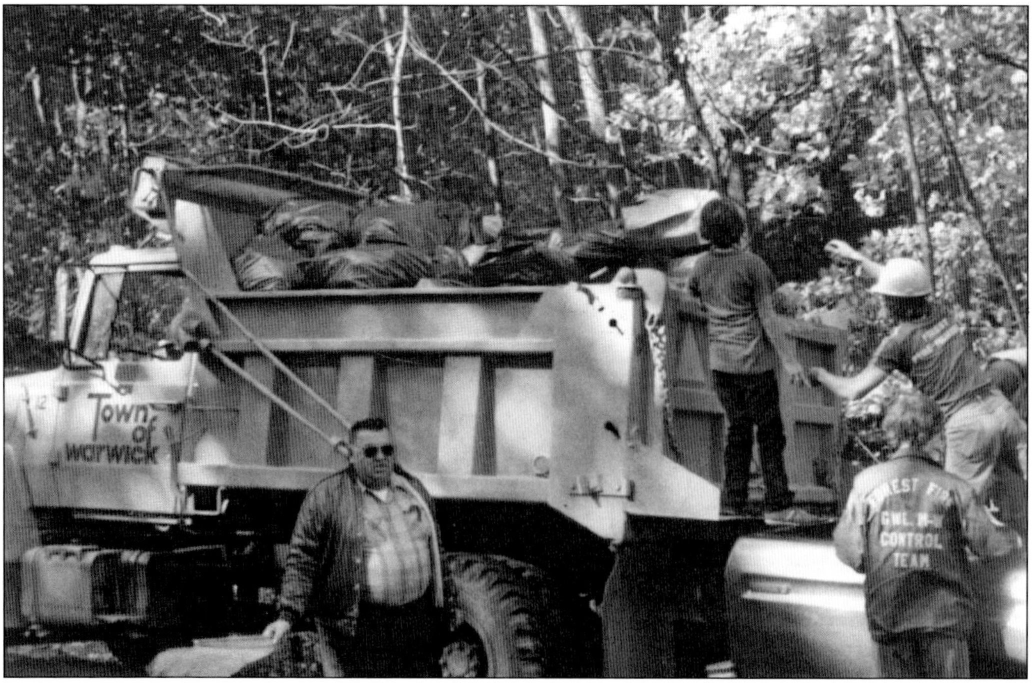

The ATC's biennial meeting in New Paltz, from May 27 to June 3, 1983, was attended by a number of trail luminaries, including Ruth Blackburn (left) and Raymond Hunt (right). Blackburn was president of the Potomac Appalachian Trail Club from 1965 to 1967 and was the outgoing ATC chair at this meeting. Hunt was a trail maintainer for three decades and the incoming ATC chair at the time of this photograph. (Courtesy of ATC.)

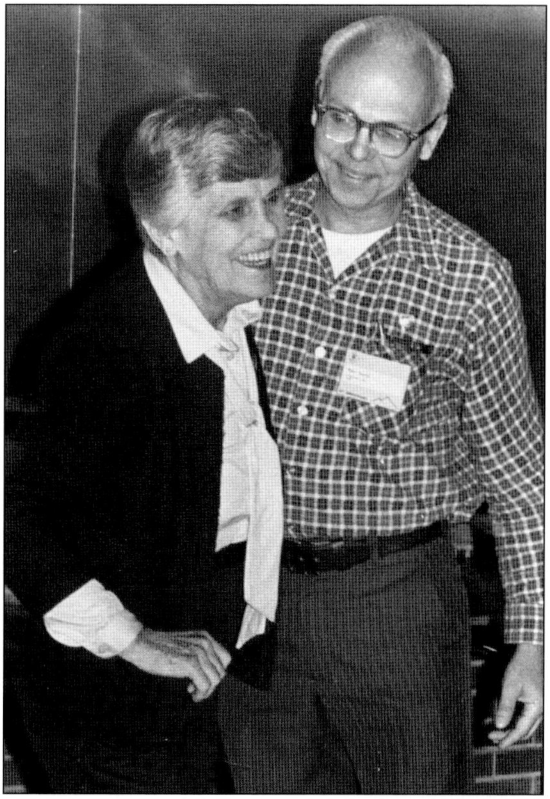

Two other people who were important figures in the history of the trail also attended the 1983 biennial meeting in New Paltz. Elizabeth Levers (left) was a chairperson of the Appalachian Trail Conference and Albert "Cap" Field (right) was the NYNJTC executive director from 1977 to 1980. (Courtesy of ATC.)

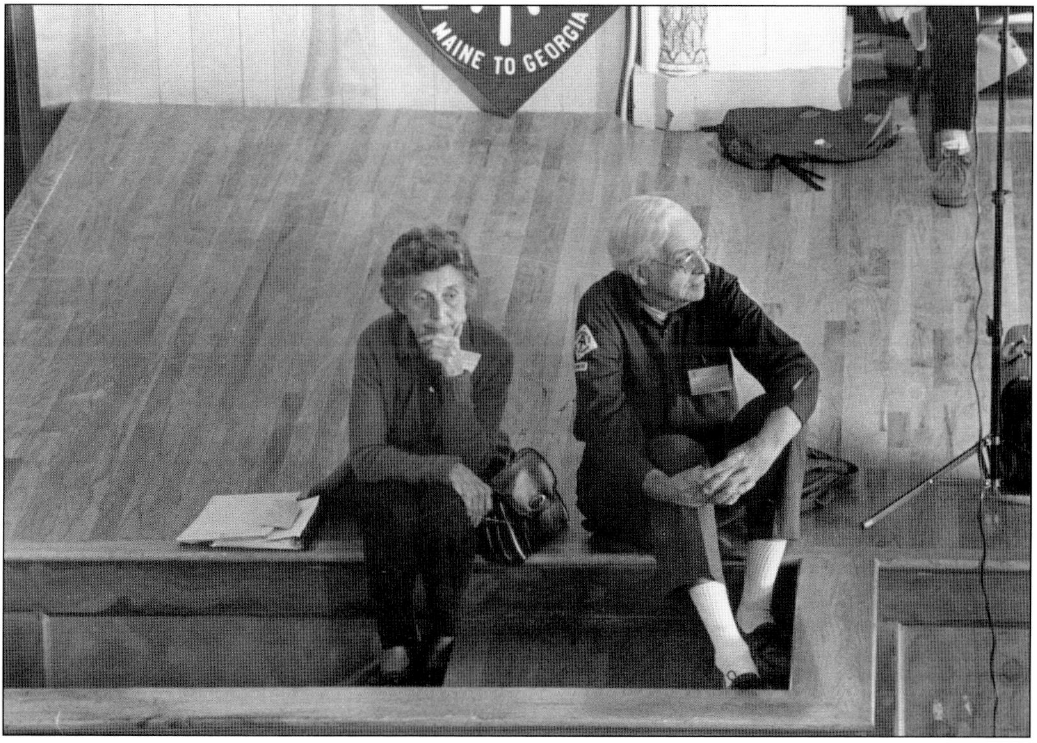

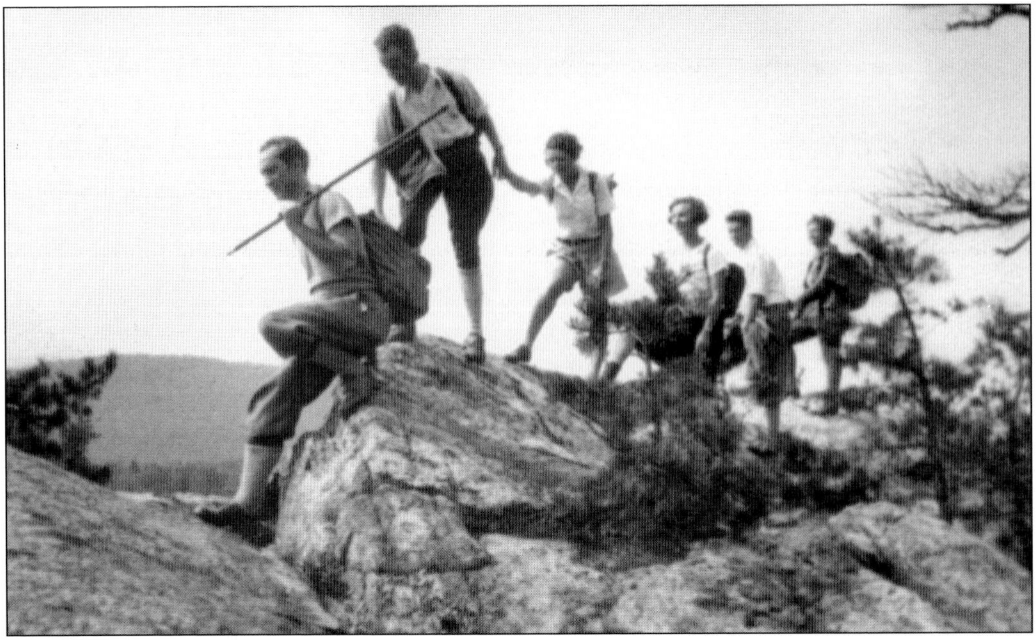

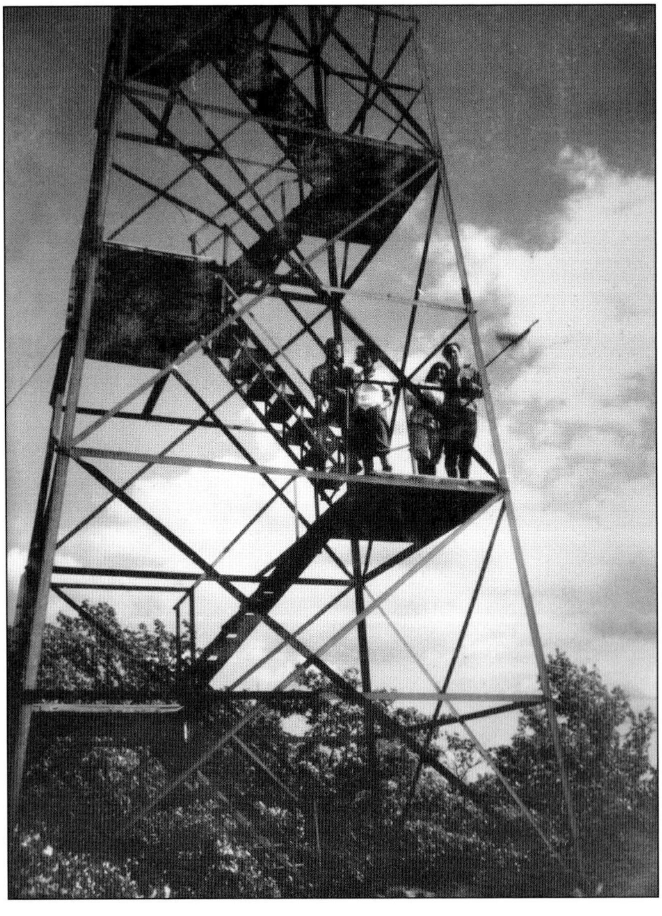

In the 1920s, William "Bill" Hoeferlin (left) led the Wanderbirds, a group he founded, across Sterling Ridge. For several decades, he published *Walking News*, providing outdoors information about New York and New Jersey. He also included some original poetry, such as "What's the sport legs were made for, / What's the purpose trails were laid for? / Well or ill, in debt or paid for / Troubles burden you, just walk them off." (Courtesy of NYNJTC.)

On May 30, 1930, unidentified hikers made the climb to the relatively new (erected in 1922) Sterling Mountain fire tower, located a short distance south of the present-day AT. The tower remains a popular destination, as the 360-degree view takes in Sterling Lake, Greenwood Lake, and, on clear days, the New York City skyline. (Courtesy of NYNJTC.)

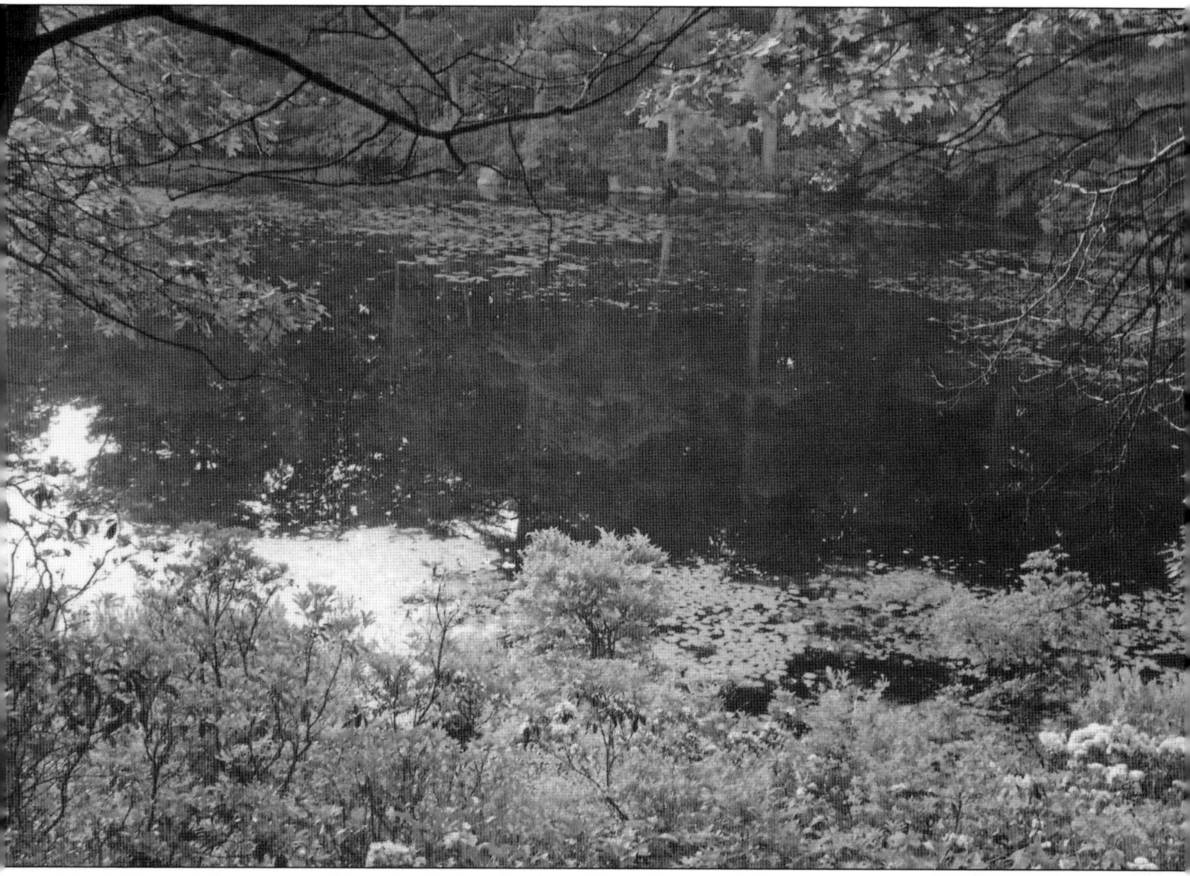

Little Dam Lake is passed by the AT in Sterling State Forest. After it came into their hands in the late 1800s, the Harriman family offered the forest as a park to New York in the 1950s. In an amazingly short-sighted move, the state refused the offer, saying the property contained too many wetlands and other problems and that the state already had all of the parklands it would ever need. Plans by new owners in the 1980s to build extensive subdivisions aroused public interest enough that New Jersey obtained 2,100 acres by condemnation. In 1996, after years of negotiations at local, state, and federal levels, the owners agreed to sell the bulk of the forest in New York at a cost of multiple millions of dollars in federal, state, and private funds. It literally took an act of Congress to save this property, which could have been obtained for a pittance when originally offered. (Courtesy of ATC.)

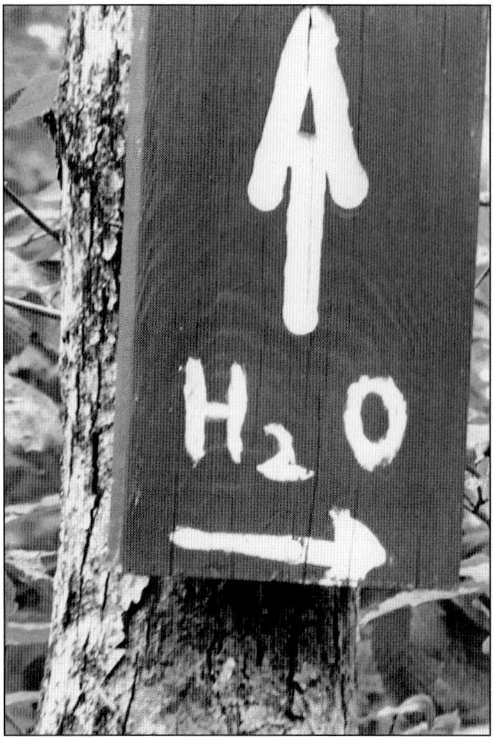

Just as directional signs play a role as people drive along a highway, they are also important on the AT. This sign near Warwick pointed out an essential need while hiking—water. Gone are the days when a hiker could drink from such sources without treating it. The increase in people visiting the AT has brought a corresponding increase in the appearance of giardia. (Courtesy of ATC.)

The Ramapo Mountain Hiking Club was one of the many clubs that were established around 1900 in New York and New Jersey. As can be seen, wool clothing was the choice of the day. The high, leather upper portion of these boots protected legs from overgrowing brush, and hobnails in the soles provided traction on soft or muddy terrain. (Courtesy of NYNJTC.)

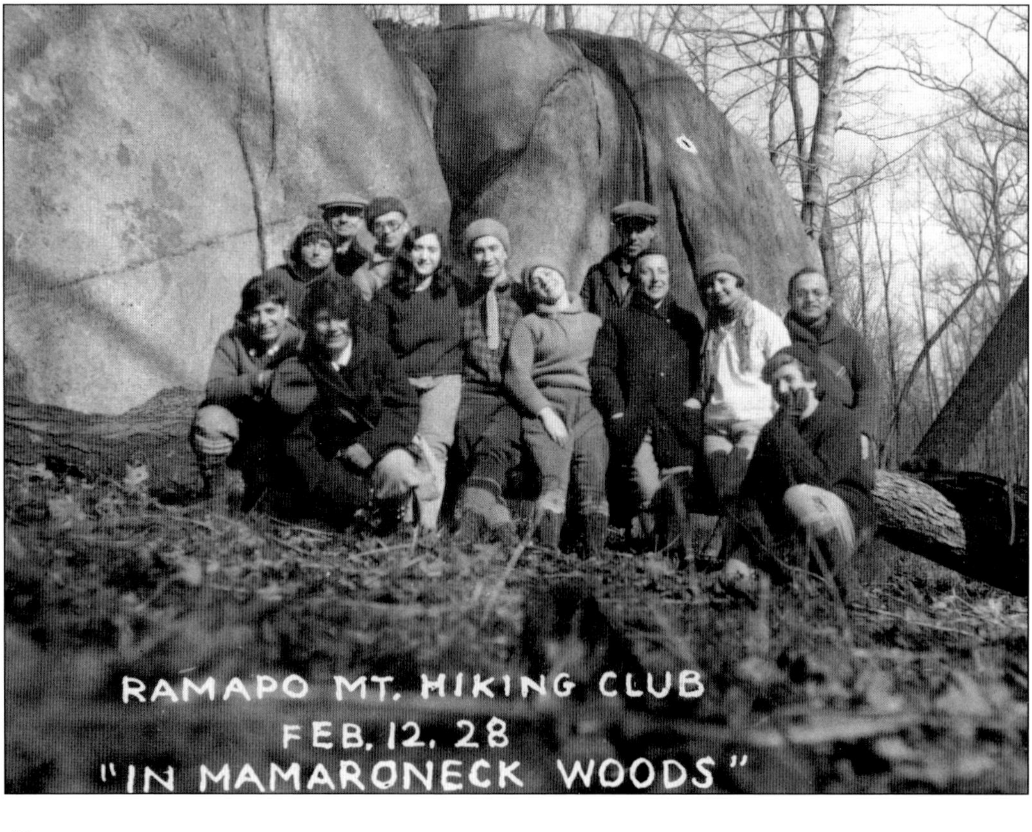

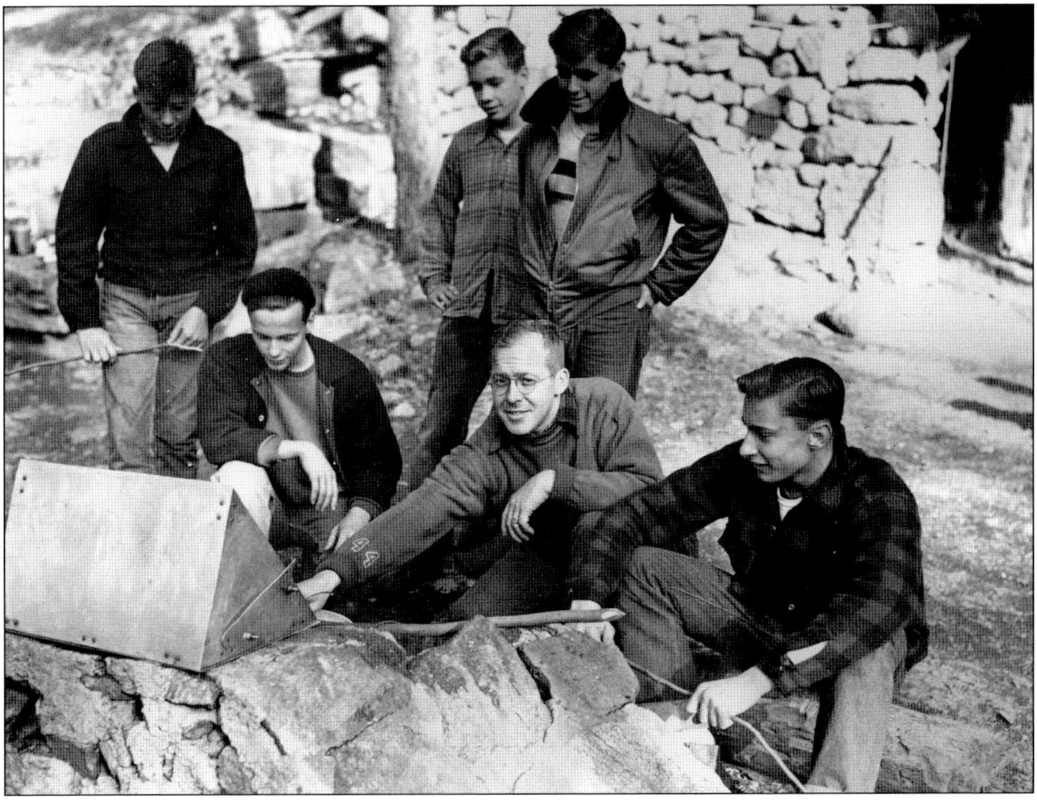

On November 6, 1949, one of Harriman State Park's official photographers, J. Boland, photographed a group from New York City cooking at Dutch Doctor Shelter, south of the AT in Harriman State Park. From left to right are (sitting) Harold Lynde Jr., William E. Austin, and Boyd Roche; (standing) Frank Couch, Robert Ellis, and John Ellis. (Courtesy of PIPC.)

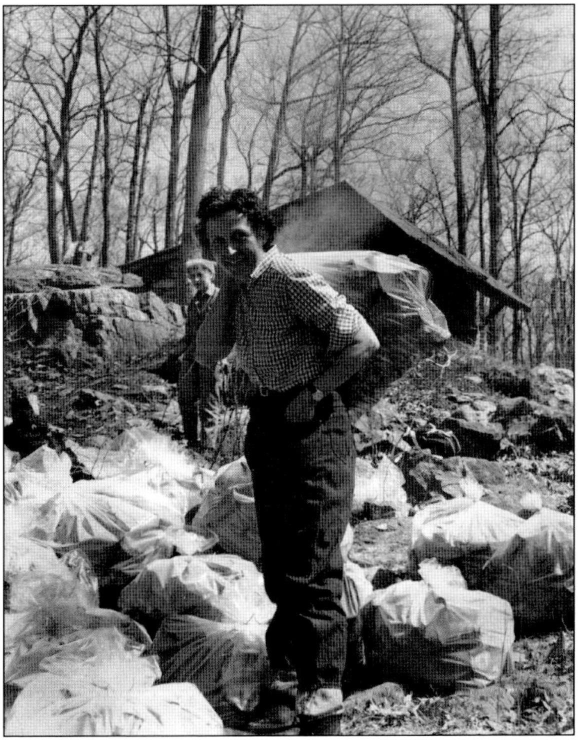

Elizabeth "Liz" Levers was photographed by Frank J. Oliver in April 1965 with the bags of trash collected at Dutch Doctor Shelter during NYNJTC's first Litter Day, an annual event she is credited with inspiring. She was active in hiking from the 1930s to the 1990s and contacted close to 150 landowners about routing the AT through their property in the early days of the trail. (Courtesy ATC.)

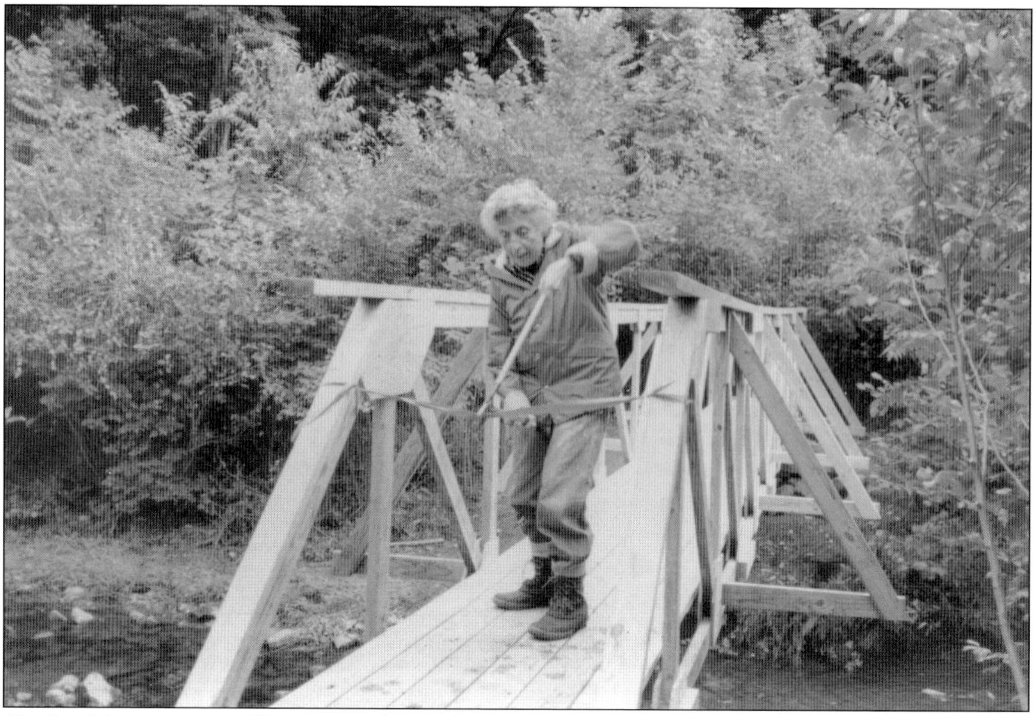

Elizabeth Levers was still active in the trail community 25 years after NYNJTC's first Litter Day. She is seen here cutting the ribbon for the opening of the bridge over Trout Brook, near Fitzgerald Falls and Lakes Road, in September 1990. Among her many other trail-related activities, she was the coeditor of the *New York Walk Book* and the first female president of NYNJTC. (Courtesy of ATC.)

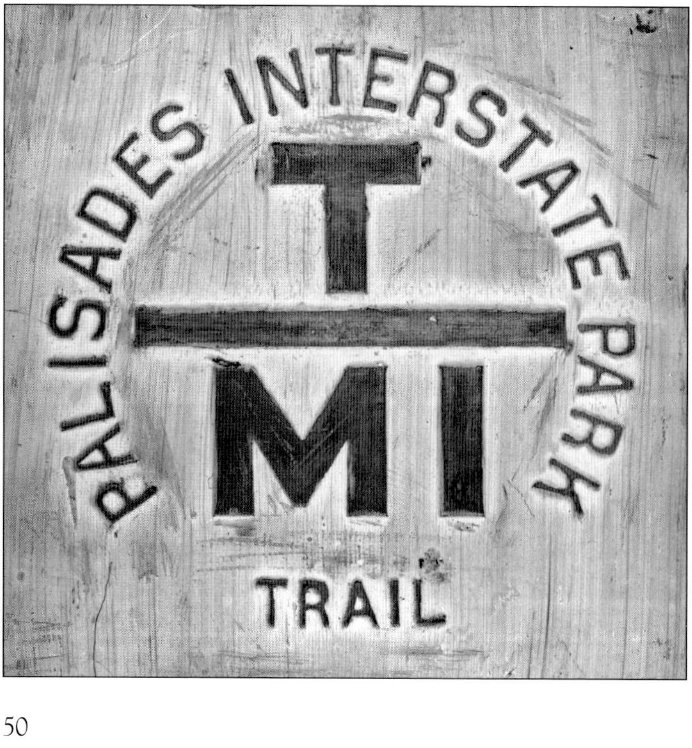

Maj. William A. Welch, the manager and chief engineer of Palisades Interstate Park, designed and hand-made the original square copper AT markers at Harriman and Bear Mountain State Parks. He also made them for other trails, such as this one for the Tuxedo-Mount Ivy Trail. In addition to aluminum AT markers also made by Welch, Arthur Perkins, ATC chairman from 1928 to 1931, prepared some galvanized iron markers with black stenciled lettering. (Courtesy of WHS.)

William Hoeferlin leaned against *Ganus Quan* ("Stone Giants") on the Tower Trail in Harriman State Park in 1936. The flared pants he is wearing are known as jodhpurs, which originated with horseback riders and the military. They were popular with hikers in the early 1900s, as the flared thighs permitted freedom of movement while the cuffs accommodated the calf-high hobnail boots. (Courtesy of NYNJTC.)

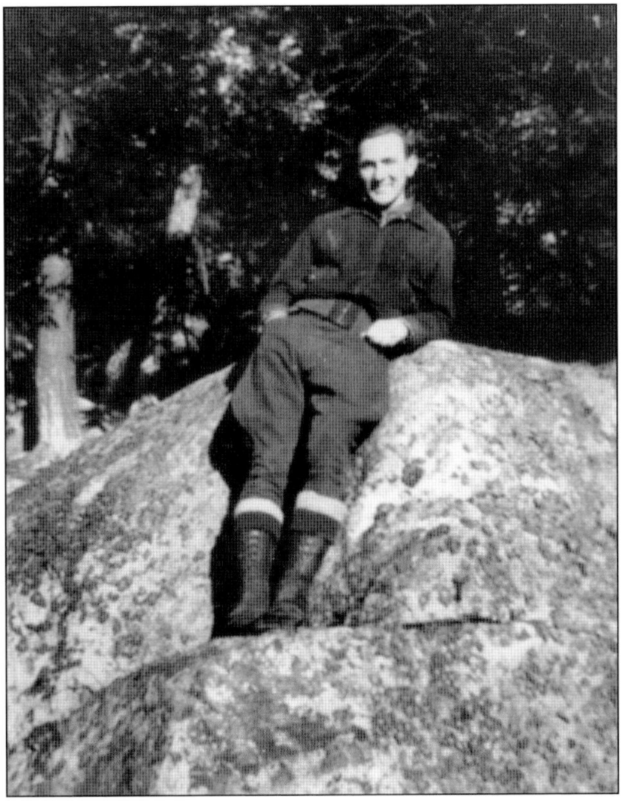

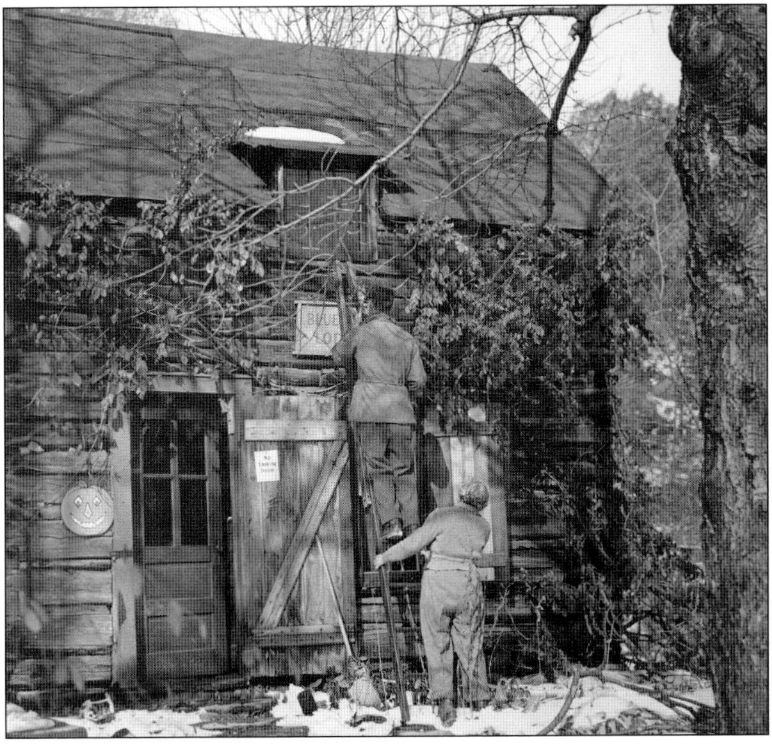

William Hoeferlin had long dreamed of owning a woodlands place, and, on November 8, 1953, he put a sign on the log cabin he had recently purchased, dubbing it Bluebird Lodge. He was active in many capacities with the NYNJTC, was the author of the *Harriman Park Trail Guide* (1944–1976), and created the *Hikers Region Maps* that covered trails from metropolitan New York to the Catskills. (Courtesy of NYNJTC.)

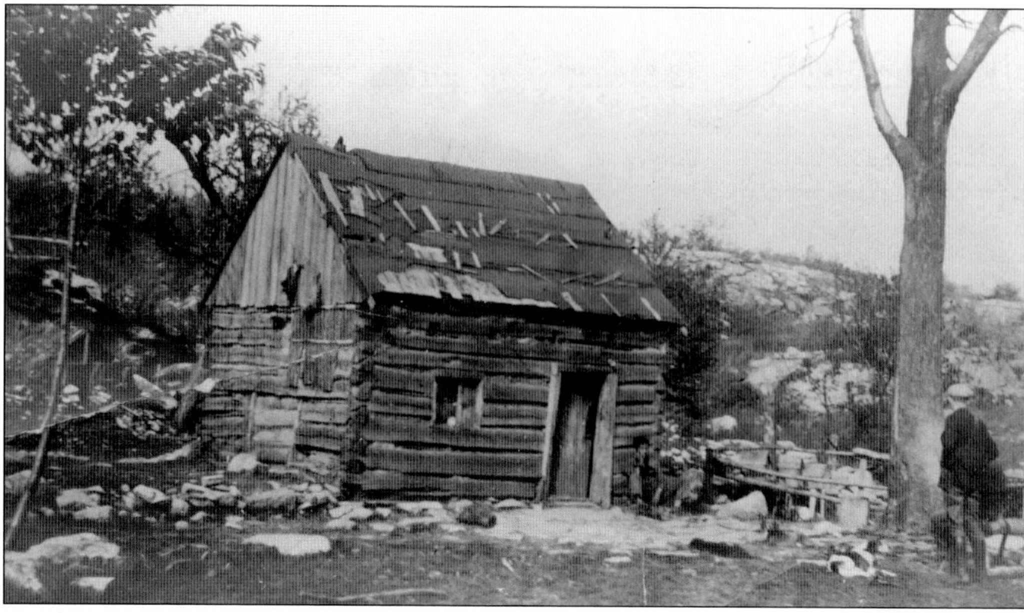

People were still living on the land when Harriman State Park was established, and some, such as the Ramsey Conklin family, were permitted to stay for several years. Members of the Conklin family lived here from 1779 to 1935, when the CCC completed work on Pine Meadow Lake. The waters flooded most of their land, but not their cabin, photographed here around 1934, which was in ruins by 1942. (Courtesy of NYNYTC.)

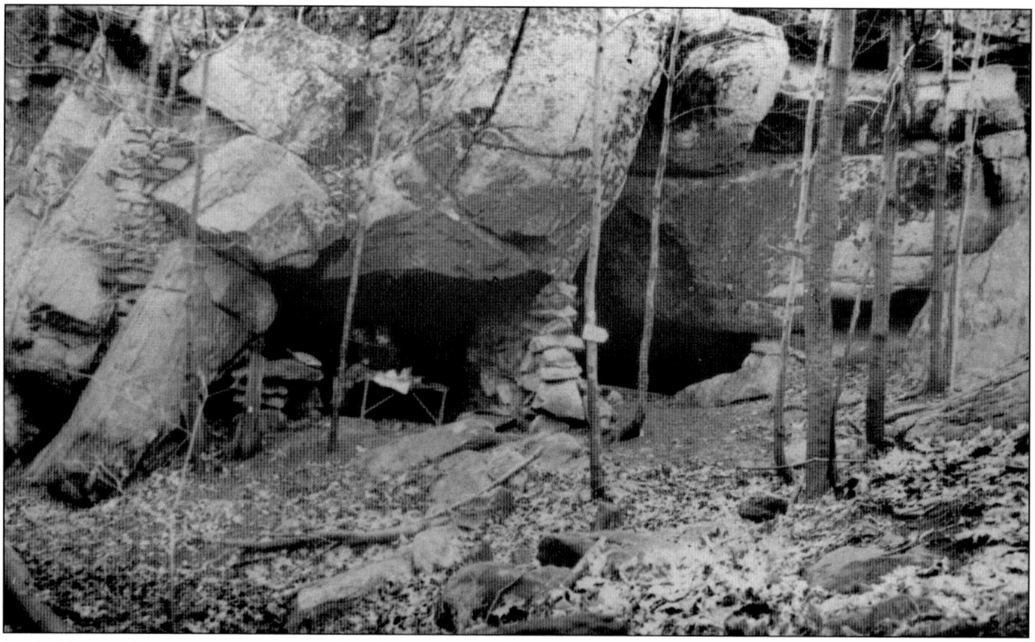

In 1922, while scouting a route for the Long Path, a 356-mile trail that passes through Harriman State Park, J. Ashton Allis found Stockbridge Cave, which officially became the Stockbridge Cave Shelter in 1928. Allis was an early member of the Fresh Air Club, formed in New York City in the 1870s, a founder of the Palisades Interstate Park Trail Conference, and an ATC secretary. (Courtesy of NYNJTC.)

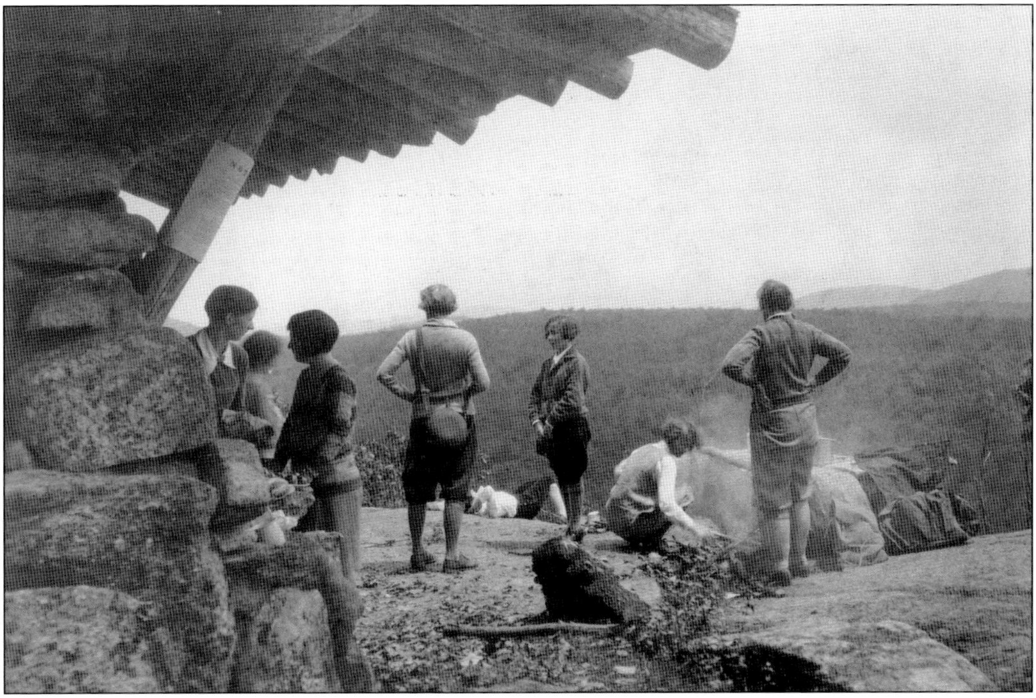

Built in 1927, Big Hill Shelter was one of the first three shelters constructed in Harriman State Park. Designed by Maj. William A. Welch, its three-sided rock walls with a built-in fireplace established the style that other park shelters would follow. This group of hikers visited the shelter in 1932. On clear days, there is a view of the New York City skyline. (Courtesy of ATC.)

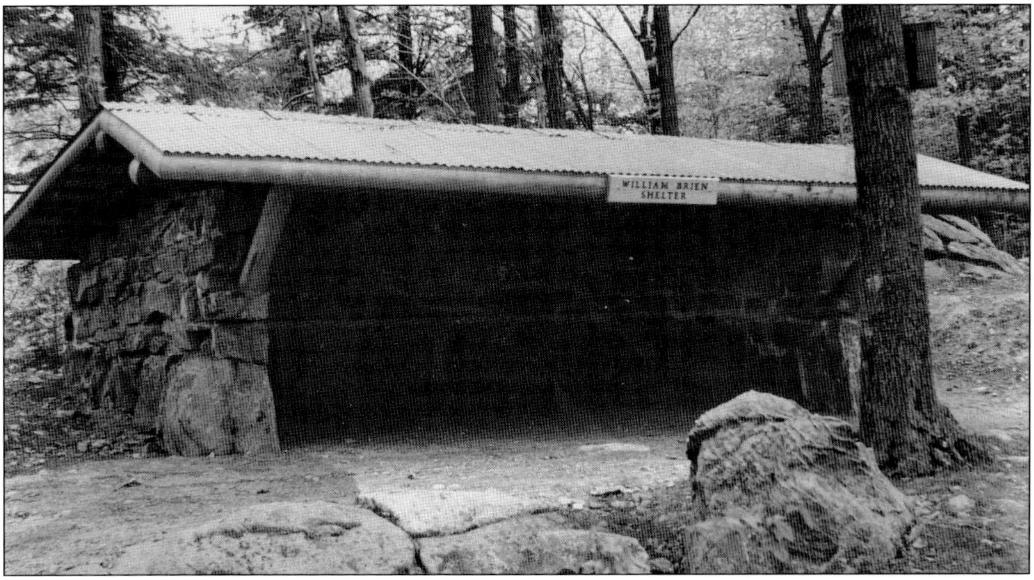

In 1957, the William Brien Memorial Shelter, named for the first president of the New York Ramblers (established in 1923), was built beside Island Pond, the first body of water northbound AT hikers encounter after entering Harriman State Park. An easy walk from nearby Arden Valley Road, the shelter was dismantled in 1973 due to vandalism. Letterrock Shelter, north of Fingerboard Mountain, was renamed in Brien's honor. (Courtesy of PIPC.)

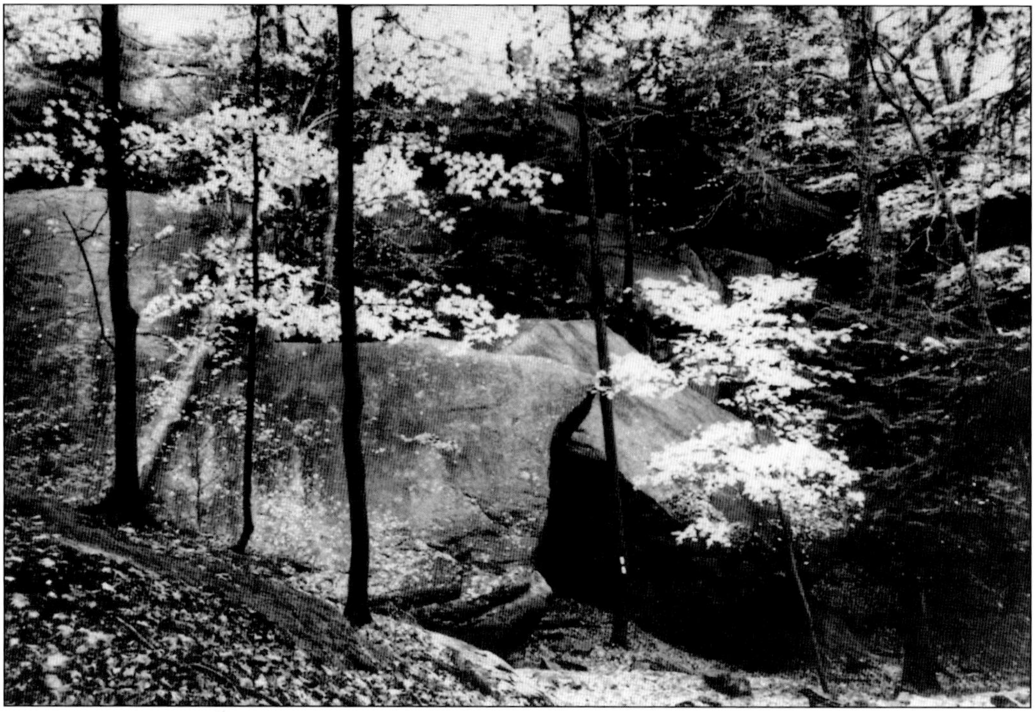

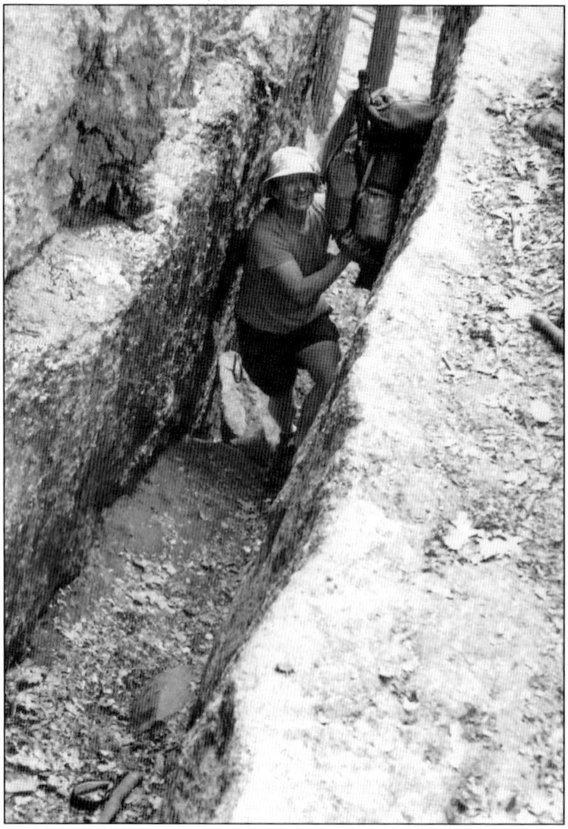

The Lemon Squeezer has been a part of the AT since the trail's first section was built and blazed in Harriman State Park in 1922–1923. First-time hikers of the area are sometimes confused that the trail's double-blaze marking indicates that they should go between the two rocks. (Courtesy of ATC.)

As generations of hikers have had to do before her, Laurie Messick Adkins had to take off and lift her pack in order to make it through the Lemon Squeezer's narrow cleft of coarse gneiss during her fourth complete hike of the AT, in 2007. (Courtesy of Leonard M. Adkins.)

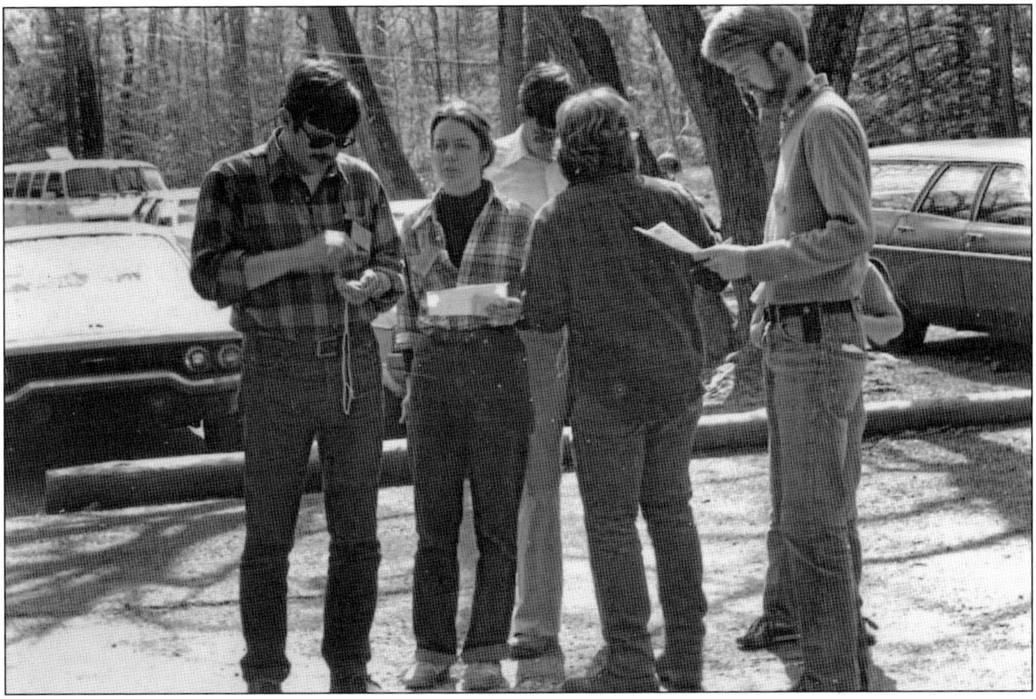

There is an almost never-ending list of undertakings that AT volunteers perform in order to build, maintain, and protect the trail. Here, in 1982, NYNJTC members prepare to take an orienteering course. Becoming skilled in map and compass work better enables volunteers to follow the AT's boundaries to monitor for encroachments or other illegal activities. (Courtesy of ATC.)

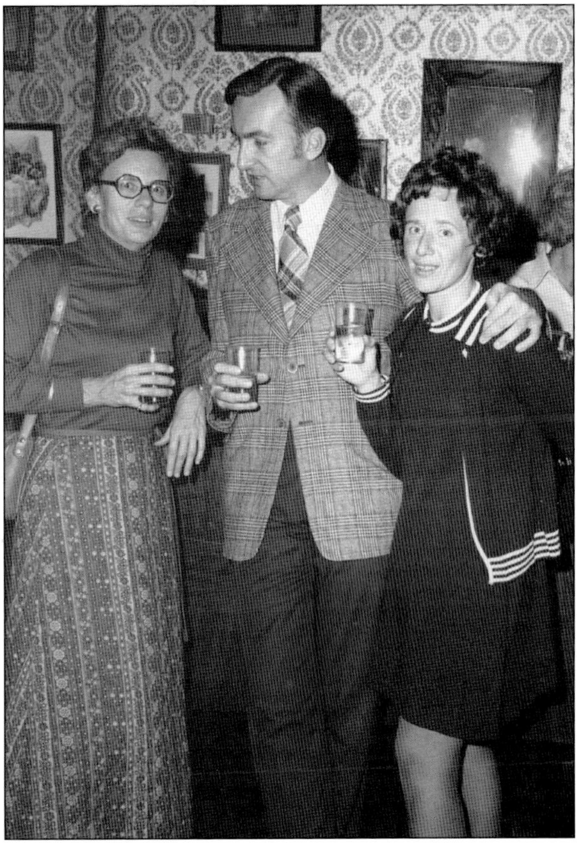

George Zoebelein (center), photographed with Ann Sutterthwaite (left) and Connie Carter (right) by Edwin W. Fitzpatrick on November 11, 1974, was president of the NYNJTC from 1964 to 1970 and ATC chair from 1975 to 1979. His background in accounting helped ATC overcome a financial deficit, and he is also credited with instituting the policy of ATC helping volunteers become more proficient in trail building and maintaining skills. (Courtesy of ATC.)

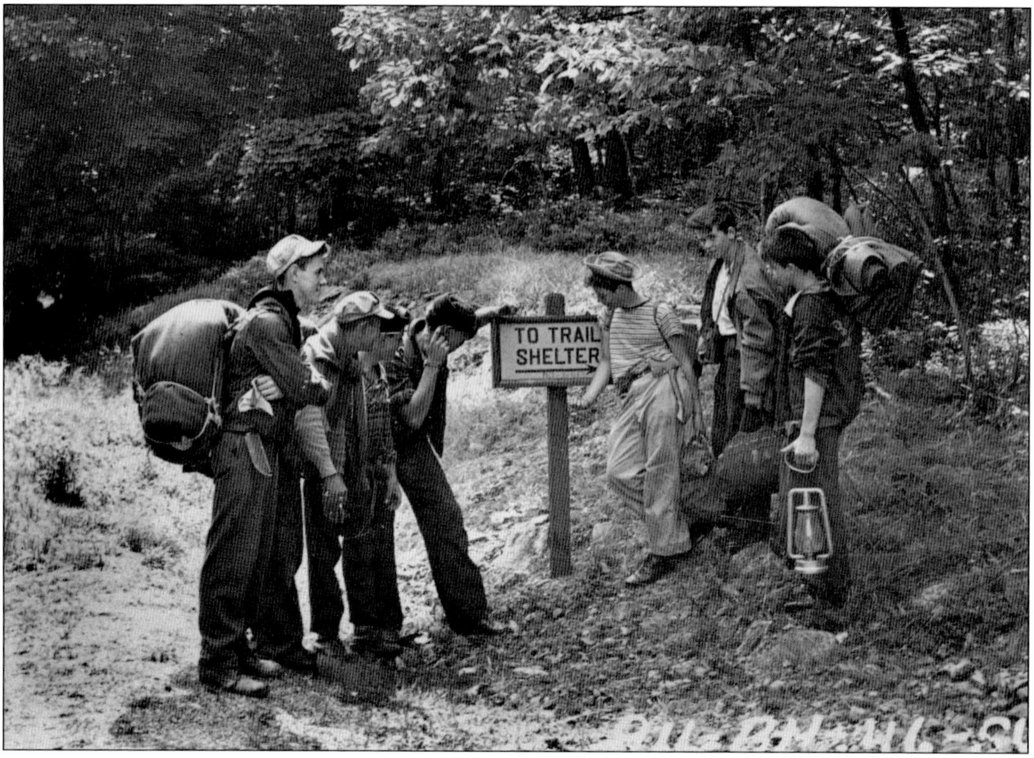

Although none of them are in uniform, a group of Boy Scouts begins their hike to Fingerboard Shelter in 1946. Boy Scouts have utilized the AT since its inception, but they have also given much back to the trail by volunteering with local AT maintaining clubs. Older boys have constructed outhouses, bridges, benches, and other structures in order to meet the requirements of becoming an Eagle Scout. (Courtesy of PIPC.)

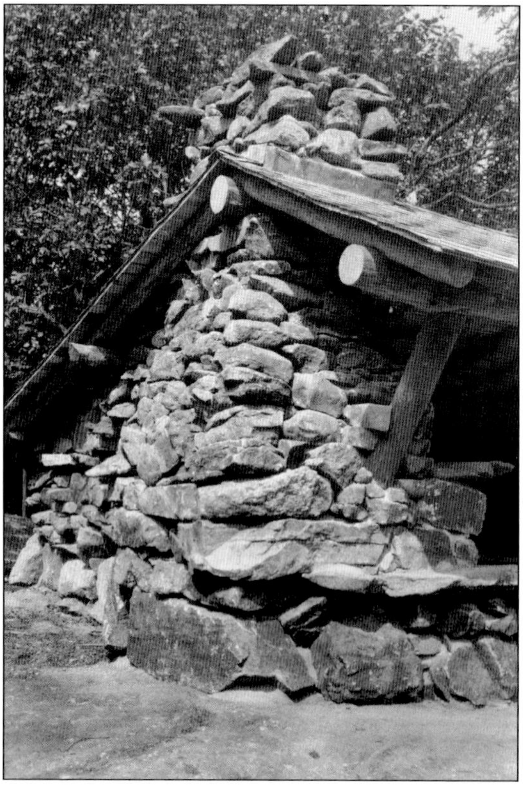

This close-up photograph of the Fingerboard Shelter, taken just after it was completed in 1928, shows the materials and methods that were employed in the making of shelters throughout Harriman State Park. Almost all of the materials, including the wood and the rocks, were gathered from nearby. A number of shelters were built by the CCC, which had close to 10 camps in or near the park from 1933 to 1942. (Courtesy of PIPC.)

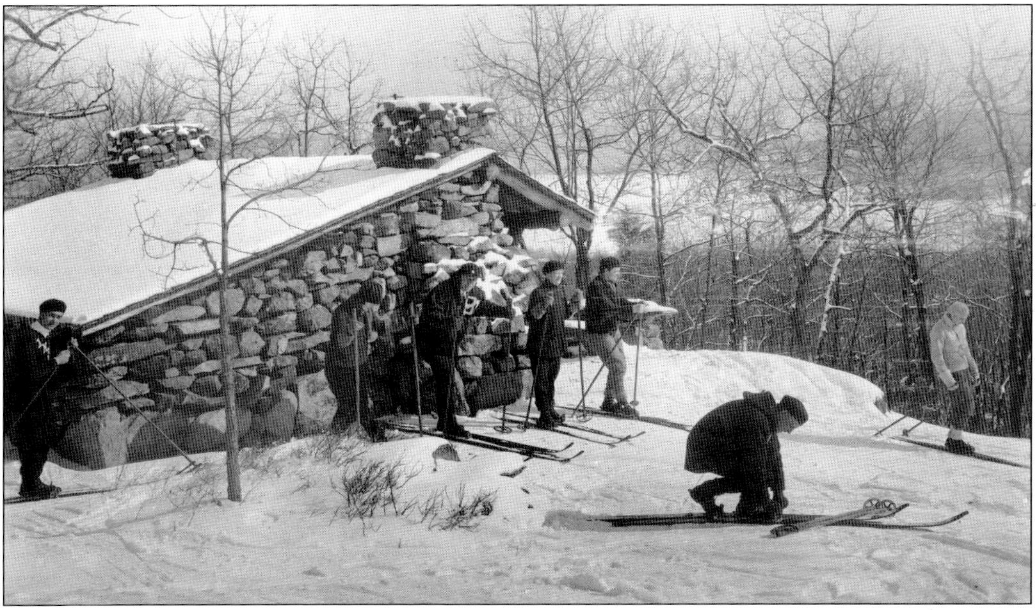

Outings on the AT are not limited to the warmer months. In the 1930s, the Bear Mountain Sports Association—the man on the far left is wearing the association's official sweater—arranged this cross-country skiing trip to Fingerboard Shelter. The association sponsored several activities, including canoeing, ice-skating, ski jumping, and swimming, in Harriman and Bear Mountain State Parks for many decades. (Courtesy of ATC.)

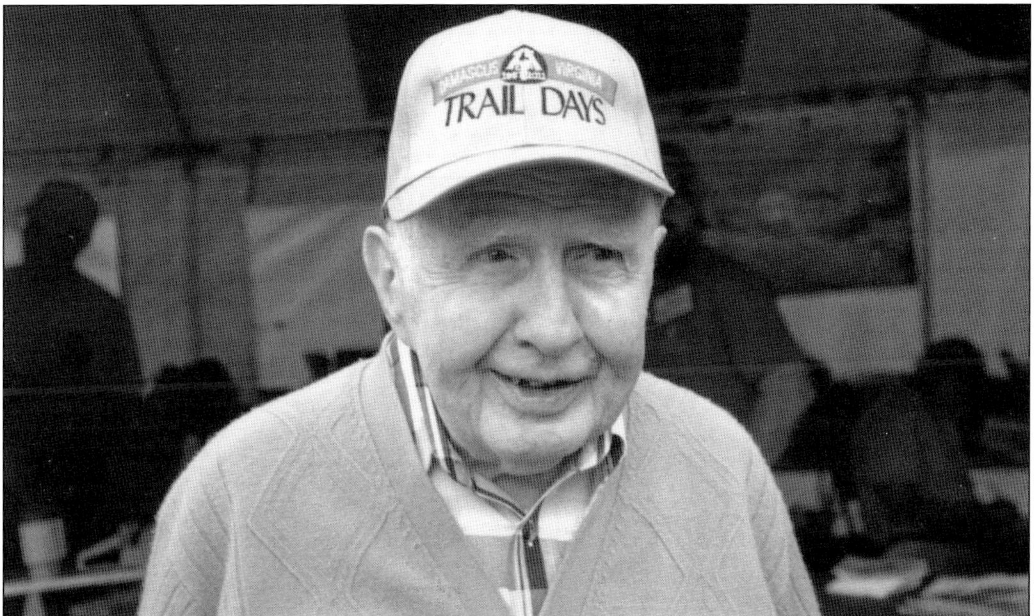

In 1951, three years after Earl Shaffer became the AT's first thru-hiker, Gene Espy, at the age of 24, became the second person to complete the trail in one continuous hike, walking from late May to late September. In a bit of serendipity, he happened to run into Chester Dzeiengielewski, who was walking southward on his way to becoming the trail's first southbound thru-hiker. (Courtesy of ATC.)

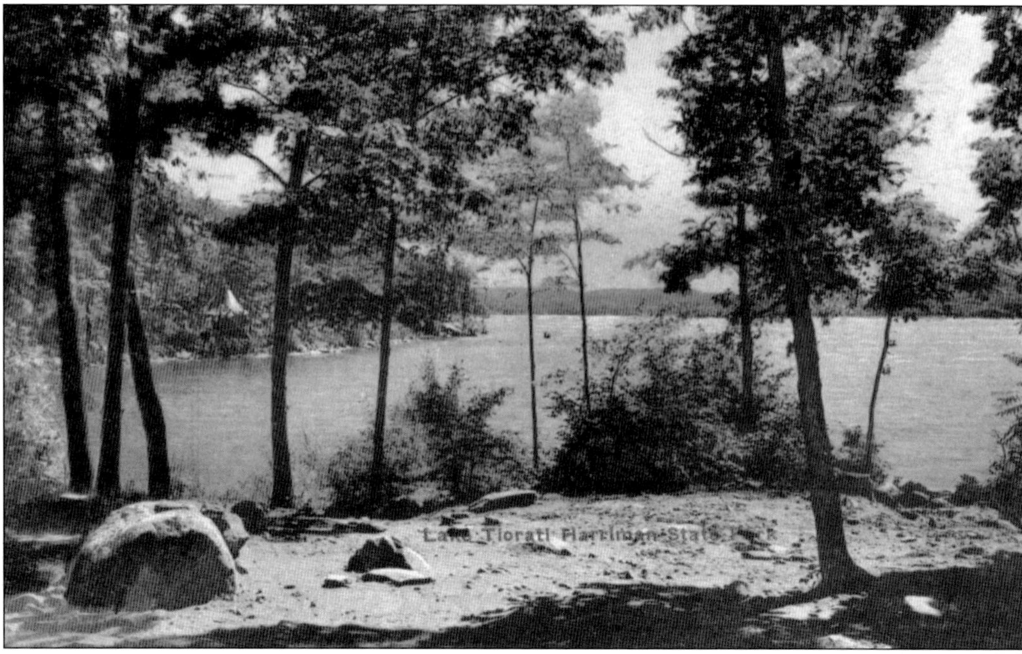

This hand-colored linen postcard of Lake Tiorati was mailed on September 18, 1947. The lake was originally two ponds known as Cedar Pond (about a half mile long) and Little Cedar Pond (a much smaller wet area), but they became one when a dam was built in 1915. (Courtesy of the Commissioners of the Palisades Interstate Park.)

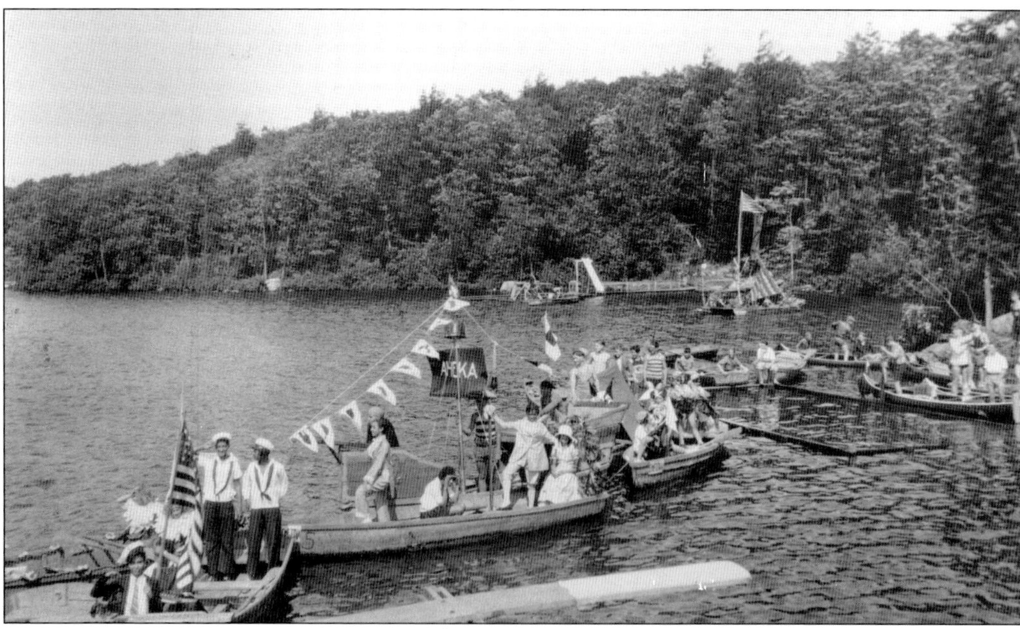

The Lake Tiorati Water Carnival in August 1927 was sponsored by Cedar Lake Camp, operated by the Young Men's and Young Women's Hebrew Association of New Jersey. Several such camps, operated by the Boy Scouts, the Girl Scouts, and religious organizations, were established on the shores of Harriman State Park's lakes. PIPC provided the needed medical and security services for the camps. (Courtesy of PIPC.)

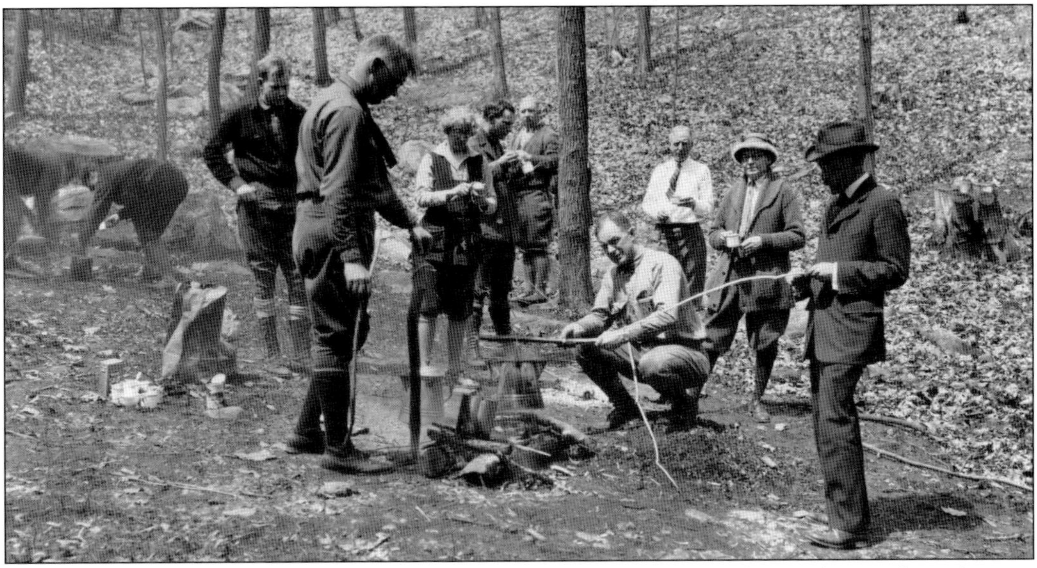

Ruby M. Jolliffe (center, behind the fire) became PIPC's first female employee when she was named director of group summer camps in 1920, a job she held for 28 years. Once called "a curious mixture of dignity and devil-may-care" by a commission employee, she created the idea of PIPC's group summer camps by establishing a YWCA camp at Blauvelt Park, on South Mountain, in 1912. (Courtesy of PIPC.)

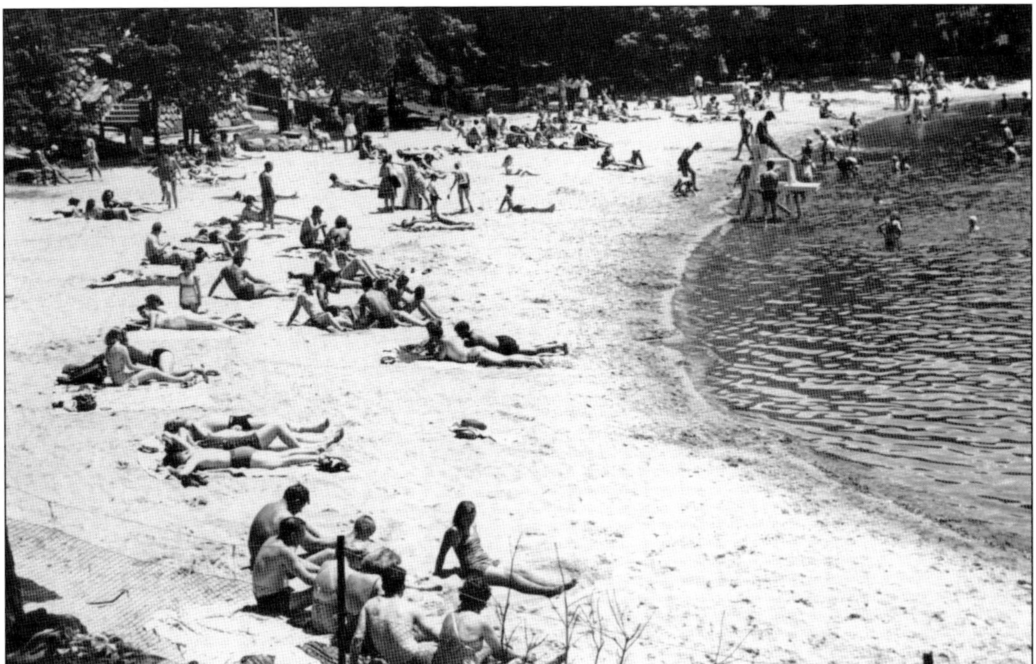

Harriman State Park photographer J. Boland captured the popularity of the Lake Tiorati beach and bathing area in 1946. Although the AT has been rerouted a number of times in the area near this body of water, the trail has always remained within a short distance of the lake, making it a popular side trip for hikers to enjoy swimming, showers, and snacks from the concession stand. (Courtesy of PIPC.)

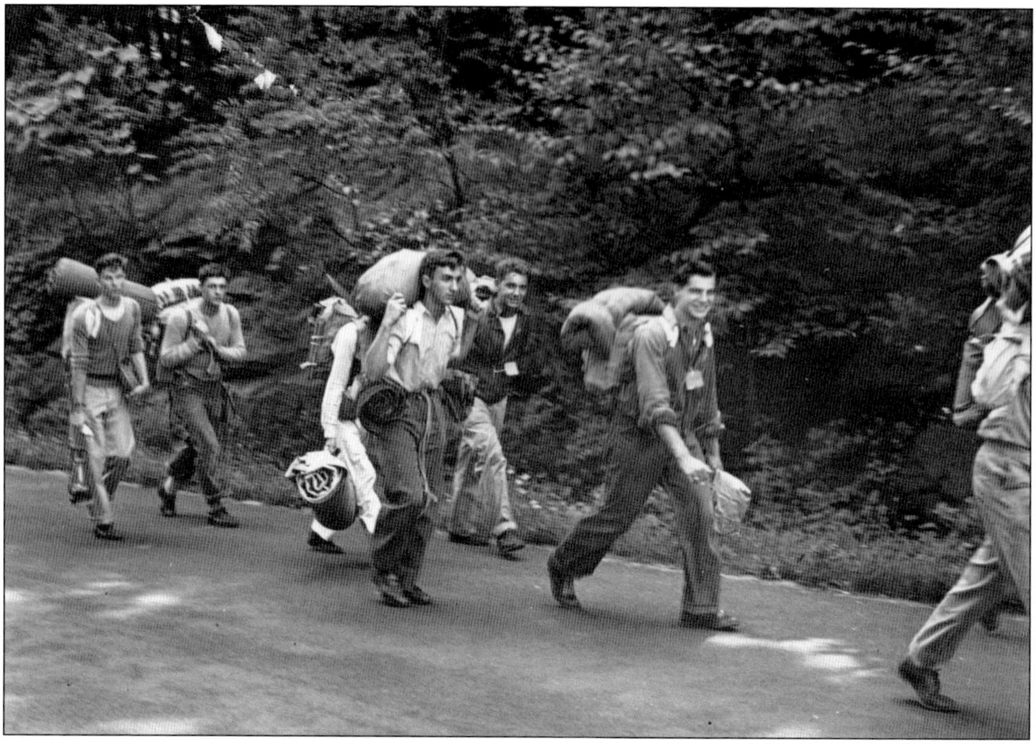

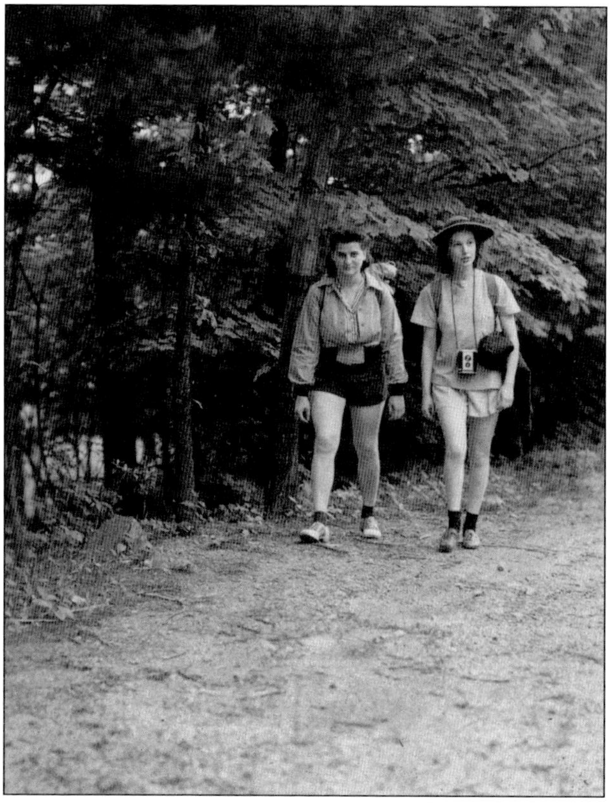

On the same day in 1946 that J. Boland photographed the many swimmers and sunbathers at Lake Tiorati (previous page), he also took this photograph of hikers setting out for a trailhead on Seven Lakes Drive. All of the young men are using soft-sided rucksacks, as aluminum frame backpacks were not available until Dick Kelty popularized them by producing them in his garage in the 1950s.

Two young women set out for a hike from Lake Tiorati in 1942. Women have always been active in hiking and maintaining the AT, but they were a small minority of those attempting thru-hikes until the late 1980s and early 1990s. They now make up approximately 25 percent of those who have reported hiking the entire trail to ATC. (Courtesy of PIPC.)

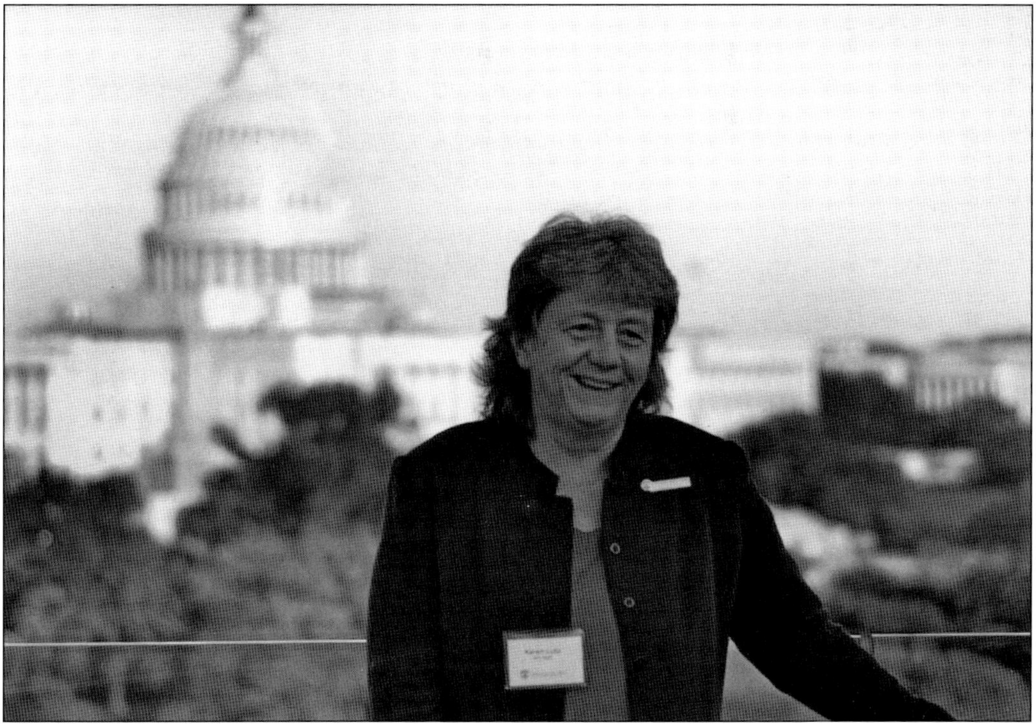

ATC has satellite offices in New England, the Mid-Atlantic, Virginia, and the southern states to maintain relations with local maintaining clubs, communities, and governments. Karen Lutz, who thru-hiked the AT in 1978, has been a regional representative and, later, the director of the Mid-Atlantic region (includes New Jersey and New York) since 1988. Lutz was photographed by Stacey Marshall during a conservation leaders awards ceremony in Washington, DC, in 2012. (Courtesy of ATC.)

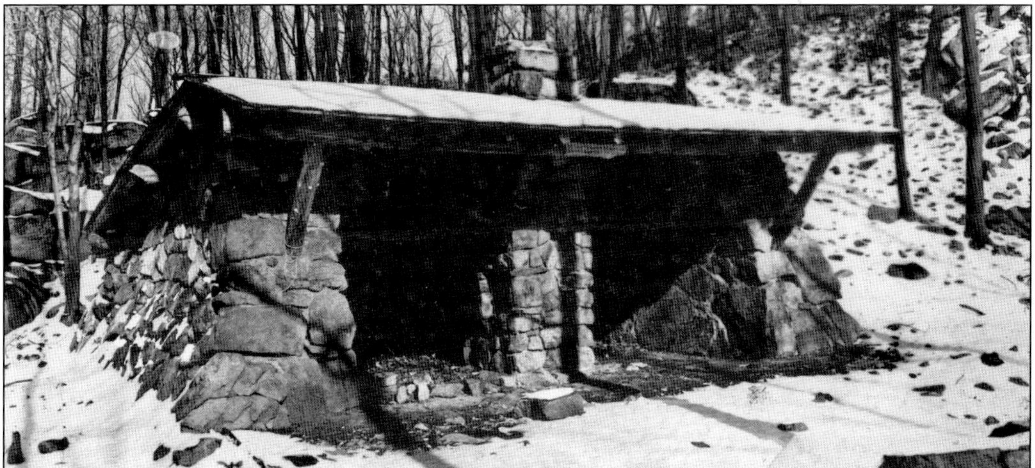

The Letterrock Shelter (now the Brien Memorial Shelter) is located on its namesake mountain and was built in 1933 by the CCC. The mountain's original name was Lettered Rock, said to have referred to Native American symbols that were painted on the rock. Another story states that a man who returned from the mountains with silver coins said he found them underneath a "lettered rock." (Courtesy of PIPC.)

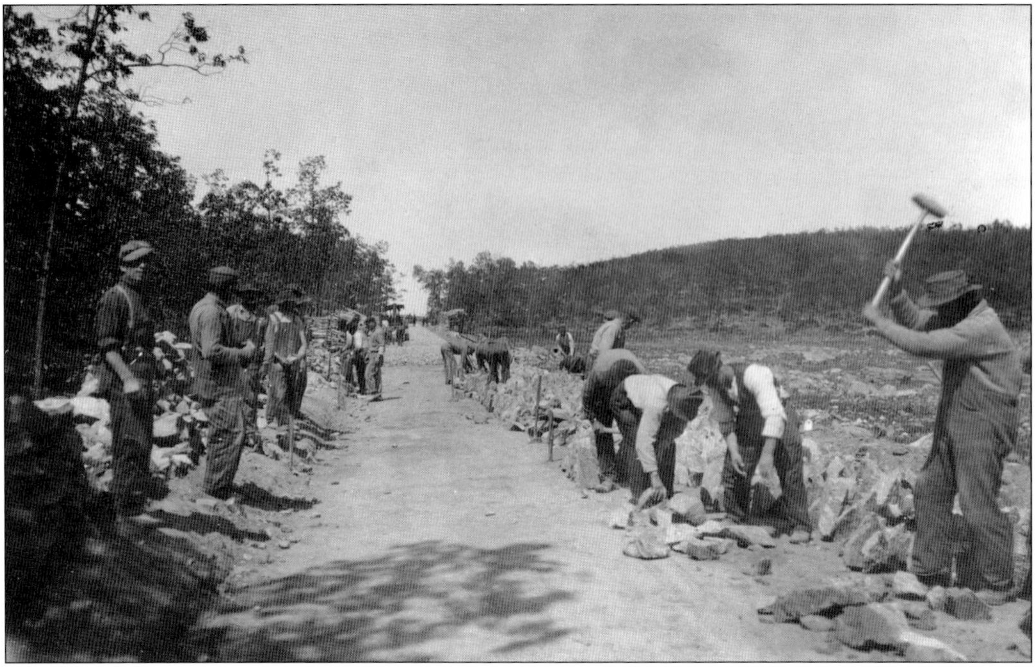

Construction of Seven Lakes Drive began in 1913 to connect the lands located within Harriman and Bear Mountain State Parks. As this 1920s photograph shows, the construction was labor intensive. The lakes the road goes by are Sebago, Kanawauke, Skannatati, Askoti, Tiorati, Silver Mine, and Queensboro. The road also provides two access points to the AT as well as a third via Arden Valley Road. (Courtesy of PIPC.)

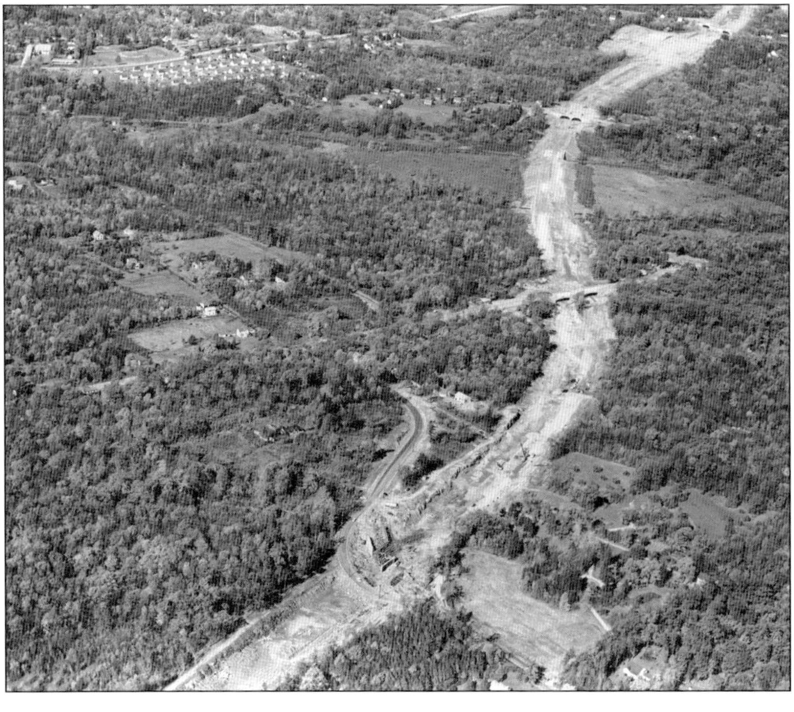

L.F. Stockmeyer of Nyack, New York, took this aerial photograph of the Palisades Interstate Parkway being constructed on October 22, 1955. Completed in 1958 at a cost of $47 million, the parkway became popular not only as a commuter route for those who work in New York City, but also as a quick route for the city's residents to reach Harriman and Bear Mountain State Parks. (Courtesy of PIPC.)

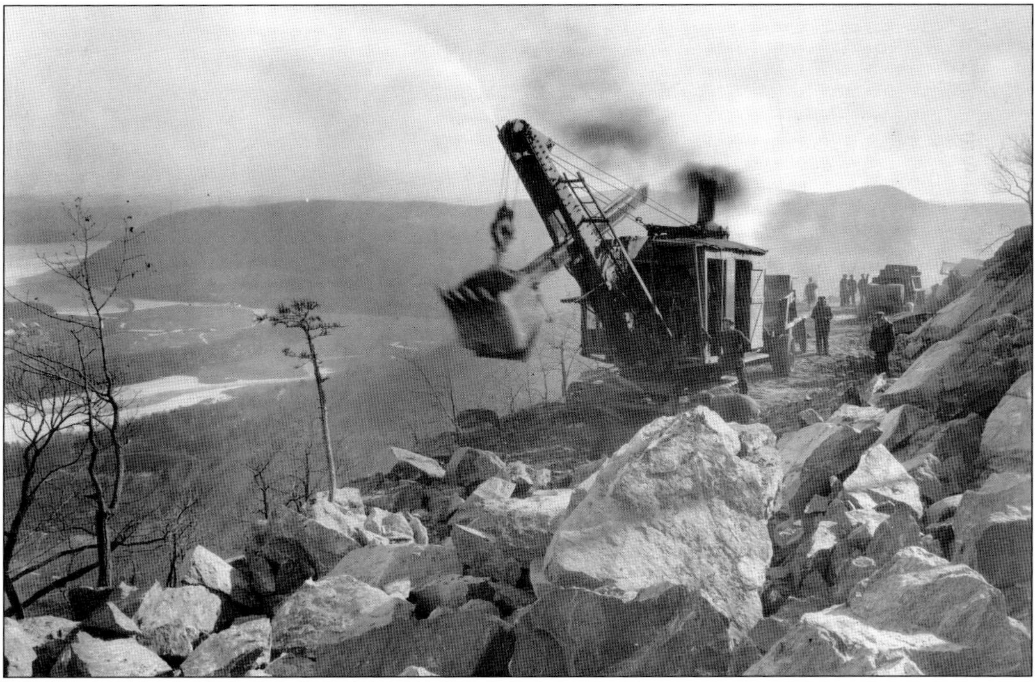

Built to honor the first chairman of the Palisades Interstate Park Commission, George Walbridge Perkins, who served from 1900 to 1920, Perkins Drive was built by workers of the Temporary Emergency Relief Administration from 1932 to 1934. This photograph is somewhat misleading because, like Seven Lakes Drive, the project was quite labor intensive, with more than 90 percent of the work being done by hand. (Courtesy of PIPC.)

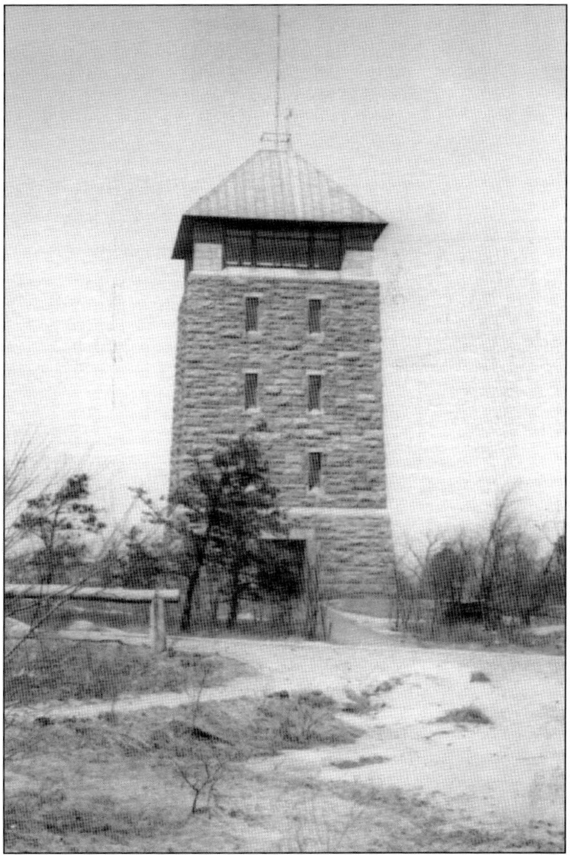

According to the Palisades Parks Conservancy, four states—New York, New Jersey, Connecticut, and Pennsylvania—are visible from the Perkins Memorial Tower, on the summit of Bear Mountain. With funds donated by George Perkins's widow and son, members of a Great Depression works project constructed the tower at the same time Perkins Memorial Drive was being built. (Courtesy of PIPC.)

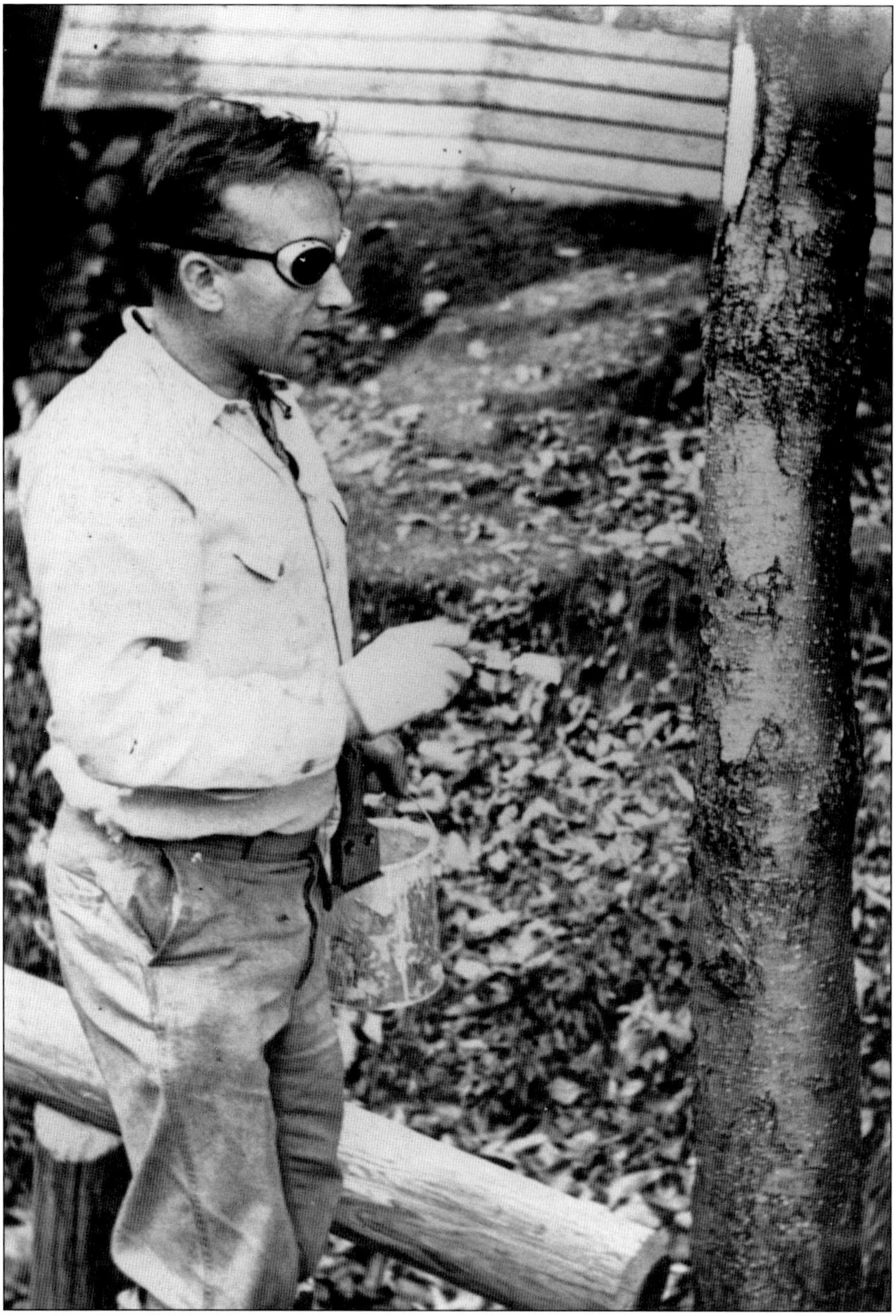

Myron Avery places a paint blaze on a tree near Bear Mountain in November 1940. He became the AT's first 2,000-miler in 1936, having walked its full length in nine years during his many scouting and work trips up and down the trail. From this experience, Avery said, "Those of us, who have physically worked on the trail, know that the trail, as such, will never be completed." This photograph was taken by Clark Fick of the Cygian Society, an outdoors club based in New York City. (Courtesy of ATC.)

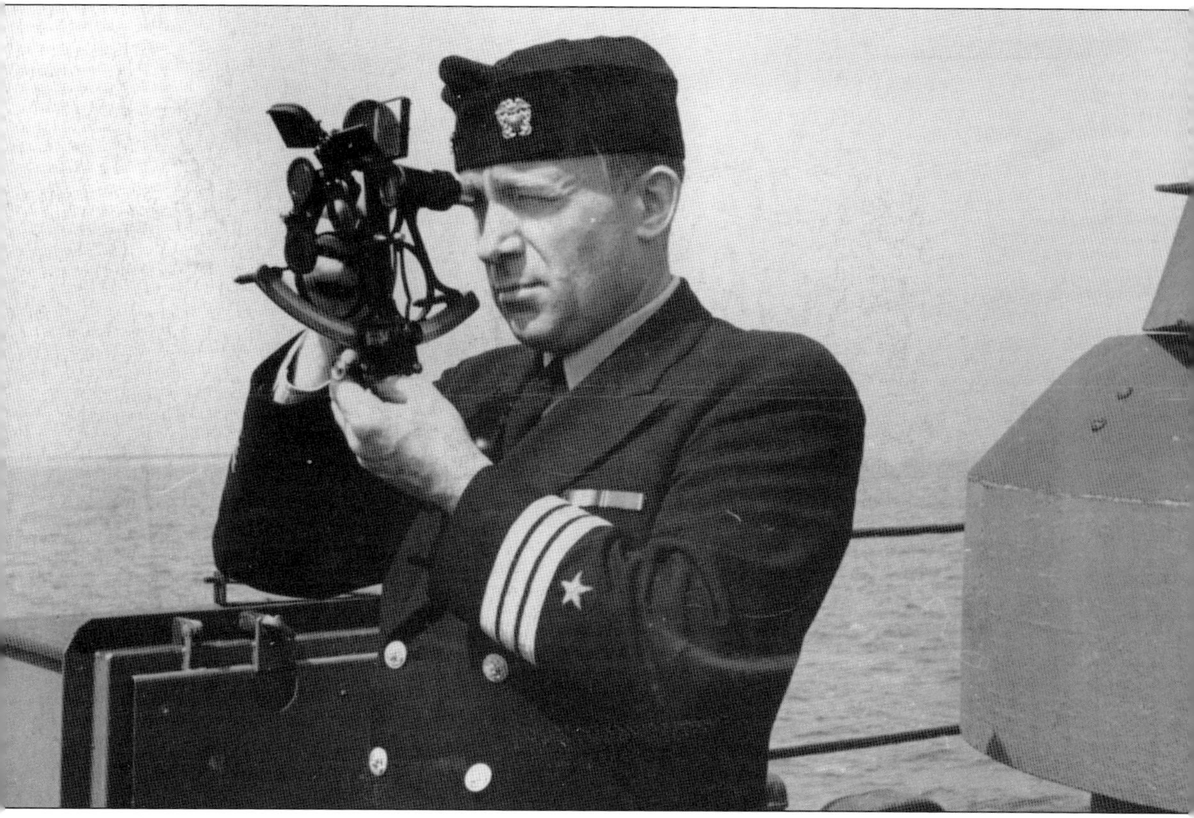

Myron Avery's many AT accomplishments are well known in the history of the trail. He served as the Potomac Appalachian Trail Club's president from 1927 to 1940; was on ATC's board of managers and executive committee, including being the conference chairman from 1931 to 1952; and functioned as the Maine Appalachian Trail Club's trails supervisor from 1935 to 1949 and then its president from 1949 to 1952. What is often forgotten is that Avery was a Harvard University Law School graduate who first worked for the US Shipping Board and was later an assistant for New York's US attorney, where he handled cases involving maritime law, many for the Navy and the Merchant Marines. He was a commissioned officer in the Navy Reserve and was called to active duty in World War II, during which time he was promoted to commander. This photograph of him was taken during a 1945 navigation cruise. (Courtesy of ATC.)

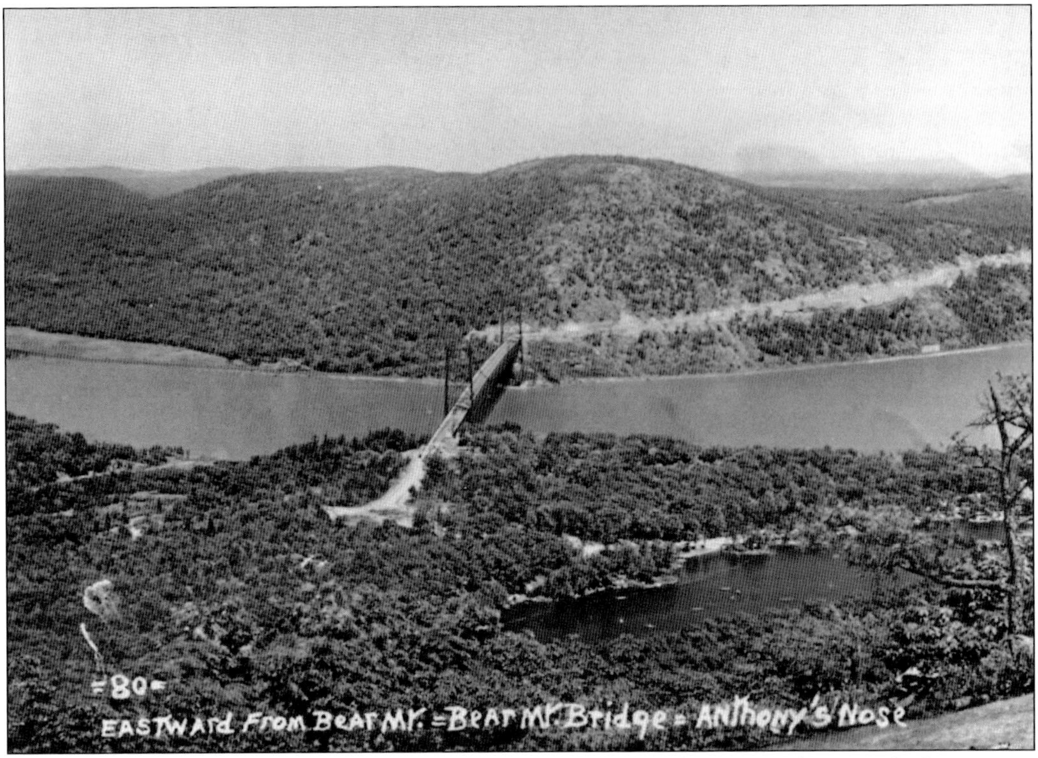

This 1930s photograph shows a small portion of the view from Bear Mountain. Anthony's Nose is across the Bear Mountain Bridge, on the east side of the Hudson River, and Hessian Lake, in the right foreground, is dotted by canoes paddled by state park visitors. (Courtesy of ATC.)

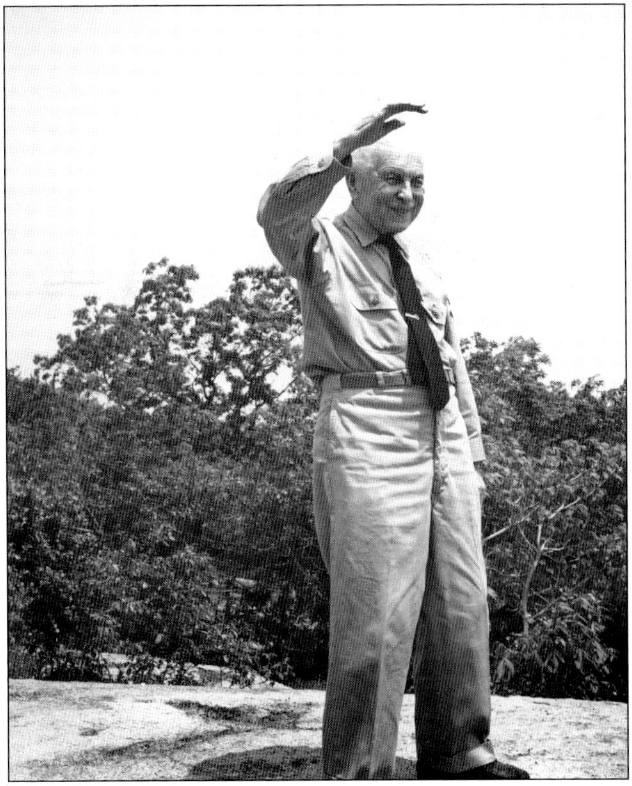

Also on top of Bear Mountain is a plaque dedicated to Joseph Bartha, the trails chairman of NYNJTC from 1940 to 1955. In addition to building and maintaining pathways for decades before he became chairman, he was also active in obtaining landowners' permissions to locate trails across their property. Bartha was 95 years old when he attended the ceremony in his honor on June 5, 1966. (Photograph by John Korbach; courtesy of PIPC.)

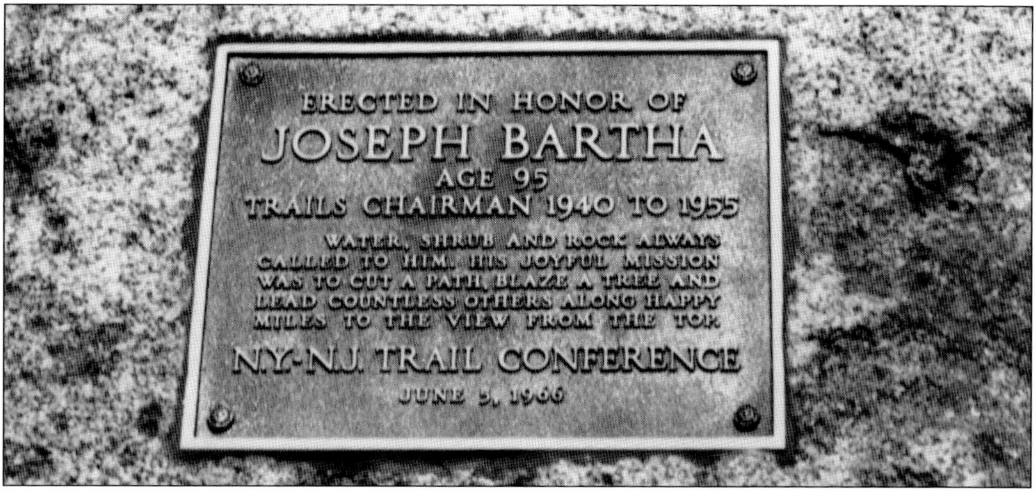

In 1944, Joseph Bartha helped William Hoeferlin measure all of the marked trails in Harriman State Park in preparation for the first edition of the *Harriman State Park Trail Guide*. Despite his advanced age at the plaque dedication, Bartha said, "The knees are still going. As long as they are not wobbling I go up into my mountains." (Courtesy of PIPC.)

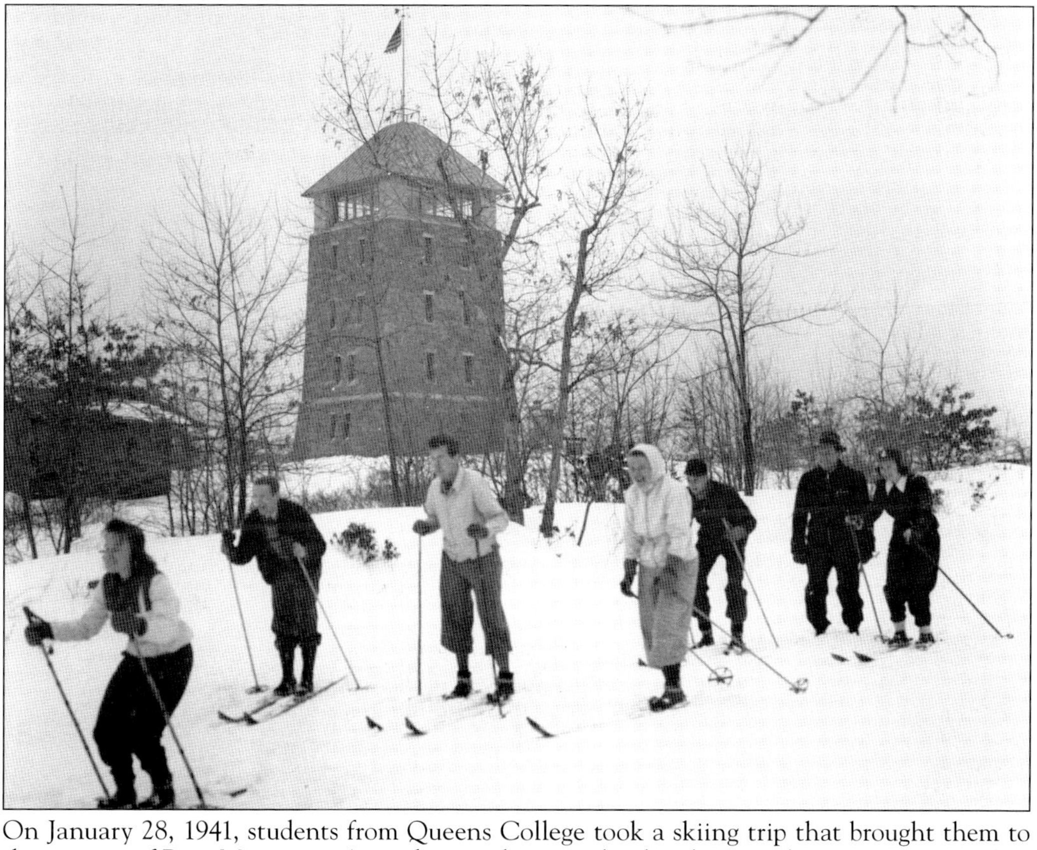

On January 28, 1941, students from Queens College took a skiing trip that brought them to the summit of Bear Mountain. According to the notes by the photographer, a Mr. Davies, they were preparing to descend the mountain when he took this photograph at 4:30 p.m. The college continues to offer skiing classes and outings. (Courtesy of PIPC.)

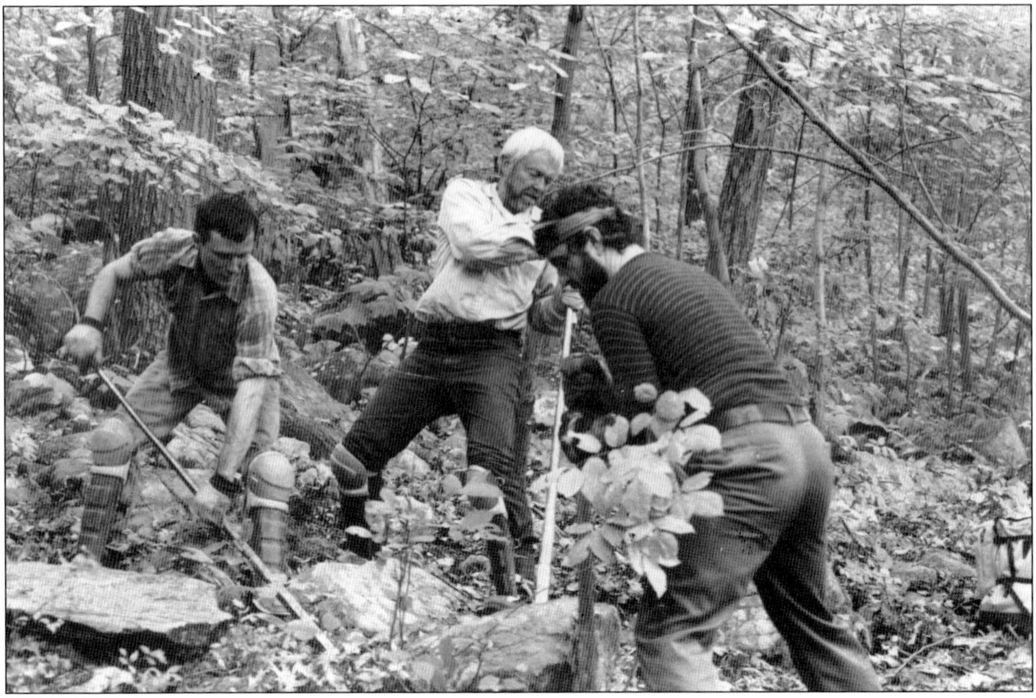

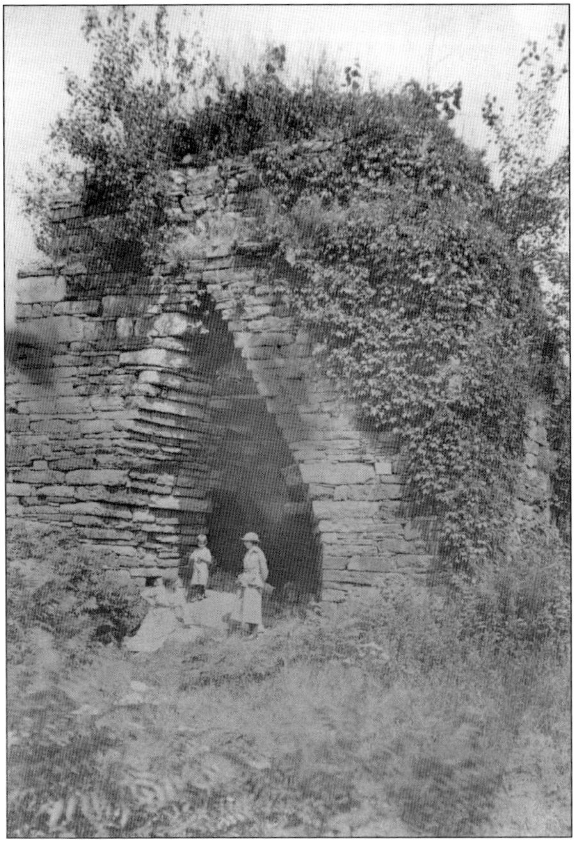

Special ATC volunteer crews, headed by trained trail bosses, help local clubs accomplish tasks, including rock work, building construction, and major relocations, which are beyond the average volunteer's expertise. The Mid-Atlantic Crew is seen here working on the trail in New Jersey and New York in 1988. From left to right, Joe ?, Mark Brumbach, and crew leader Sid Bucher pry loose a boulder to be used in trail construction. (Courtesy of ATC.)

When the AT opened across Bear Mountain on October 7, 1923, it went down the mountain's north side to Popolopen Creek, an area of active iron mining and smelting from the late 1700s to the early 1900s. Photographed in the 1920s and still standing today, the Queensboro Iron Furnace, at the confluence of Popolopen and Queensboro Creeks, operated from around 1780 to the mid-1800s. (Courtesy of PIPC.)

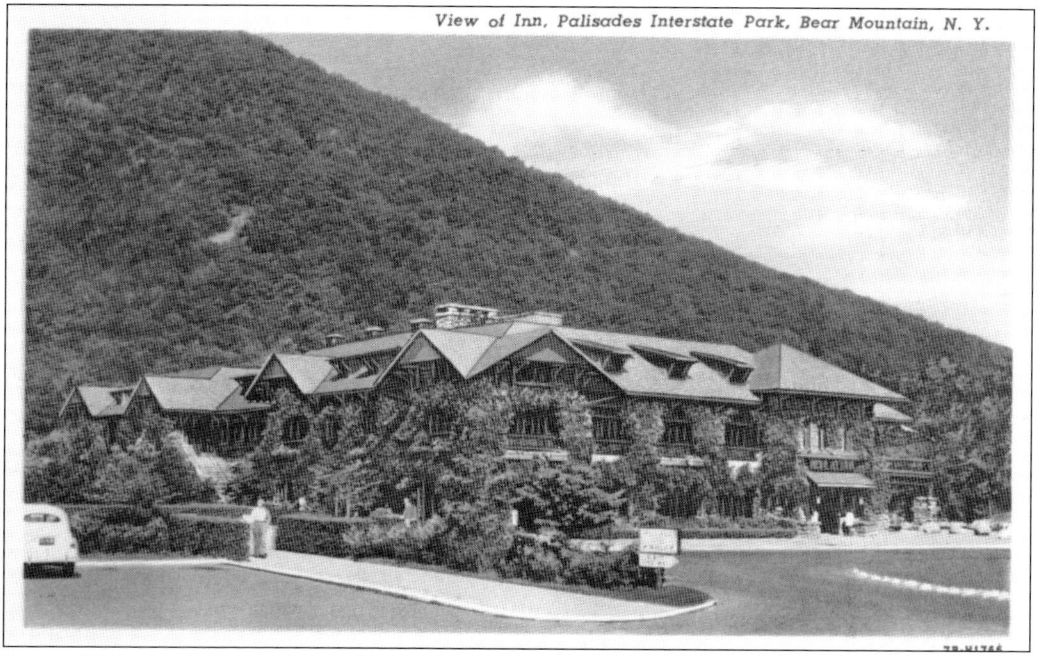

In the 1930s, the AT was relocated onto the more eastern-facing slope of Bear Mountain, enabling it to go by the Bear Mountain Inn. The inn, constructed of giant boulders and large chestnut logs, was opened to the public on June 27, 1915. The room rate at the time was $4.50 a night, which included breakfast, lunch, and dinner. In 2014, rates start at $259, without meals. (Courtesy of Curteich-Chicago.)

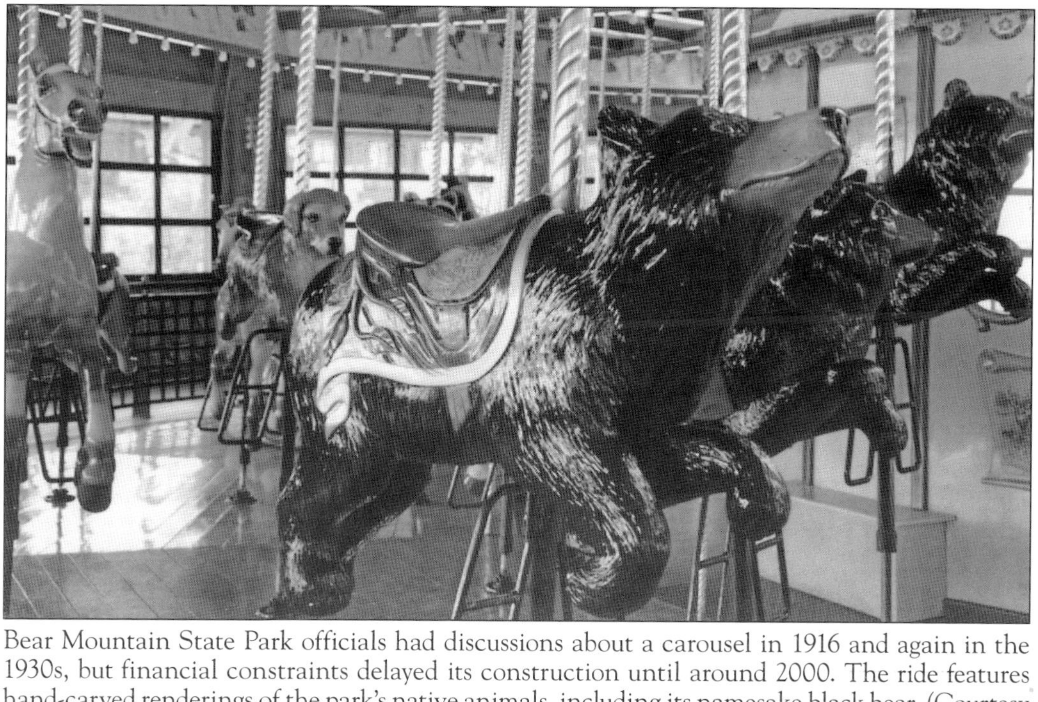

Bear Mountain State Park officials had discussions about a carousel in 1916 and again in the 1930s, but financial constraints delayed its construction until around 2000. The ride features hand-carved renderings of the park's native animals, including its namesake black bear. (Courtesy of Guest Services, Inc., and ATC.)

Committee of Arrangements

for

THE APPALACHIAN TRAIL CONFERENCE

1941

General Chairman .... FRANK PLACE
Banquet .... JOSEPH BARTHA
Camping .... MURRAY H. STEVENS
Exhibits and Literature .... BENJAMIN SIMINOW
Hikes and Excursions .... CHARLES F. LUSCHER
Hospitality .... J. ASHTON ALLIS
Publicity .... FRANK J. OLIVER
Reservations .... WILLIAM BURTON
Reception .... ANGELIQUE RIVOLLIER

Chairman of the Board of Managers ...... MYRON H. AVERY
THE APPALACHIAN TRAIL
(A Mountain Footpath from Maine to Georgia.)

Dinner

TENTH BIANNUAL
APPALACHIAN TRAIL CONFERENCE

Friday, May Thirtieth, 1941
BEAR MOUNTAIN INN
Palisades Interstate Park, New York

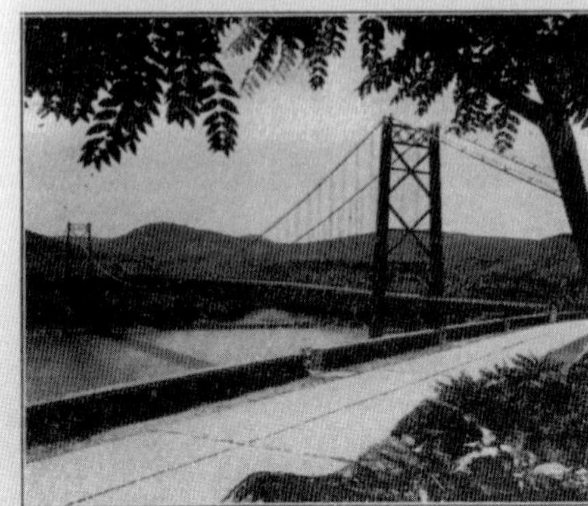

Vista Harriman Bridge, Bear Mountain, N. Y.

Although the dinner brochure above says that the meeting of the Appalachian Trail Conference at the Bear Mountain Inn in 1941 was the "Tenth Biannual Meeting," the conference did not hold biannual meetings, and it was not until the 1970s that regularly scheduled biennial meetings were established. The back page is an example of the many roles trail volunteers are willing to take on. NYNJTC trails chairman Joseph Bartha headed the banquet committee; NYNJTC president William Burton handled reservations; NYNJTC's treasurer J. Ashton Allis arranged hospitality; and Frank Place, a president of the Tramp and Trail Club, volunteered for the duties of the banquet's general chairman. While today's meetings do have speakers and presentations, they are not as formal as this one, which centered on the evening meal (below). (Both, courtesy of ATC.)

Program

TOASTMASTER
Frank Place
Chairman New York-New Jersey Trail Conference

SPEAKERS

John Sieker
Chief of the Division of Recreation and Lands
U. S. Forest Service

Subject: ***National Forests and the Appalachian Trail.***

Carl P. Russell
Supervisor of Research and Interpretations
National Park Service

Subject: ***National Parks and the Appalachian Trail.***

Menu

Georgia Shrimp Cocktail

Celery Olives

Puree of Jersey Tomatoes

Broiled Delaware Shad and Roe

or

Charcoal Broiled Sirloin Steak

Baked Potatoes from Maine

Early New York State Peas

Mixed Green Salad from the Carolinas

Native Dressing

Fancy Ice Cream, New England States

Southern Cookies

Coffee

General meetings of the ATC include hikes, excursions, and informative workshops and are usually attended by many of the trail's local maintaining clubs. Here, members of the Potomac Appalachian Trail Club, which was based in Washington, DC, at the time and maintains the trail in Virginia, West Virginia, Maryland, and Pennsylvania, participate in one of the outdoors activities at the 1941 ATC meeting at Bear Mountain State Park. (Courtesy of PIPC.)

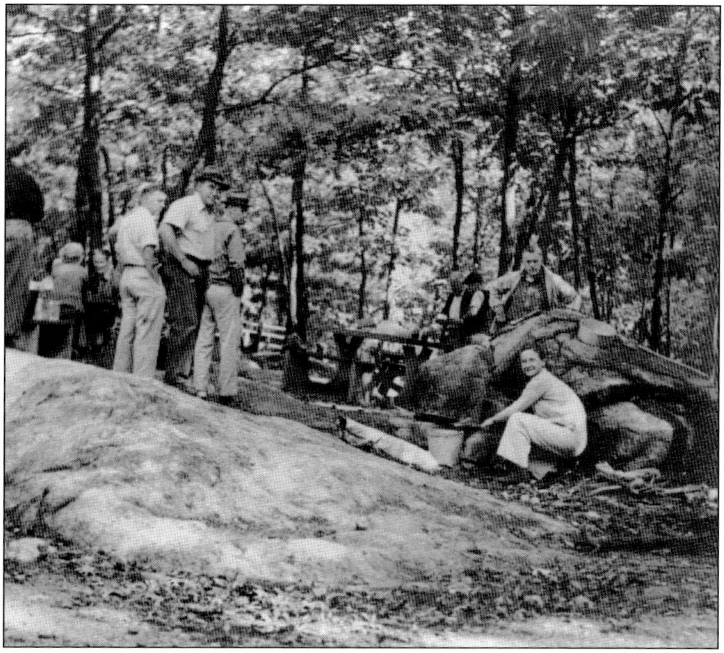

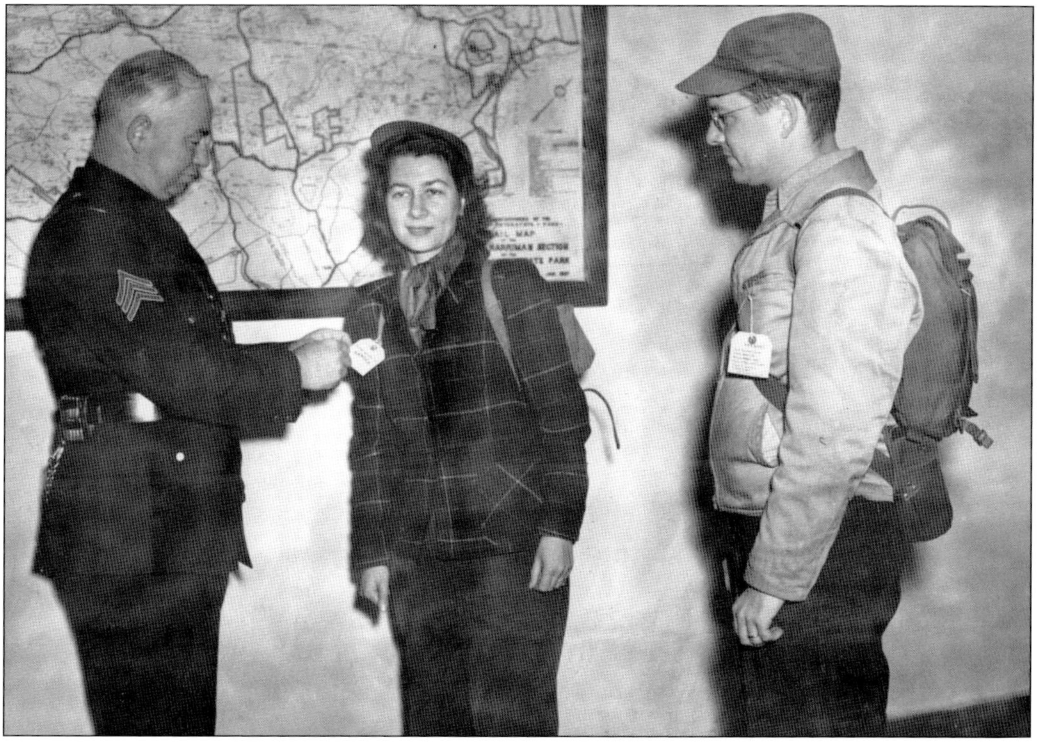

Bear Mountain State Park kept such detailed records that what took place at the police desk in the Administration Building on November 6, 1949, is still known today. A state park police officer, a Sergeant MacGuire (left), officially registered hikers Mr. and Mrs. Ben Warriner of 65 Clark Court, Rutherford, New Jersey, by providing them with registration and identification tags. (Photograph by J. Boland; courtesy of PIPC.)

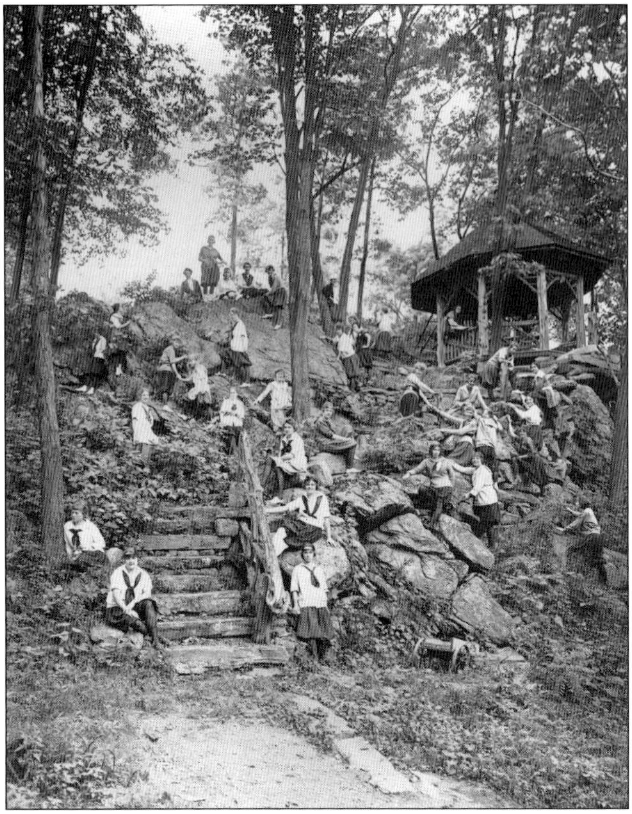

Nearly three dozen Girl Scouts in full uniform pose inside, below, and next to this gazebo around 1920. Because of its location close to Bear Mountain State Park's playground, the gazebo was heavily used through the years and appeared in many family outing photographs. (Courtesy of PIPC.)

This 1914 photograph of the Bear Mountain State Park parking lot provides evidence that, despite the relatively primitive roads of the day, the park was popular almost a decade before the AT was built and a year before the Bear Mountain Inn opened to the public. The photograph is also significant for the conspicuous absence of the Bear Mountain Bridge across the Hudson River. (Courtesy of PIPC.)

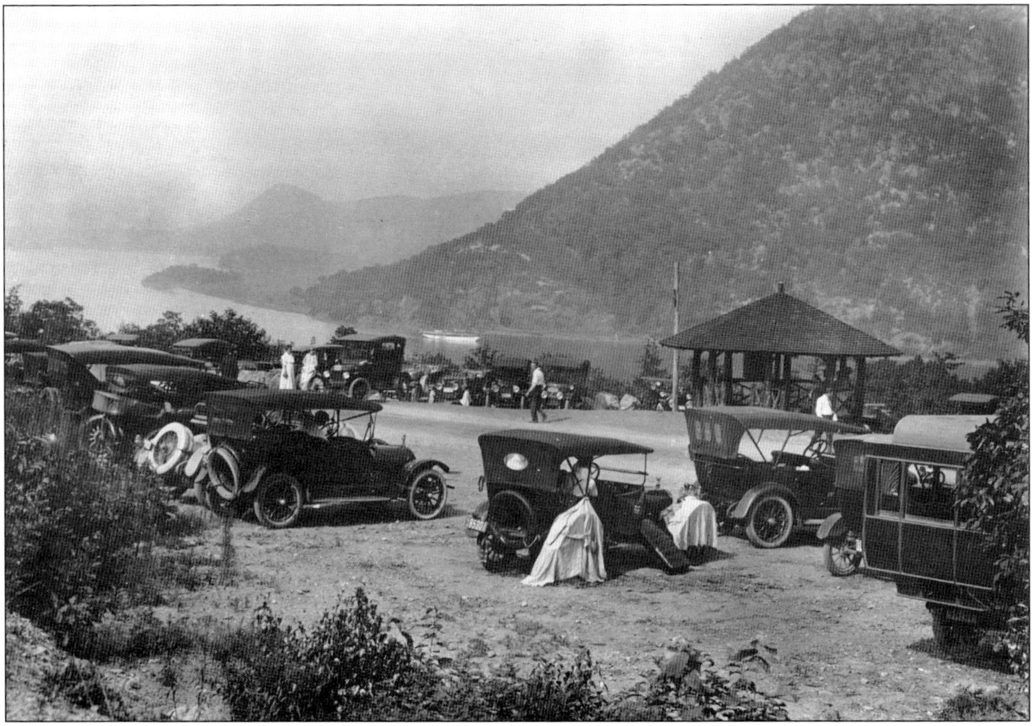

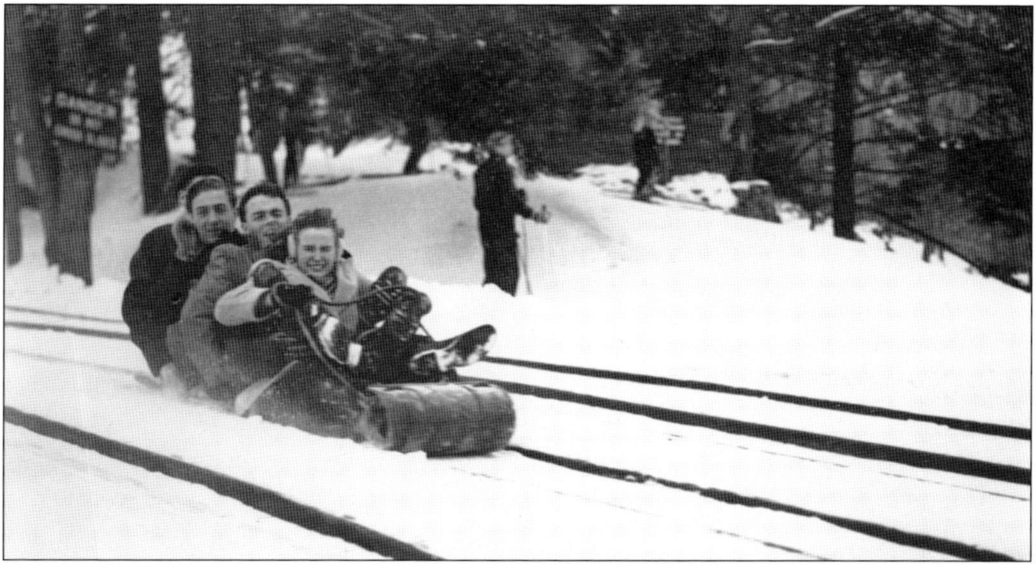

As with many places in winter, Bear Mountain State Park barely had any visitors during the colder months. In order to attract more people, the park instituted its winter sports program during the winter of 1922–1923. Soon, guests could engage in tobogganing, skiing, ice skating, sleighing, snowshoeing, and ski jumping, resulting in more than half a million visitors in the winter of 1928–1929. In January 1948, photographer Harvey McGeorge captured the image above of tobogganers coming to the end of their run. The ski jump attracted athletes from around the world and is said to have been the site of more ski jump competitions than any other place in the United States when it closed in the 1970s. The photograph below, taken by J. Boland on February 19, 1950, attests to the park's ski jump popularity. (Both, courtesy of PIPC.)

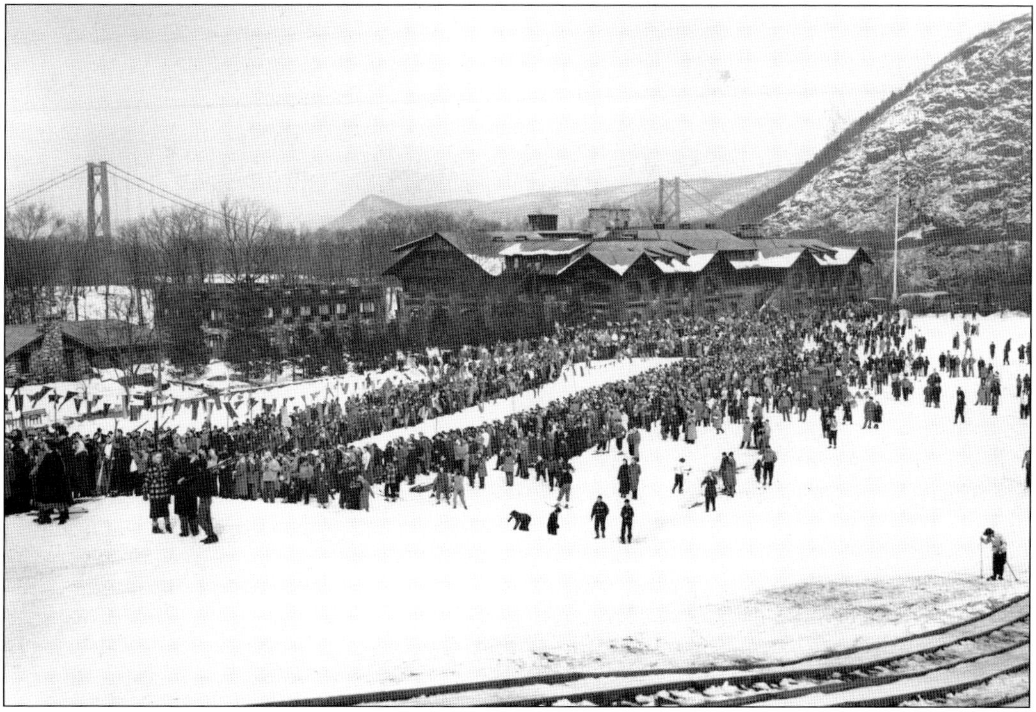

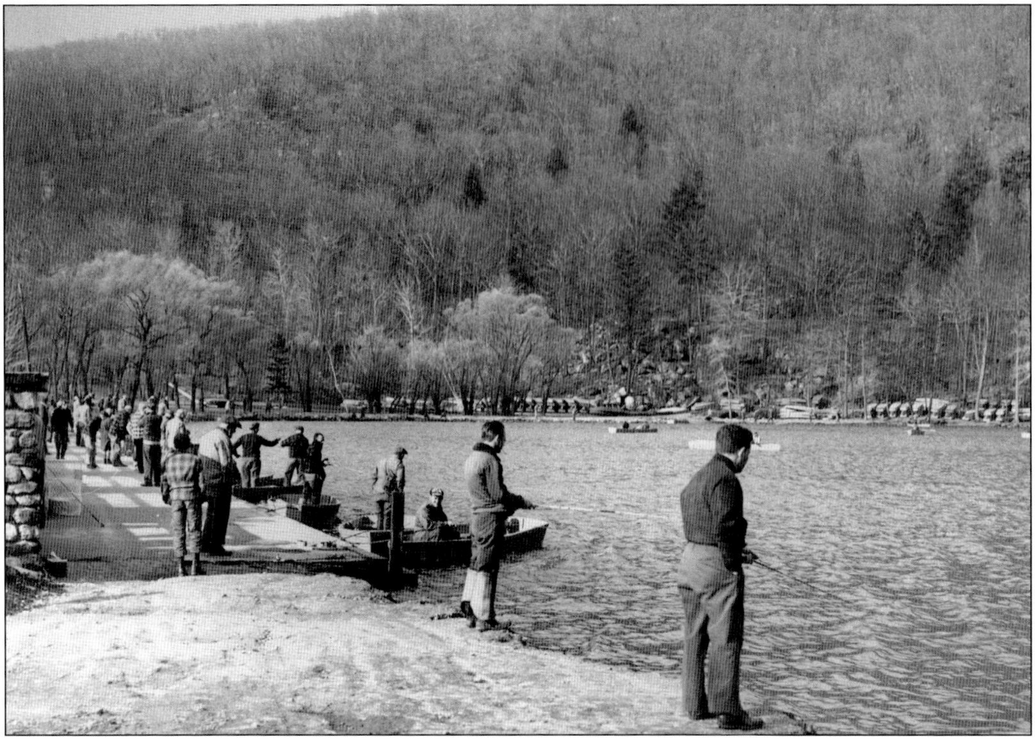

Anglers cast their lines hoping for a catch on opening day of trout season at Hessian Lake on April 4, 1949. Today, trout fishing is permitted year-round, and bass, sunfish, and perch are also caught here. The bodies of so many Hessian soldiers were in the lake after the attack on Fort Clinton in 1777 that its original name of Sinnipink was eventually changed to Hessian. (Courtesy of PIPC.)

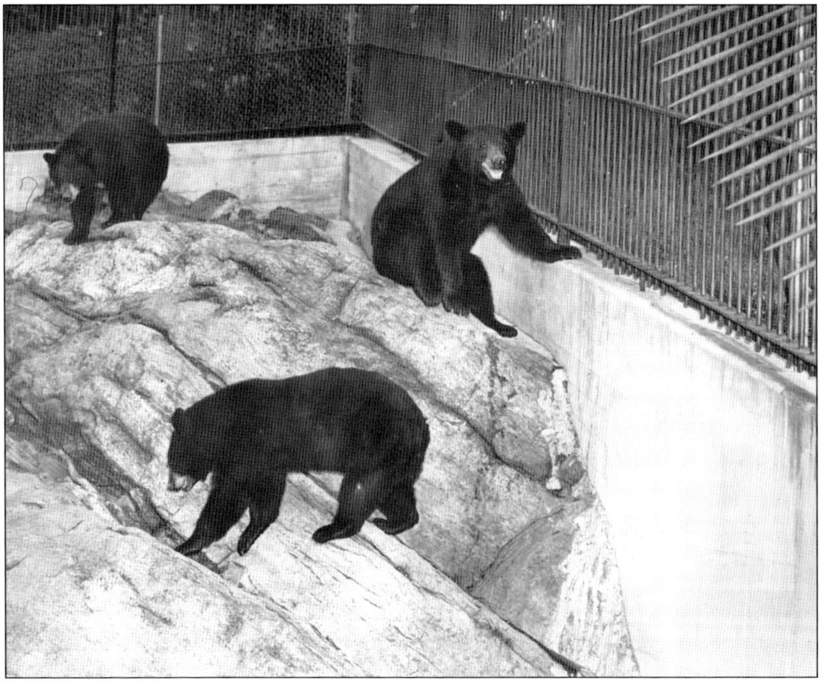

The Trailside Museums and Zoo, through which the AT passes, was opened in 1927 and ensure that thru-hikers will see a bear—these three were photographed in 1950—during their journey. The bear's den is also significant for another reason: it is at about 124 feet above sea level, the lowest point of the entire trail. (Courtesy of PIPC.)

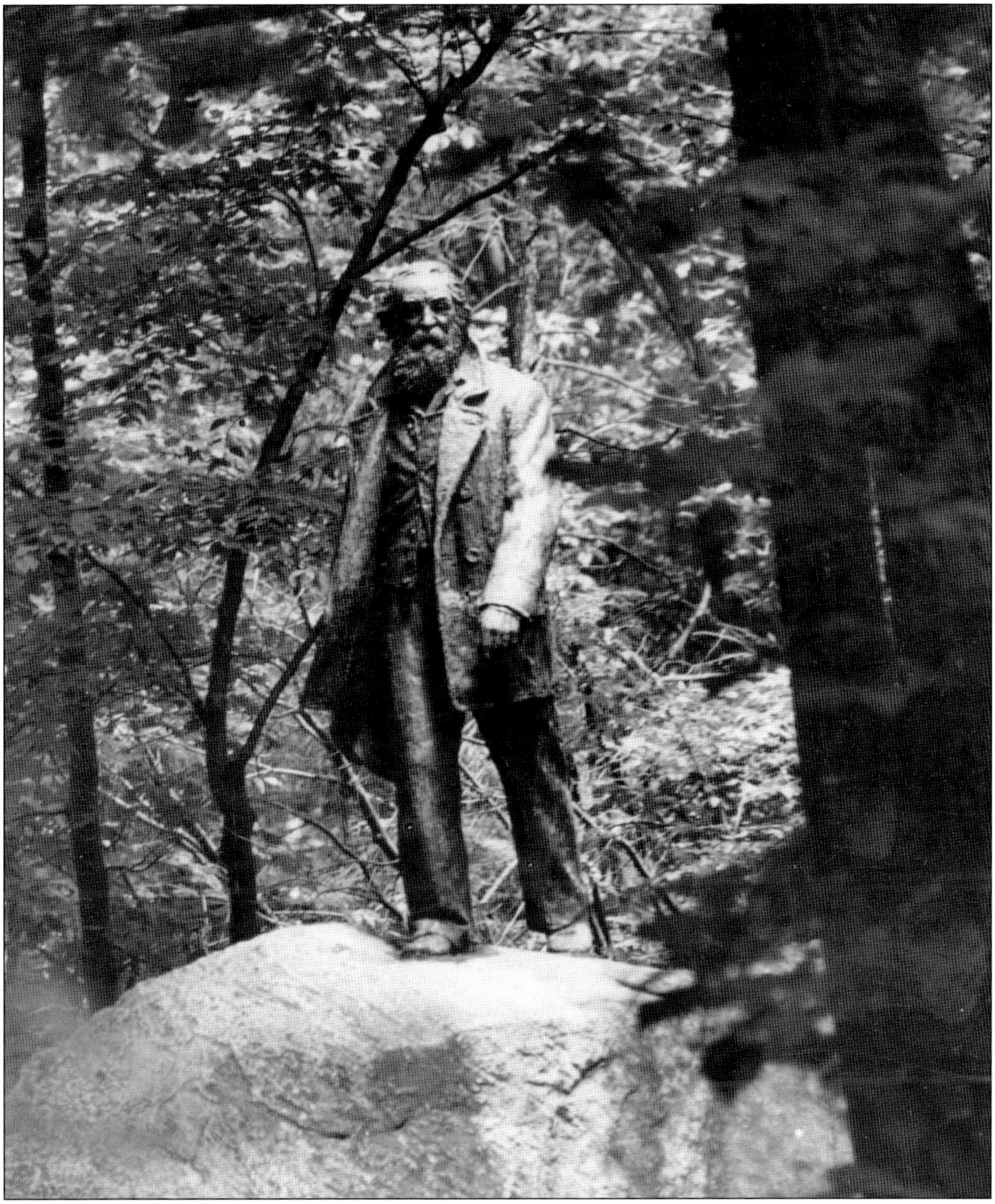

Averell Harriman commissioned the statue of Walt Whitman that stands near the entrance to the Trailside Museums and Zoo, fittingly placed beside the long-distance AT in 1940. Whitman's 1856 poem "Song of the Open Road" includes the following section: "Afoot and light-hearted, I take to the open road, / Healthy, free, the world before me, / The long brown path before me, leading wherever I choose. / Henceforth I ask not good-fortune—I myself am good fortune; / Henceforth I whimper no more, postpone no more, need nothing, / Strong and content, I travel the open road . . . From this hour, freedom! / From this hour I ordain myself loos'd of limits and imaginary lines, / Going where I list, my own master, total and absolute . . . Now I see the secret of the making of the best persons, / It is to grow in the open air, and to eat and sleep with the earth." (Courtesy of PIPC.)

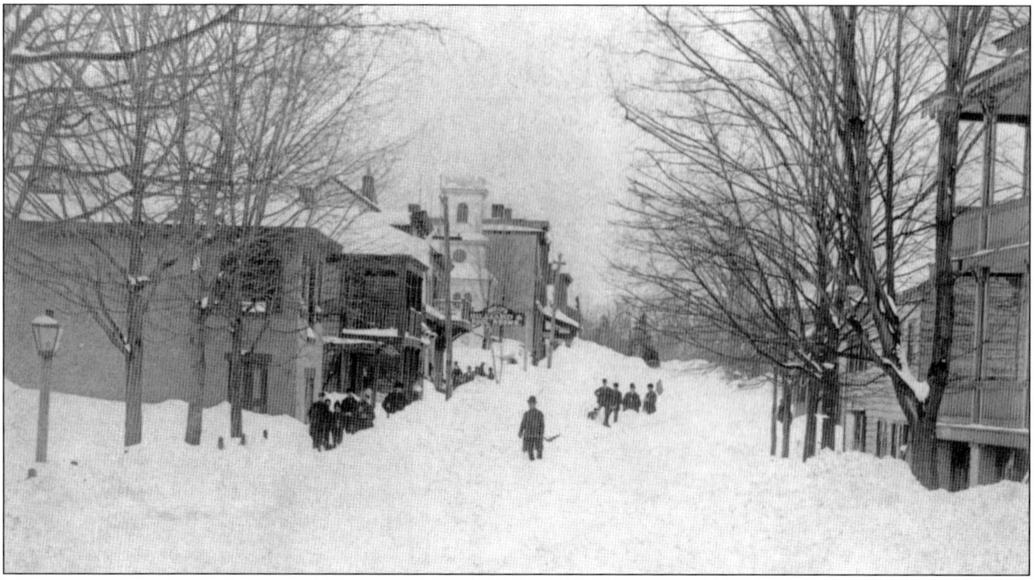

New York can receive vast amounts of snow, but this 1888 storm was one of the most severe in American history. This photograph of the village of Highland Falls, just a few miles north of Bear Mountain, vividly depicts how much snow fell, covering the first floor of some of the buildings. Winds of 45 miles per hour created drifts close to 50 feet high. (Courtesy of PIPC.)

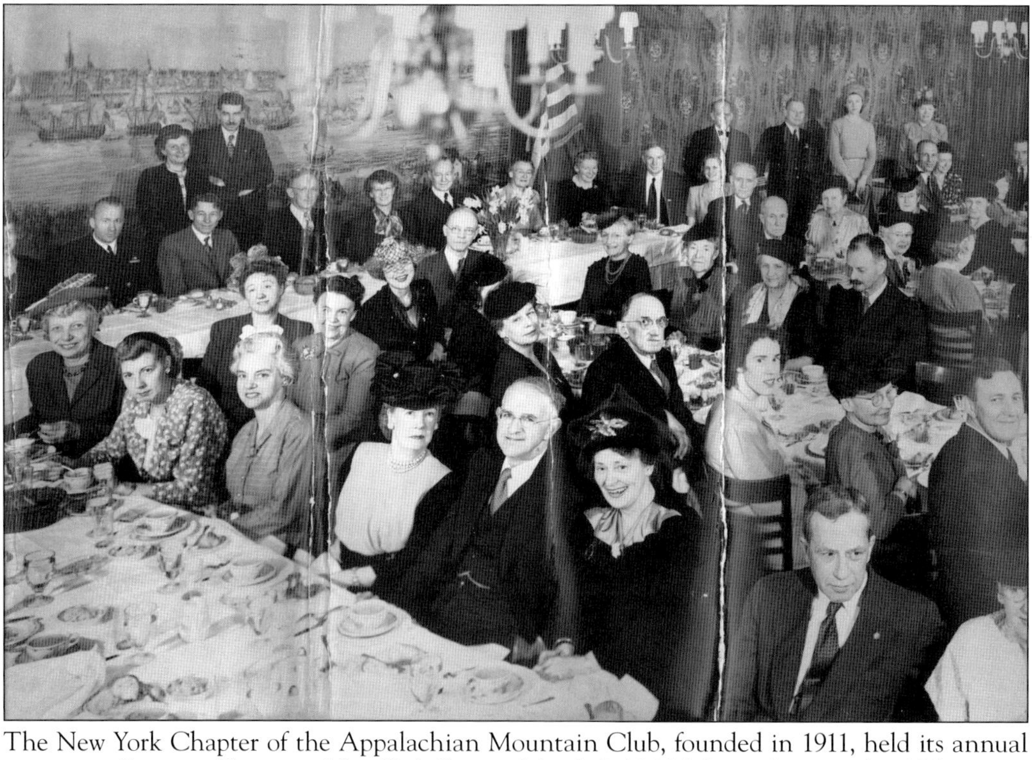

The New York Chapter of the Appalachian Mountain Club, founded in 1911, held its annual meeting at Fraunces Tavern in New York City on March 3, 1946. Myron Avery, in his 15th year as ATC chairman, is seated on the left at the head table. The tavern, which has been in operation since 1767, is where George Washington bid farewell to his troops in 1783. (Courtesy of ATC.)

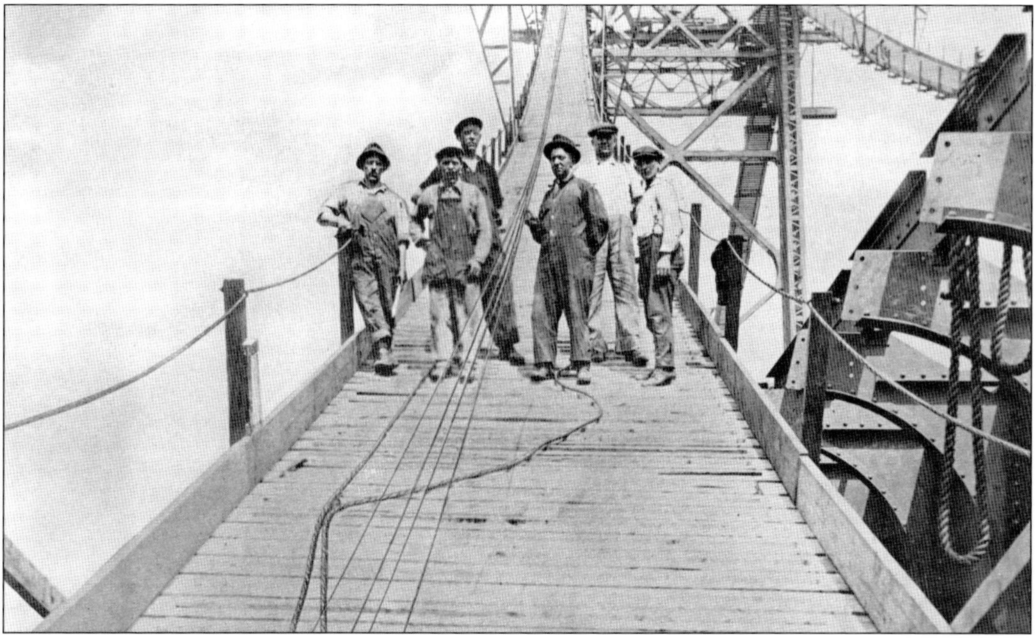

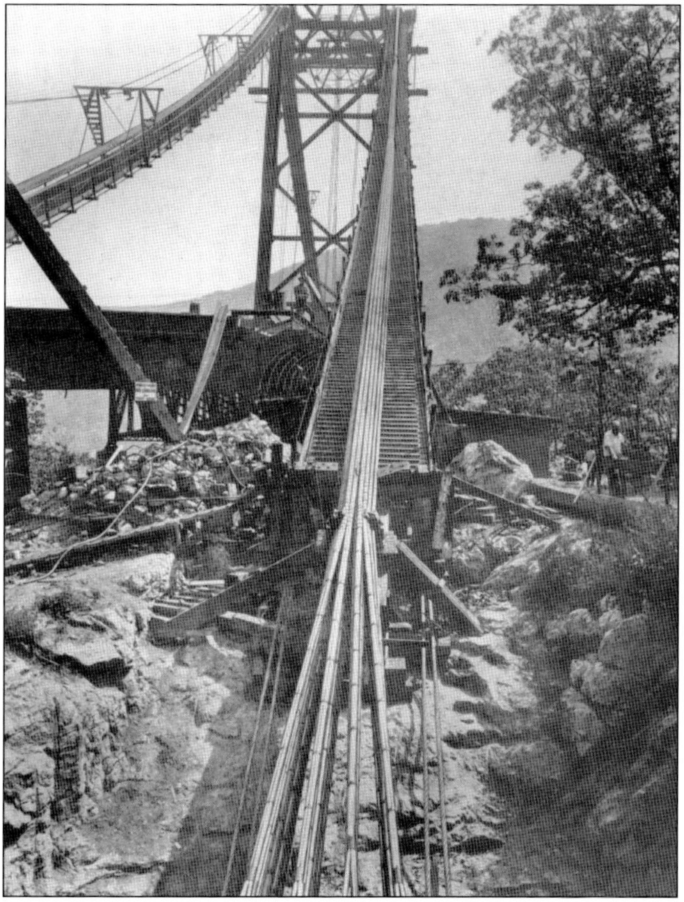

The Bear Mountain Bridge was the longest suspension bridge in the world and the first such structure to have a concrete deck when it opened on Thanksgiving Day, November 27, 1924. The idea for the bridge, and a bit of preliminary construction, was begun in the 1860s and 1870s by private corporations, whose efforts ended with financial troubles. In 1922, the Bear Mountain Hudson River Bridge Corporation was established to complete the project. As the bridge was being built, workers used wooden walkways (above) that connected the deck to the top of the towers. The large suspension cables that hold up the bridge are actually a mass of individual cables (right), each consisting of more than 7,000 individual galvanized wires, which were squeezed and bound together in place by the workers. (Both, courtesy of PIPC.)

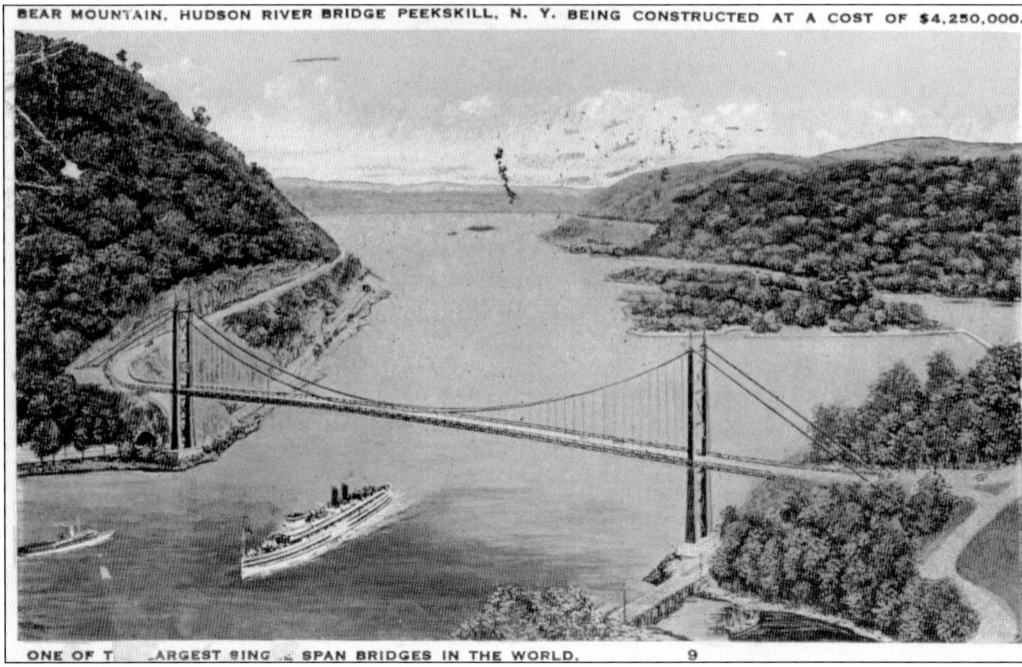

This postcard was mailed on August 15, 1924, three months before the Bear Mountain Bridge opened. The bridge was the vital link joining the AT south of the Hudson River to the trail continuing northward. Although the bridge was never self-sustaining, it originally had a toll that even hikers had to pay. Earl Shaffer paid 5¢ on his historic 1948 hike. (Courtesy of J. Ruben.)

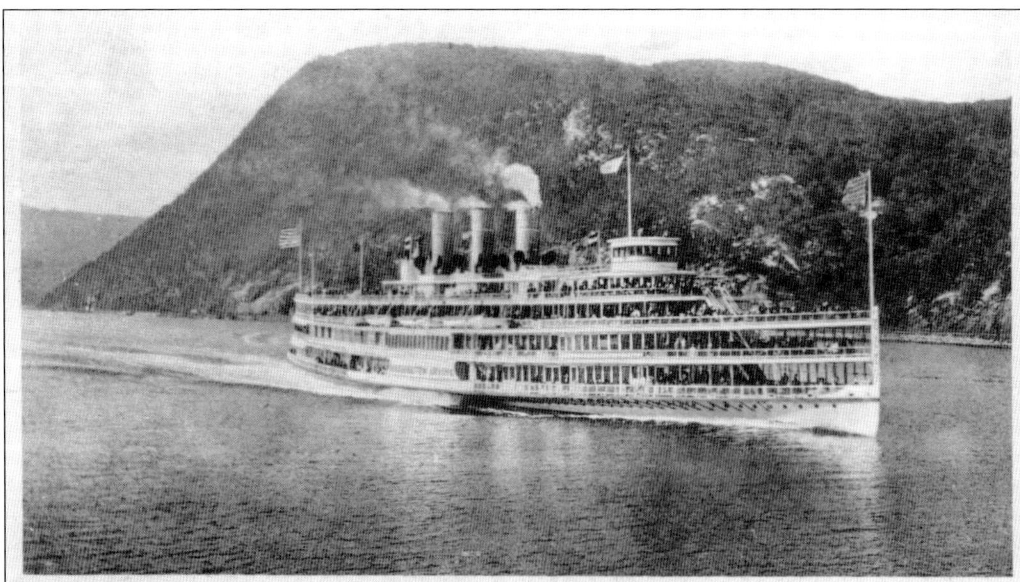

Companies (and, soon after, PIPC) began running steamship excursions to Bear Mountain as early as 1910, delivering passengers from and to New York City. The *Washington Irving*, the Hudson River Day Line's largest ship, operated from 1913 to 1926, when it sank after colliding with a barge. On the east side of the river, the AT originally went to Anthony's Nose; it is now a side trail. (Courtesy of the Hudson River Day Line.)

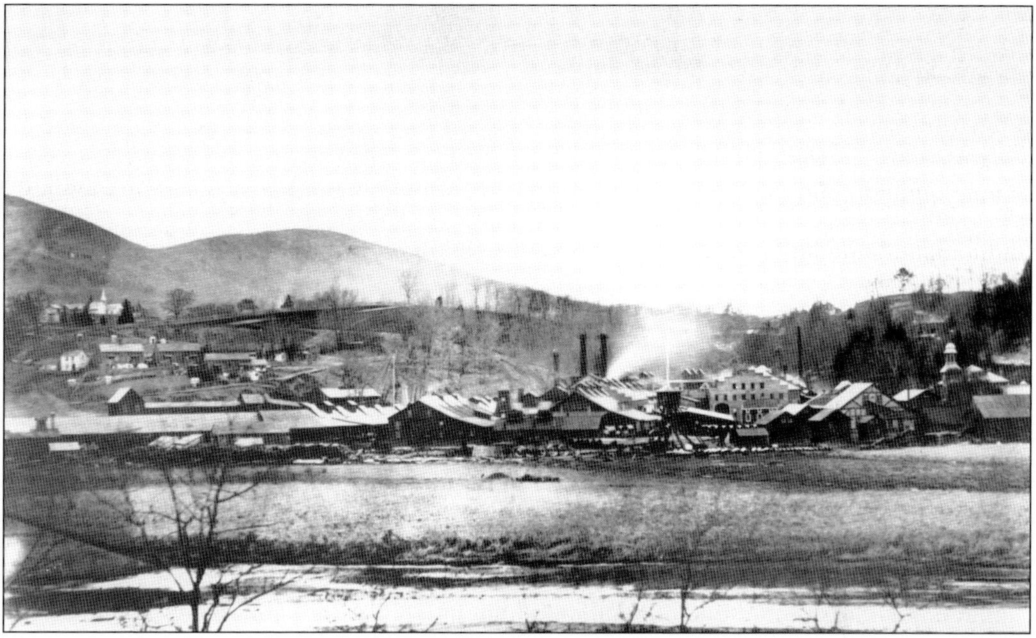

North of Anthony's Nose, another side trail leads to a view of West Point, which looks much different today than it did when this photograph of the West Point Foundry was taken in the early 1900s. The foundry was established in 1818 to supply America's military with artillery, the most famous being Parrott rifles. It also produced steam engines, locomotives, and water system pipes. Operations ended in 1911. (Courtesy of ATC.)

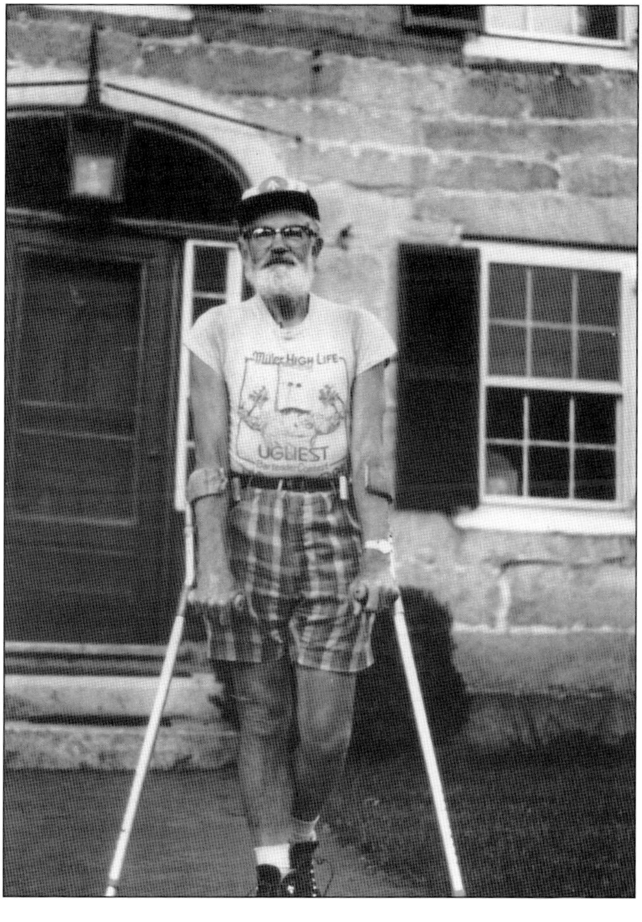

Robert Barker hiked the AT three times in the 1980s despite having multiple sclerosis. Using crutches that had been modified to give him more stability, he went through six crutch tips during his second 2,000 miles, a southbound trip from Maine to Georgia. Barker was friends with one of the AT's other standout hikers, William Irwin, who became the first blind thru-hiker in 1990. (Courtesy of ATC.)

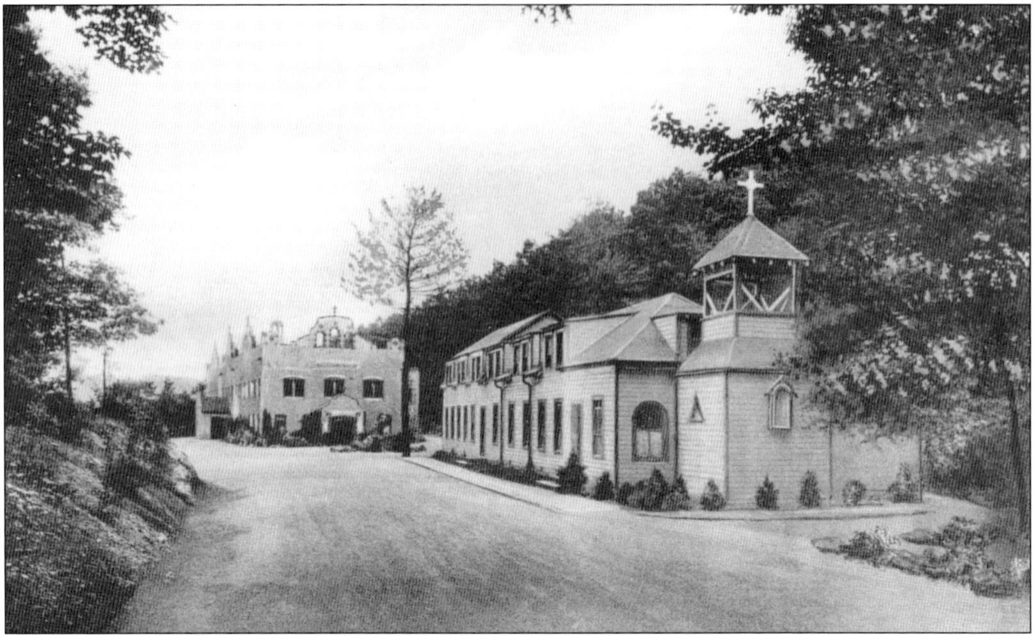

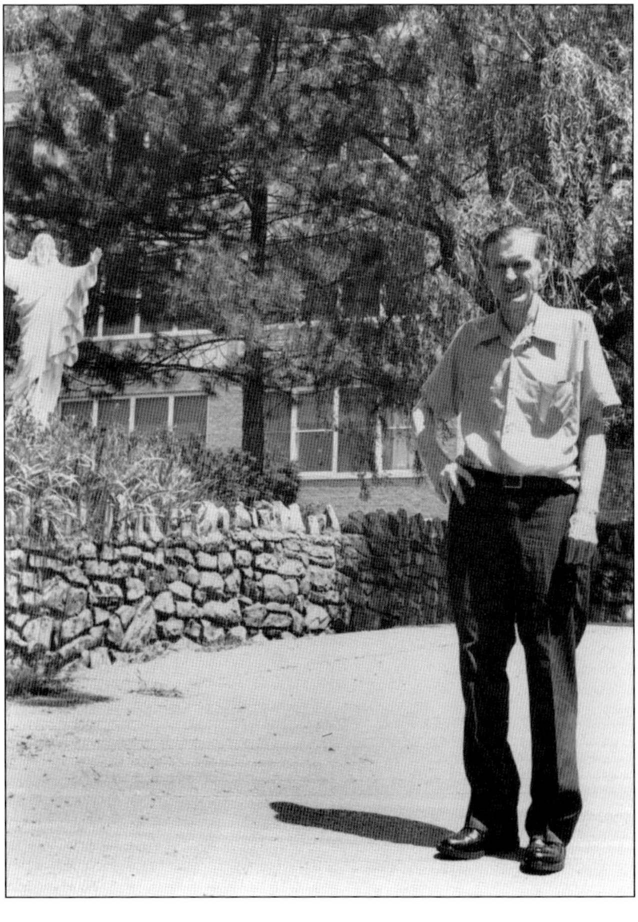

Graymoor, a few minutes' walk from the AT, was established around 1900 by the Franciscan Friars of Atonement and the Franciscan Sisters of Atonement. Members of both orders take vows of poverty and service to others. The early-1900s postcard above shows the St. Christopher's Inns, with the older one in front and the newer one in back. They provide housing and other services for men in need. From 1974 to 1994, Graymoor hosted AT hikers, providing all-you-can-eat meals (and inviting them to "raid" the kitchen during the night), a simple friar's cell (room with bed, table, and lamp), and laundry. In the 1970s and 1980s, Father Bosco (left) was the overseer of the hiker ministry. Increasing hiker numbers forced Graymoor to discontinue the policy, but it does still permit camping on its property. (Above, courtesy of Ave Maria Hour, Graymoor; left, courtesy of ATC.)

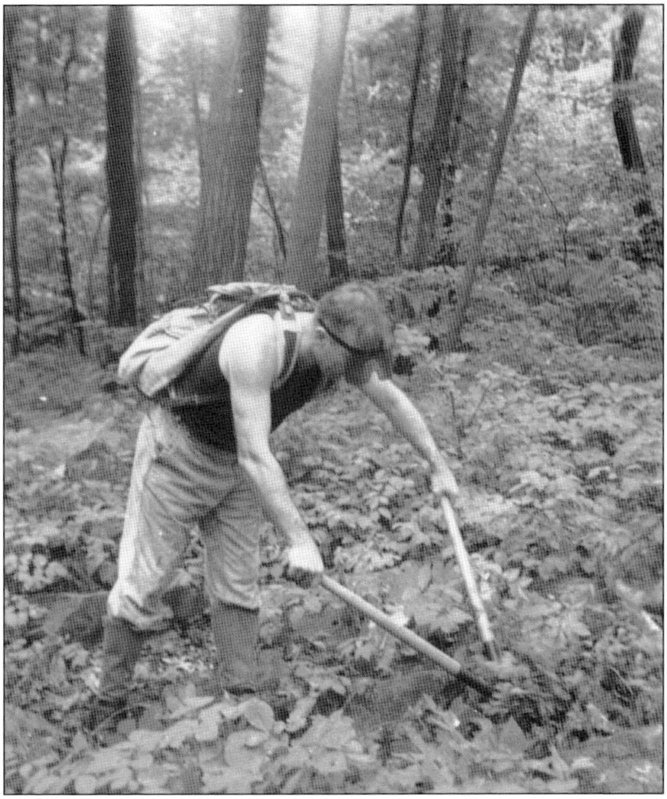

It appears that Myron Avery, at one time or another, did just about every kind of task that volunteers have ever performed on the AT. At right, in 1941, he was photographed by C.E. Dornbusch clipping brush in Clarence Fahnstock State Park. Below, Frederick S. Best photographed the Raymond H. Torrey Memorial Shelter, which once stood near the summit of Shenandoah Mountain in the state park. Torrey is a trail legend, having been an early trail builder and maintainer, a founding member and chairman of the NYNJTC, and the coauthor of the *New York Walk Book*. From 1920 until his death in 1938, Torrey informed the public about outdoors and hiking news in his *New York Evening Post* column "The Long Brown Path." (Right, courtesy of ATC; below; courtesy of SHS.)

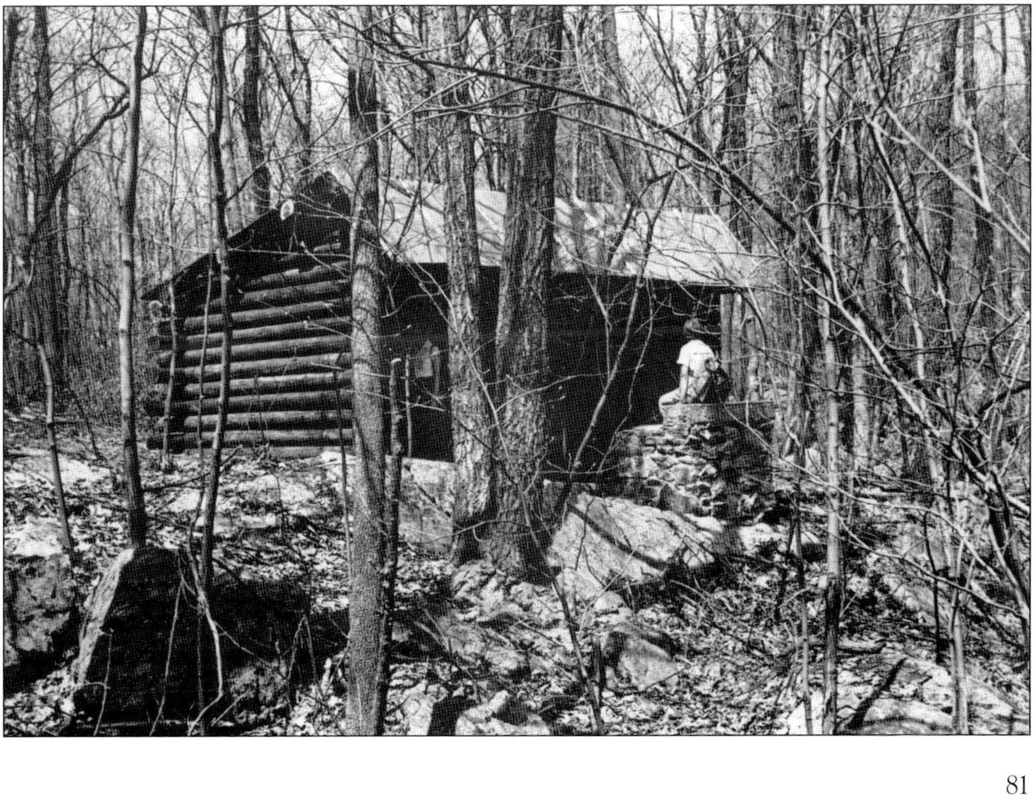

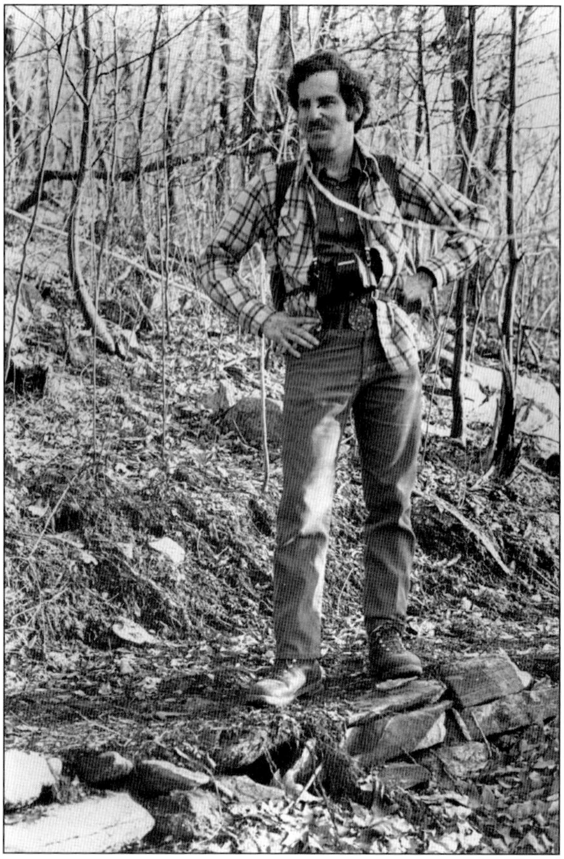

Ron Rosen (at left and below) typifies the long-term dedication of AT volunteers. Beginning by maintaining a section of the trail in the 1970s, he has been an overseer of the construction of trail shelters, established workshops to train volunteer trail corridor monitors, and attended meetings and gone into the field working to move the trail off roads and into the woods in eastern New York. Along with other volunteer work he has done, he has been chairman of the Dutchess/Putnam Appalachian Trail Management Committee (an affiliate of the NYNJTC), served on other trail management committees, and written and obtained grants for public education about the AT. Rosen was given an honorary life membership in ATC during the conference's 38th biennial meeting in 2011 and was named ATC volunteer of the month in March 2012. (Both, courtesy of ATC.)

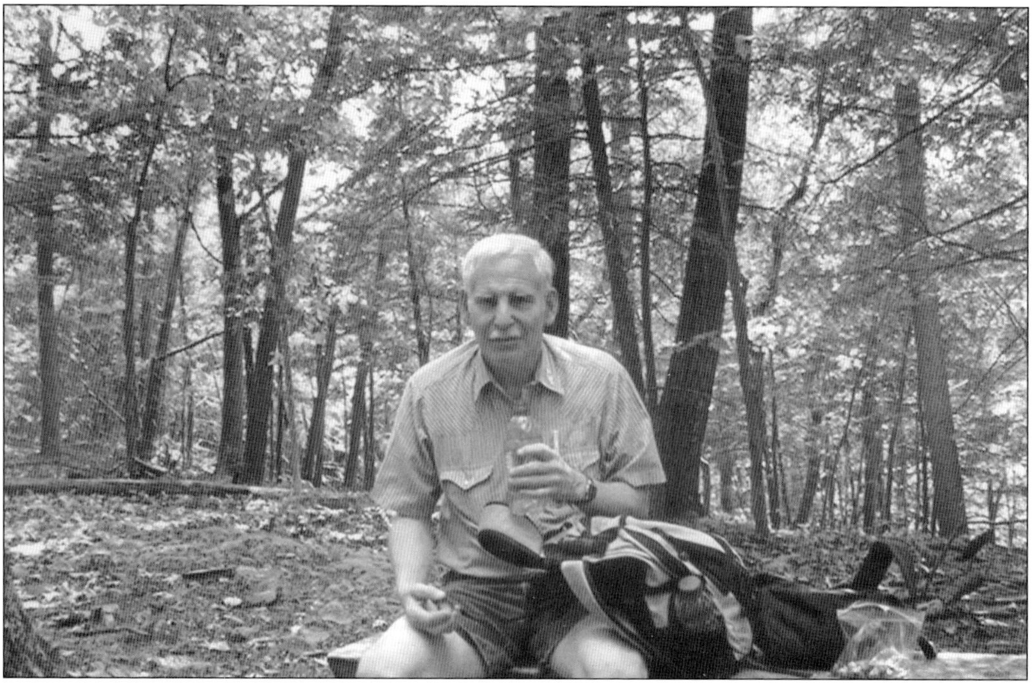

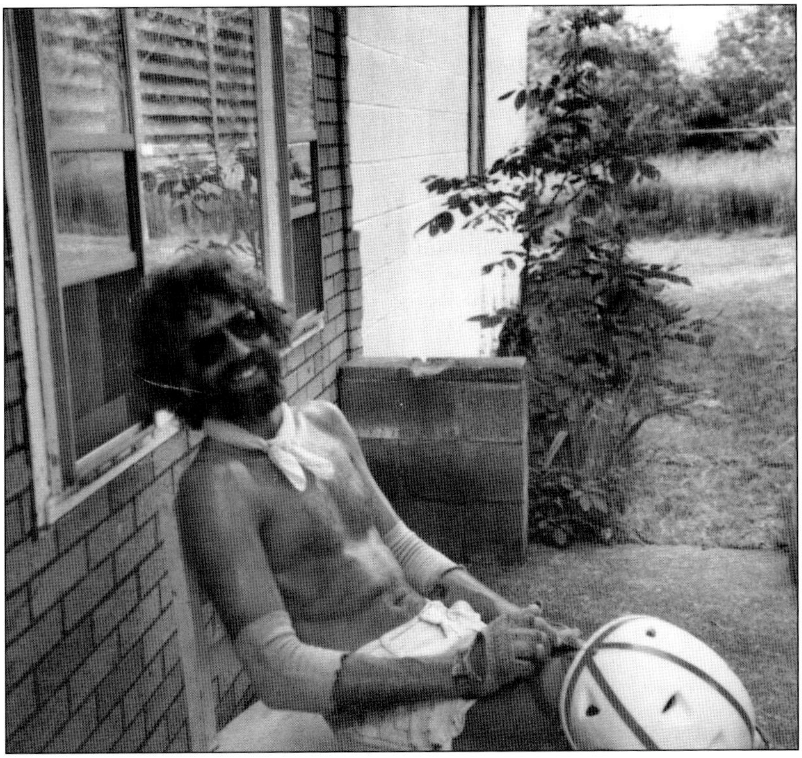

Ralph Ferrusi, photographed by Laurie Messick in 1982, was a driving force behind convincing the National Park Service to allow volunteers to convert into a trail shelter a building it had acquired when purchasing land to protect the trail. Ferrusi was the 311th person to hike the AT when he completed it in 1975. After a 22-year series of section hikes, he completed it again in 2000. (Courtesy of Laurie Adkins.)

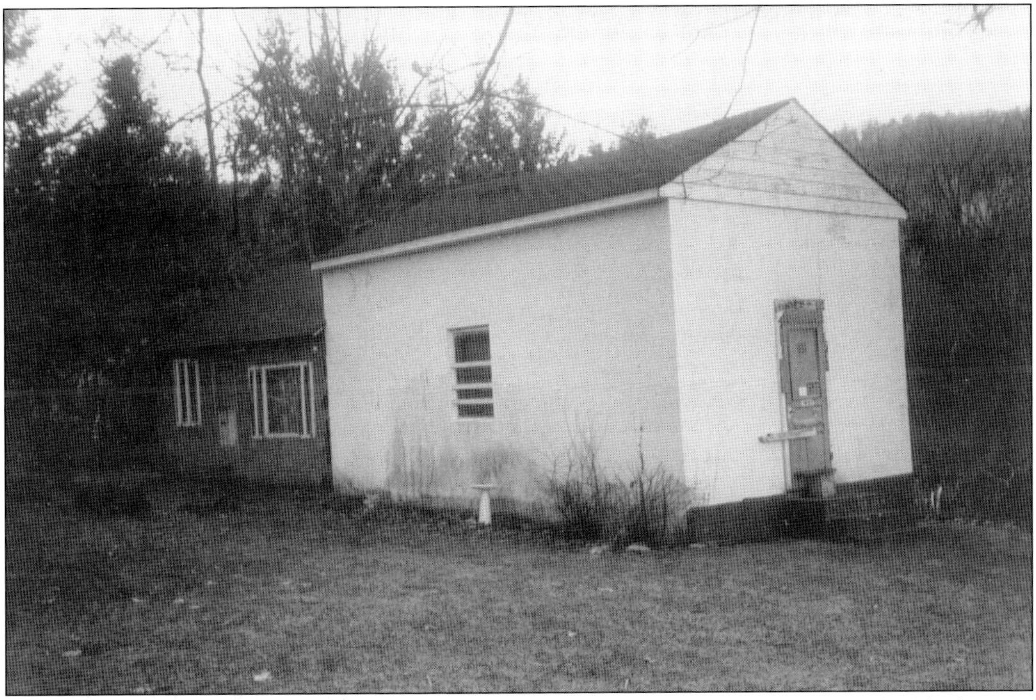

The Ralphs Peak Hikers Cabin (RPHC) was a small old home with one large cinder block room attached to a small wooden room that had an electric stove in it. However, there was no electricity in the building when it was opened to hikers in the early 1980s. (Courtesy of RPHCV.)

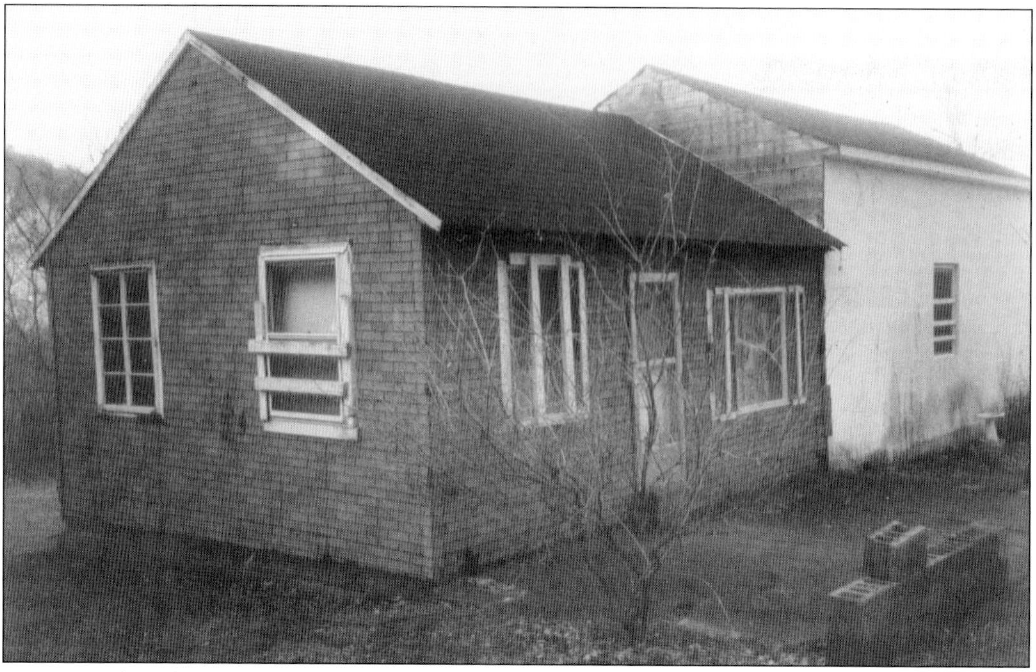

Because of its deteriorating condition, the wooden back portion of the RPHC, seen in the foreground, was removed a few years after the cabin had been established as a shelter. The Shenandoah Shuttle, a donated bicycle, enabled hikers to pedal to the nearby general store to resupply and obtain fresh sandwiches. (Courtesy of RPHCV.)

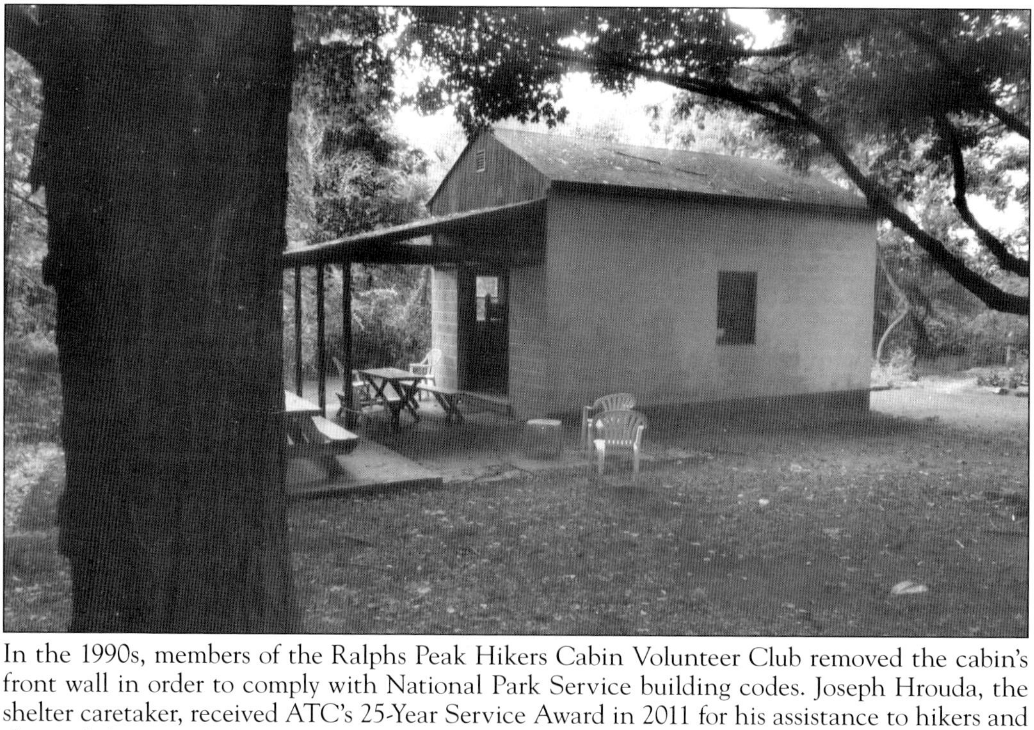

In the 1990s, members of the Ralphs Peak Hikers Cabin Volunteer Club removed the cabin's front wall in order to comply with National Park Service building codes. Joseph Hrouda, the shelter caretaker, received ATC's 25-Year Service Award in 2011 for his assistance to hikers and the trail. (Courtesy of Leonard M. Adkins.)

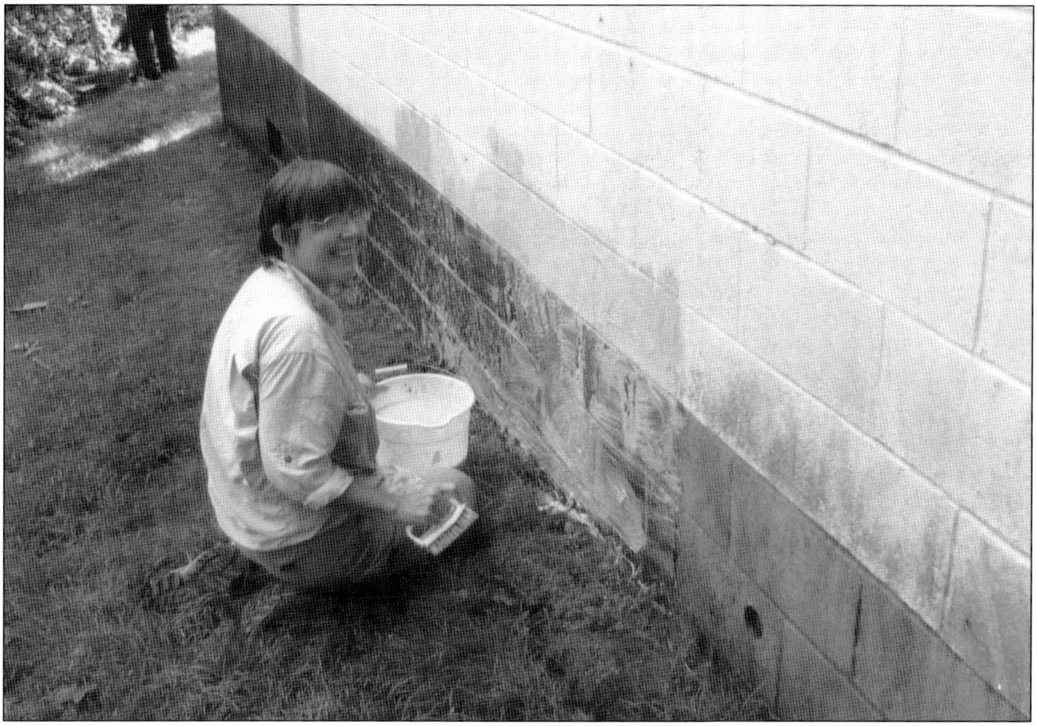

AT volunteers do all sorts of jobs. Ginny Owen, who has hiked the AT twice, among other long-distance trails, arrived for the Appalachian Long Distance Hikers Association's work weekend at RPHC in 2009 and was asked to scrub mold off the cabin. The association formed in 1983 to enable hikers to remain in contact when not on the trail and to help on various trail projects. (Courtesy of RPHCVC.)

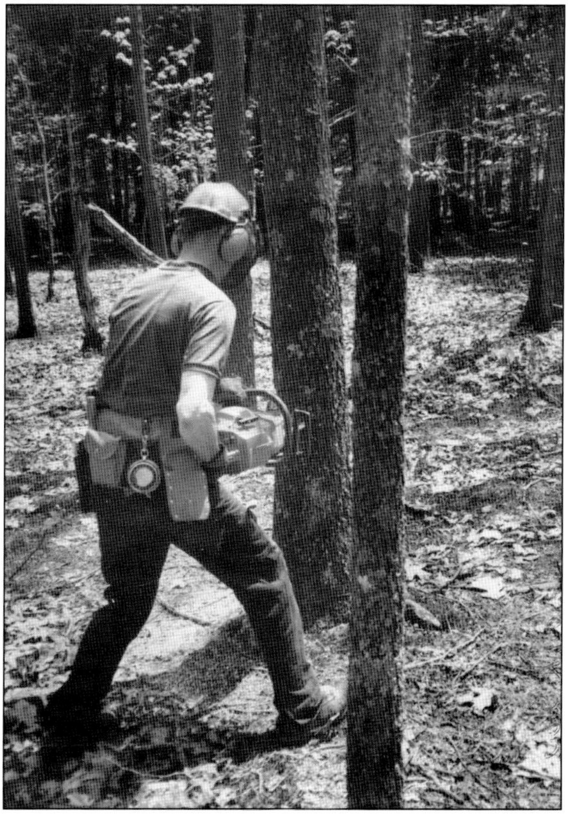

To be compliant with regulations, AT volunteers who wish to use a chain saw must take introductory and refresher courses on how to safely use the machines. The development of new techniques is a reason refresher courses are required. Here, during a workshop in May 1996, despite volunteers having been previously trained to never use the saw's tip, Jeff Putnem demonstrates the effectiveness and safety of the plunge cut. (Courtesy of CT-AMC.)

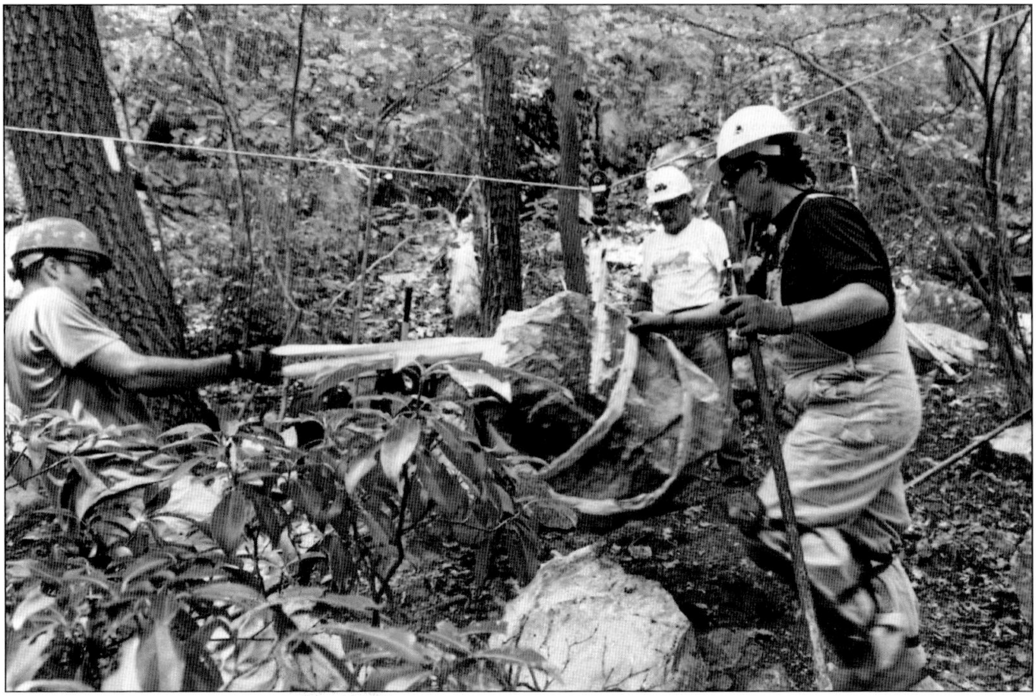

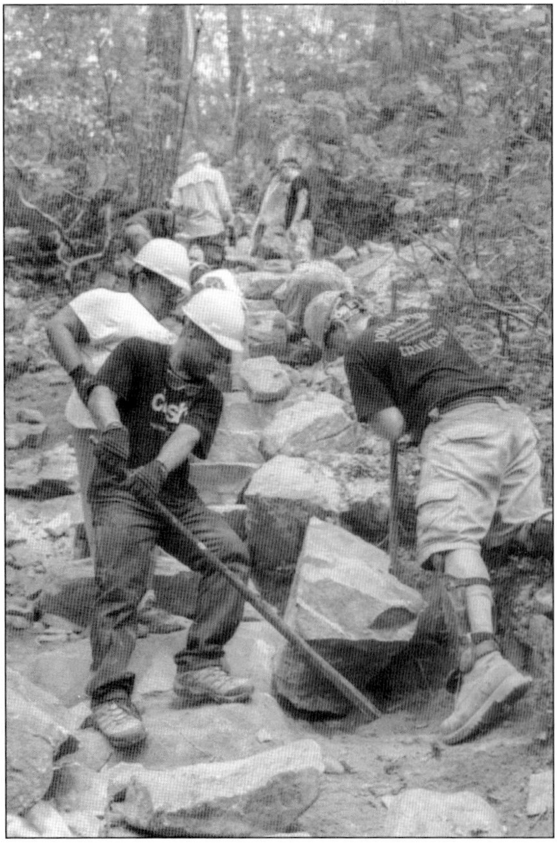

Like volunteers of the Mid-Atlantic Crew, associated with ATC, those of the Jolly Rovers, affiliated with NYNJTC, provide assistance and expertise with trail work that would be beyond the abilities of the local maintaining clubs, specifically rock work like the type seen above. In 2012, the Jolly Rovers assisted RPHCVC in building a stable and aesthetically pleasing rock staircase on a steep section of trail (left). Today, NYNJTC has 10,000 members who maintain more than 1,000 miles of trails in the metropolitan New York City area. It is also the umbrella organization for close to 100 other affiliated outdoors groups with more than 100,000 combined members. (Both, courtesy of Fred Sterns.)

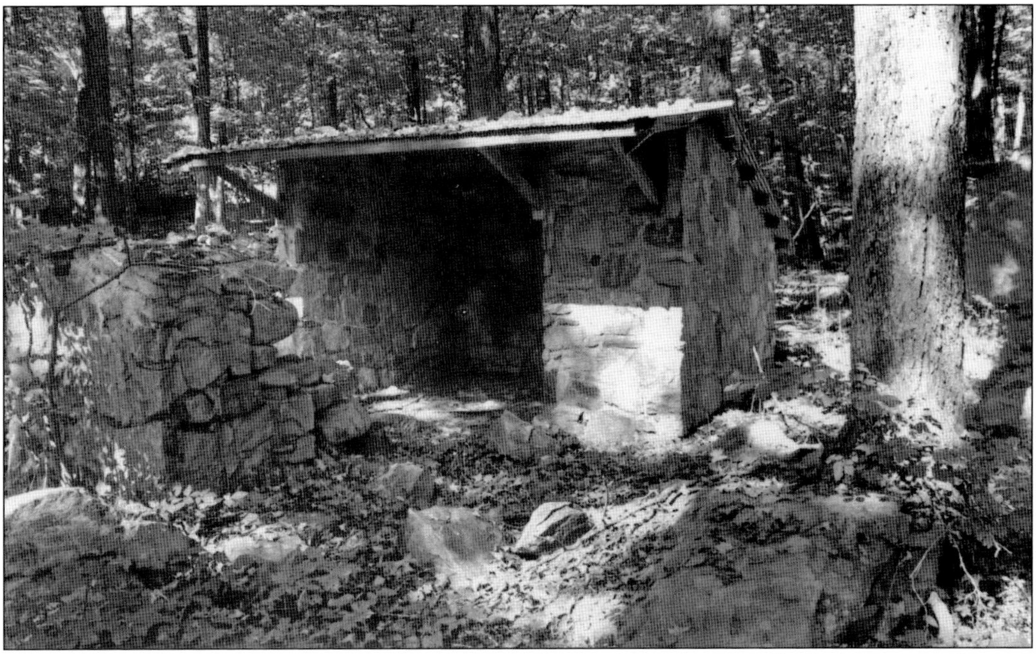

In 1958, there were only a few homes in the area where the Farmers Mill Shelter was built, next to Williams Crossroad on land donated by H.M. Lester. Housing developments soon sprang up to surround the shelter, and hikers in the 1970s and into the early 1980s walked by fashionable homes. Neighborhood children would run out to meet and walk with the hikers, often generously providing them with candy, cookies, and other snacks. Hikers who stayed overnight could also watch matches on the lighted tennis court constructed just a few yards below the shelter. Despite being abandoned after the trail was relocated in 1982, the shelter (above) and its accompanying outhouse (below) were still standing when Bill and Amy Bancroft photographed them in 2013. (Both, courtesy of Bill and Amy Bancroft.)

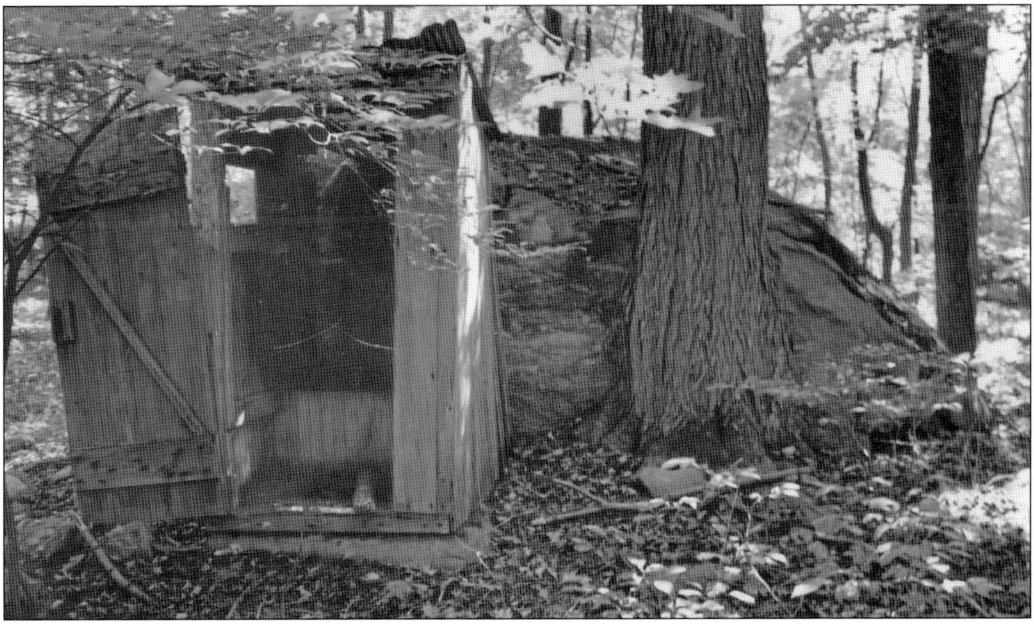

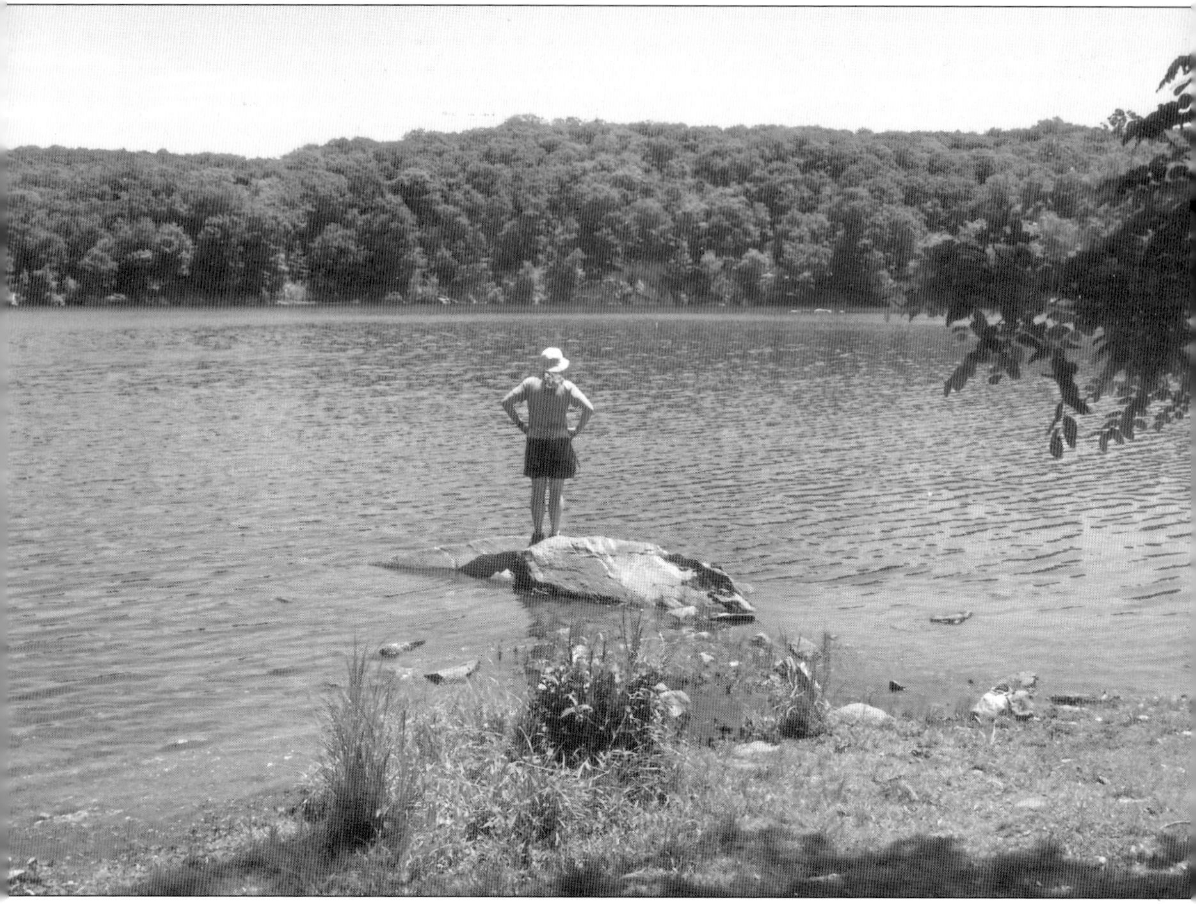

Lakes are a significant feature near the AT in eastern New York. Nuclear Lake received its name from a research facility along its shore that, in 1972, suffered an explosion that blew out windows in a lab, sending an unknown amount of plutonium across the land and into the lake. Subsequently, the buildings were taken down and the area was extensively tested and found to be safe. The AT had been rerouted beside the lake by the time this photograph was taken in the late 1900s. Prior to the mid-1980s, the AT went on roads by another lake, Edward R. Murrow Memorial Park, in Pawling. The town government permitted hikers to stay at a pavilion above the lake, even allowing them to swim and shower for free. The park's concession stand was also a draw for hikers. (Courtesy of Leonard M. Adkins.)

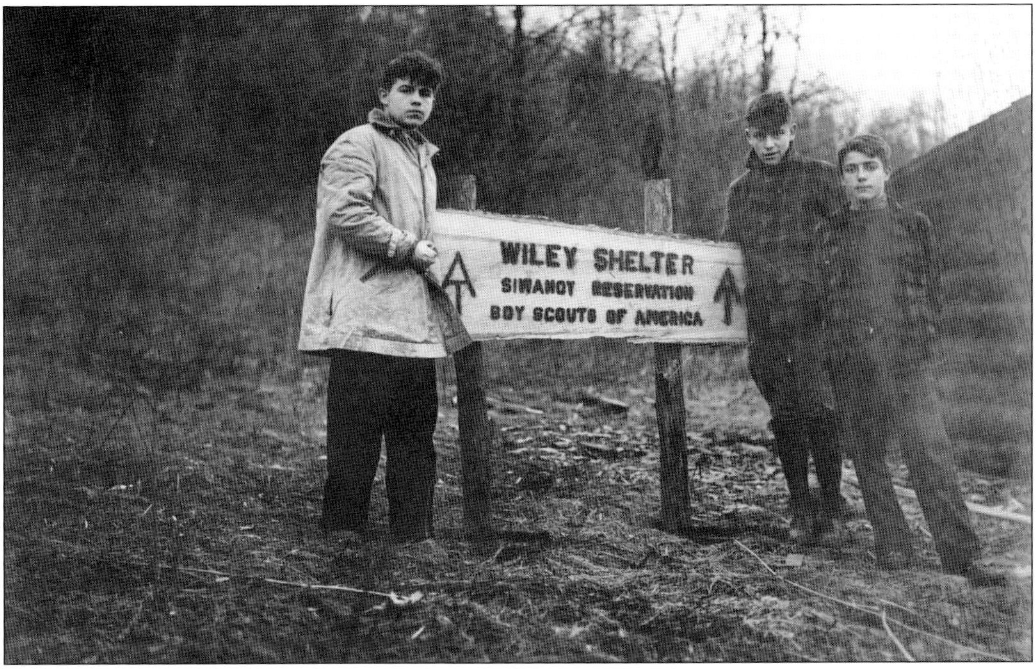

Above, in 1941, Boy Scouts posed beside the sign for the Wiley Shelter, named for a person who helped construct it, William O. Wiley of the Tramp and Trail Club. When it formed in New York City on September 11, 1914, annual dues for the club were $1.50. The shelter is located on land that was once a part of Boy Scout Camp Sinoway, opened in 1926. The camp was popular year-round until the 1980s, when attendance started to drop. Most of the property was sold and became upscale housing in the late 1990s and early 2000s. Thanks to the protection of the AT, the shelter and the land around it look much the same as they did when Myron Avery took the photograph below, soon after the shelter was completed in 1940. (Both, courtesy of ATC.)

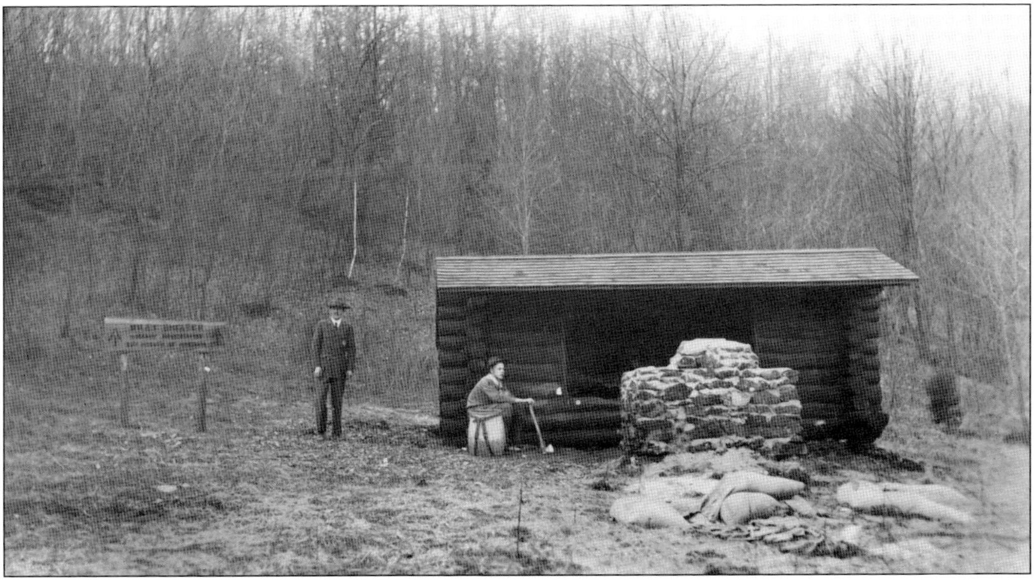

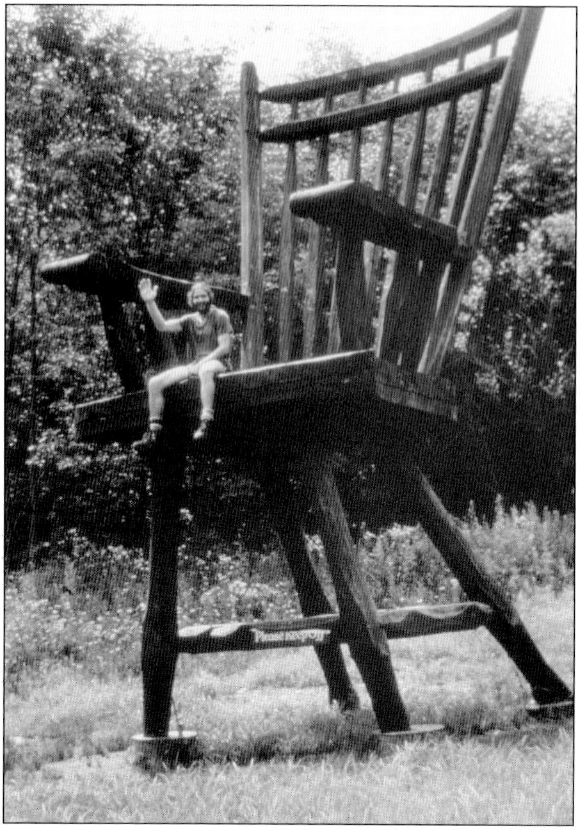

Following many of the same roads it had followed since it was first blazed in the 1920s and 1930s, the AT crossed Ten Mile River on a highway bridge at Webatuck, going by a furniture manufacturer. Even though a sign said, "Please keep off," many hikers, including Albie Pokrob, seen here in 1980, could not resist sitting in the giant chair. A major relocation subsequently moved the trail. (Courtesy of Warren Doyle.)

Northward from the Ten Mile River crossing, the AT followed Dogtail Corners Road for more than a mile, with little room for hikers to get off the pavement to avoid automobile traffic. Once on woods roads and finally onto a pathway, the trail ascended to Schaghticoke Mountain, where it left New York and entered Connecticut. (Courtesy of Leonard M. Adkins.)

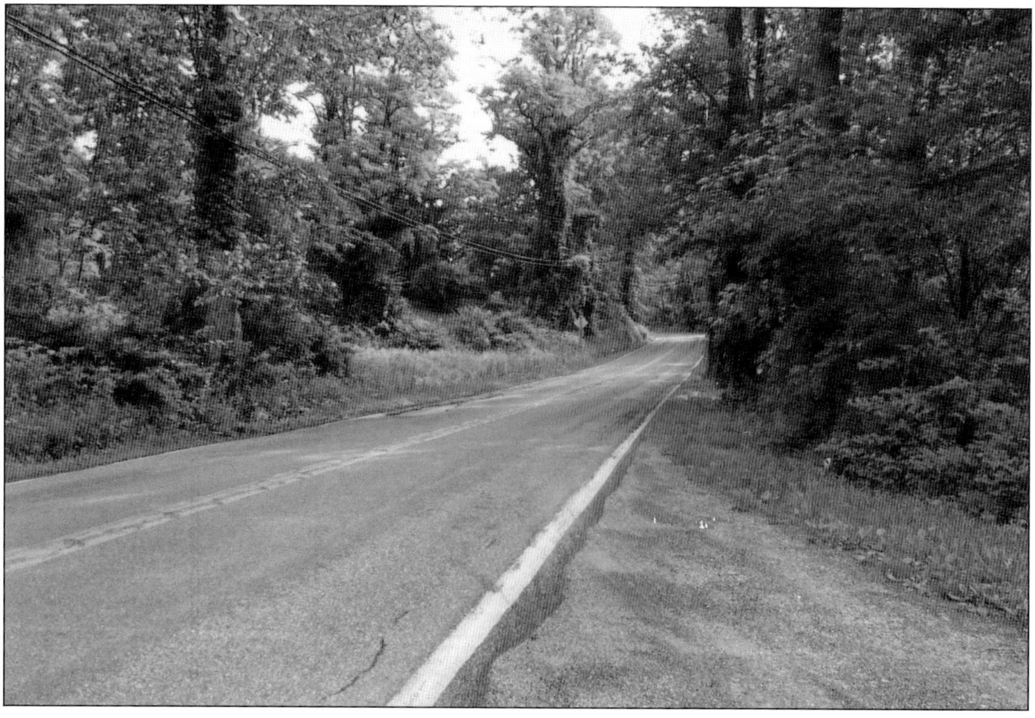

Three

Connecticut

Entering Connecticut, the AT crosses Ten Mile River and briefly goes back into New York before passing through the Schaghticoke Indian Reservation, the only Native American lands the trail is located upon. Zigzagging over Mount Algo and Calebs Peak, the trail descends St. Johns Ledges to begin one of its longest level stretches, a walk of nearly five miles along the Housatonic River.

Originally, the trail crossed the Housatonic to make a traverse of the forests through the Litchfield Hills. Due to concerns over increased development, it was relocated in 1988 to stay on the western side of the river and pass through the highlands of the Housatonic State Forest for views of the Taconic Mountains to the west and the Housatonic Valley to the east. The original route is now part of the Connecticut Blue Trail System and connects back with the AT near where the trail recrosses the Housatonic River to hook up with a nature trail south of Falls Village. The stone ruins along this pathway were part of a canal system built in 1851 to bring water to a hydroelectric plant that was to provide the power to turn Falls Village into a huge industrial center. In what today would surely be grounds for a lawsuit, the plan failed because the builders of the canal had neglected to use mortar to hold the rock walls of the canal together.

At Great Falls, the trail again crosses the Housatonic River and then ascends to grand vistas of the Housatonic Valley, the Taconic Mountains, and, on clear days, Mount Greylock in Massachusetts, 50 miles to the north. The trail gains the heights of the Taconic Range as it crosses over barefaced Lions Head and, for the first time since Maryland, rises above 2,000 feet atop Bear Mountain (2,316 feet), the highest mountain entirely in Connecticut (the state's highest point is on the southern slope of Mount Frissell as it rises into Massachusetts).

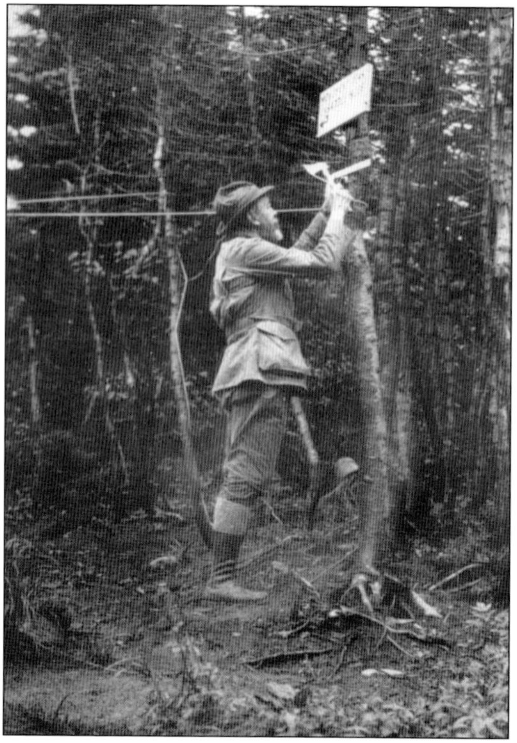

Even those who held the highest positions within the trail community and ATC in the early days of the trail went out to physically work on it. Judge Arthur Perkins of Connecticut, appointed ATC chairman in 1928, was often found working on the trail. Here, in 1927, he nails a sign to a tree to mark a newly scouted section. This photograph was taken by a Mr. Wright. (Courtesy of ATC.)

Nestell "Ned" Kipp Anderson (right), wearing his trademark bandana, lived and farmed in Sherman and is credited with scouting, contacting landowners, building, and maintaining almost all of the AT in Connecticut from 1929 to 1949. He was often accompanied by Myron Avery (seated on the rock in the center). On the left is Howard Evans, and George Helmke is behind Avery. (Photograph by Frederick S. Best; courtesy of SHS.)

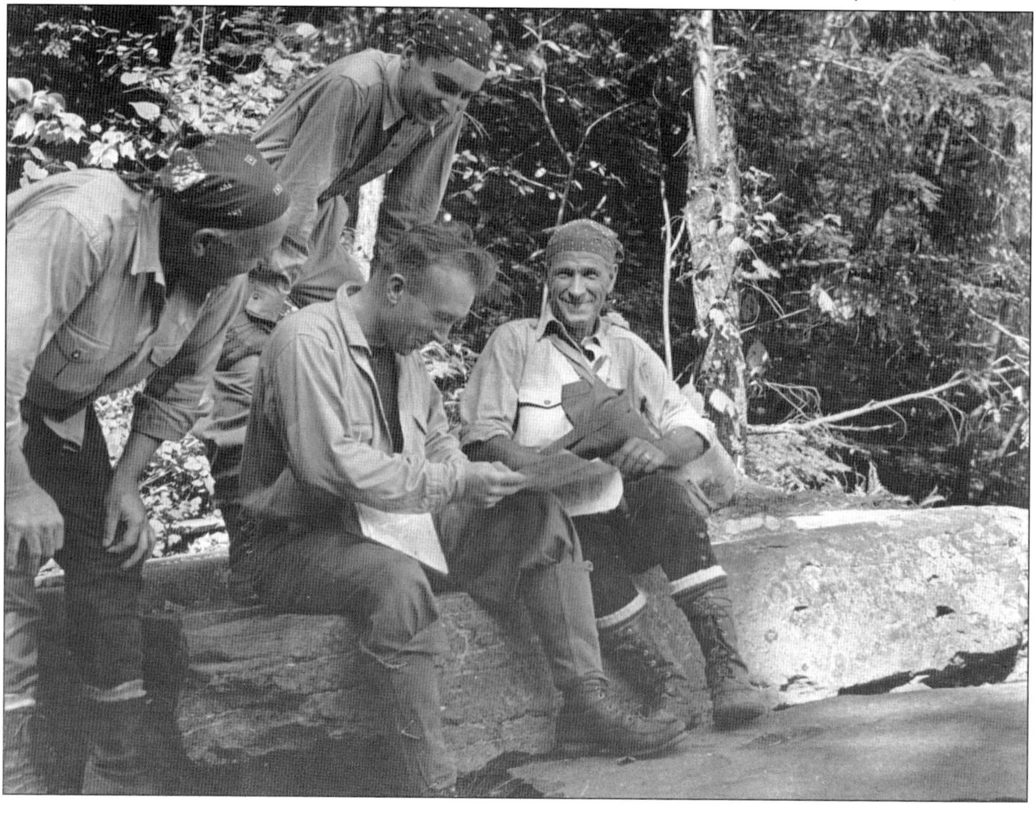

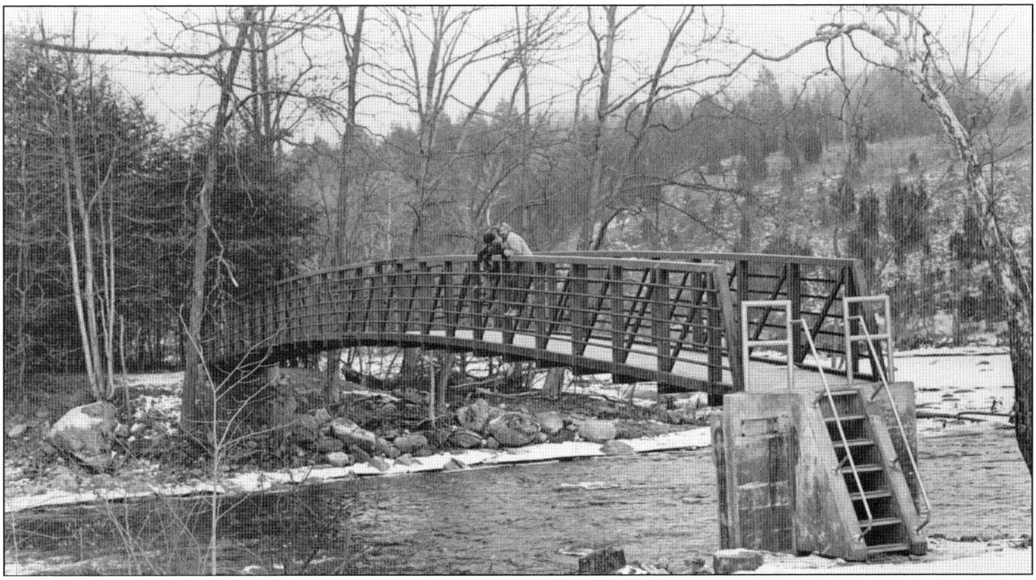

The completion of the Ned Anderson Memorial Bridge across the Ten Mile River in 1983 enabled a relocation to take the trail off of miles of roads. It also eliminated trail miles in New York while adding some in Connecticut. The prefabricated steel reinforced bridge was lifted into place with a crane. The Naromi Land Trust and AMC donated the bridge's $50,000 cost. (Courtesy of ATC.)

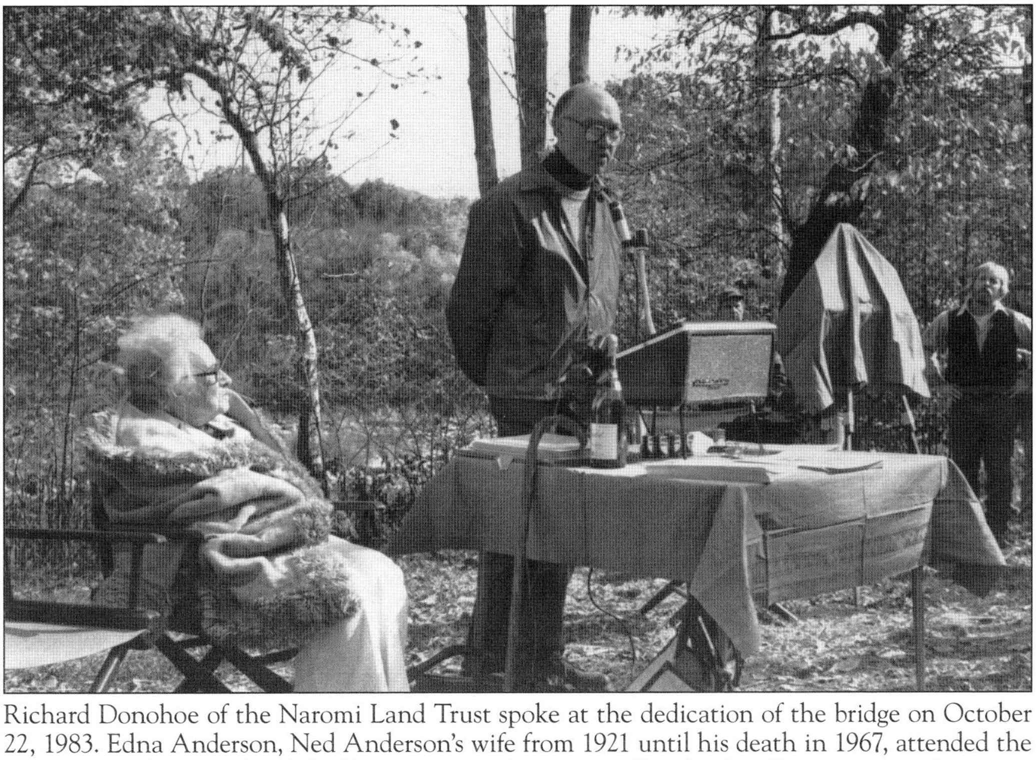

Richard Donohoe of the Naromi Land Trust spoke at the dedication of the bridge on October 22, 1983. Edna Anderson, Ned Anderson's wife from 1921 until his death in 1967, attended the ceremony and is seated at left. She participated in many of her husband's activities and outings. (Courtesy of ATC.)

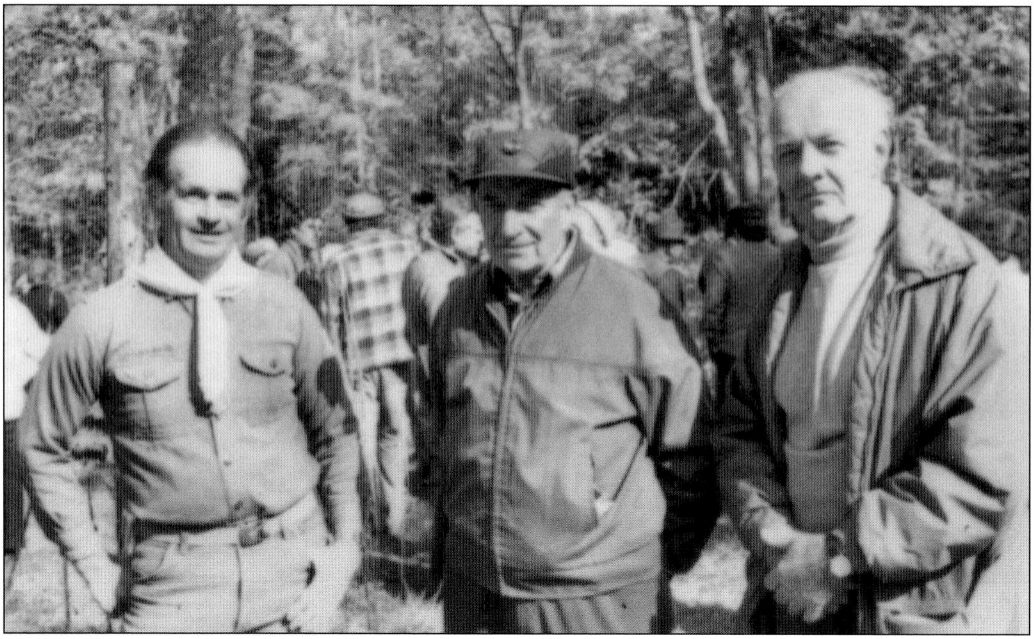

Three of Ned Anderson's original Boy Scouts from the 1930s, who had helped him scout and build much of Connecticut's AT, attended the ceremony dedicating the Ten Mile River Bridge in his honor. From left to right are Marshall Munch, Albert Soukoup, and Kenneth Rogers. (Courtesy of SHS.)

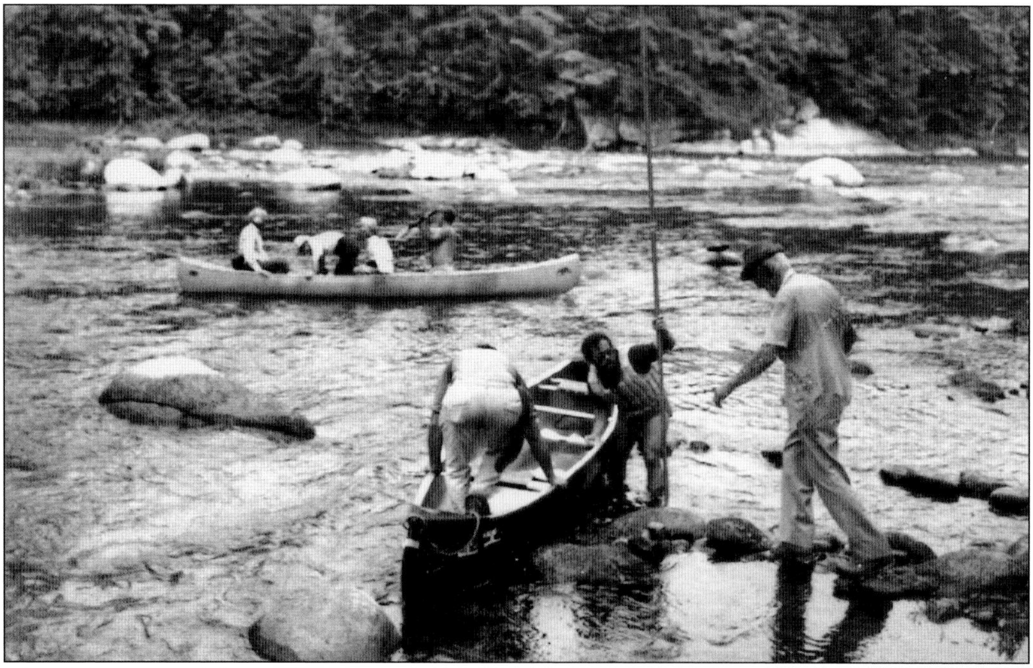

The dedication of the Ned Anderson Memorial Bridge in October 1983 occurred before the bridge was put in place, on December 5 and 6 of that year. Since there was no bridge, some ceremony attendees celebrated the day by crossing the river in canoes. (Photograph by Dereka Smith; courtesy of ATC.)

This hand-carved paddle was made to commemorate Ned Anderson's first overnight camp with his Boy Scouts, on April 25, 1931, at Rhodes Ravine. In attendance were Chester Boyd, Arvid Alfredson, Emerson Osborn, Kenneth Rogers, Robert Judd, Clayton Cass, and Arrin English. Anderson also helped build a cabin for the Scouts at Spring Lake in Sherman. (Courtesy of SHS.)

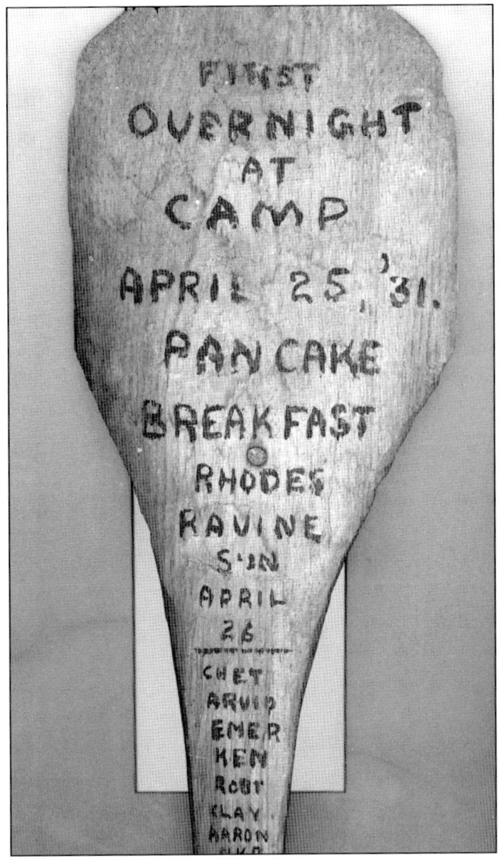

In 1932, Ned Anderson organized the Housatonic Trail Club, which, according to its bylaws, was created "to explore the mountains for scientific and artistic purposes . . . to bring together for co-operation all those interested in forests and mountains and to develop trails and camp sites." In 1940, some of the members posed for a photograph at Anderson's home on Brae Burn Farm. Anderson is second from the right. (Courtesy of SHS.)

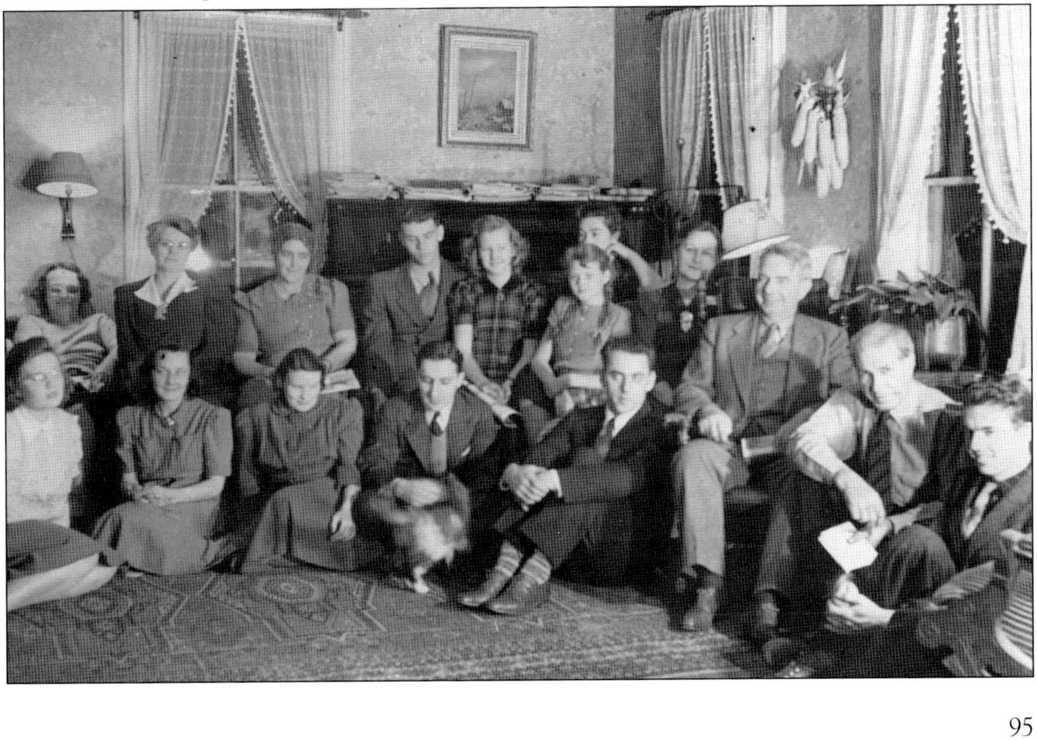

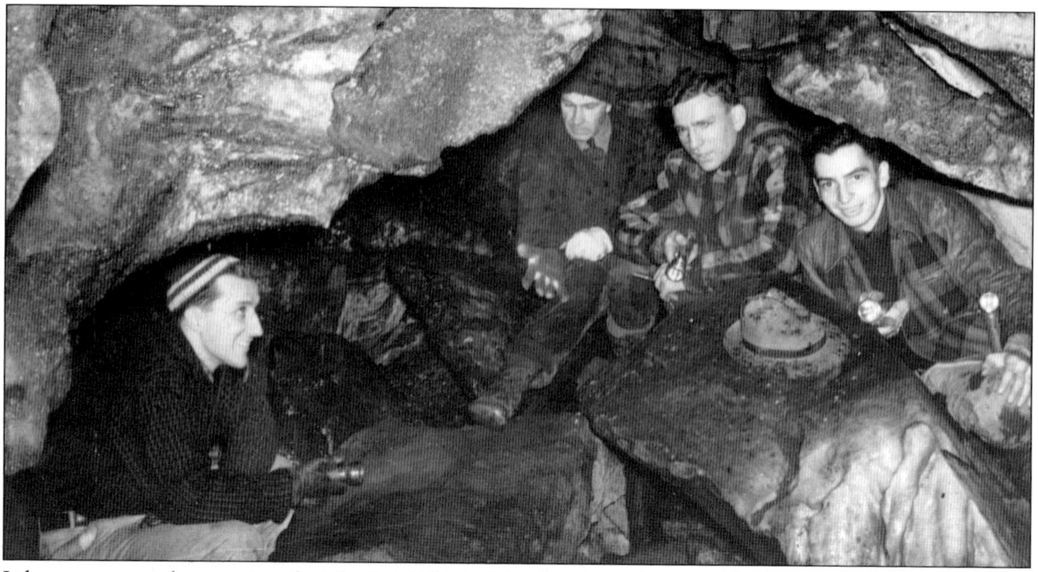

Like many people associated with the AT, Ned Anderson did not just hike. An avid spelunker, he also led the Housatonic Trail Club, as well as informal groups, on underground outings. In 1941, (from left to right) Joseph Ruddley, Anderson, Fred Heitcamp, and George Helmke went to the Tory Cave, close to New Milford. The name is derived from a British loyalist, known as Tories, who hid in the cave during the Revolutionary War. (Courtesy of SHS.)

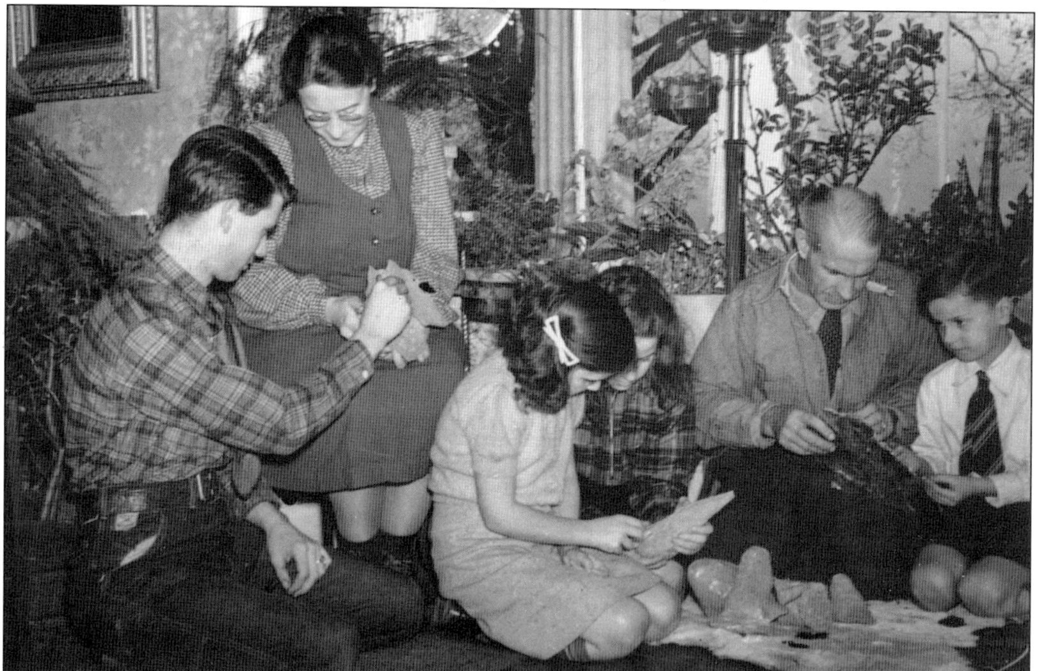

The biography *Ned Anderson: Connecticut's Appalachian Trailblazer/Small Town Renaissance Man*, written by Doris Tomaselli, shows that Anderson (second from right) was a dedicated family man. He was photographed giving a geology lesson to, from left to right, his son Theodore Anderson III; his wife, Edna; and his daughter Alice Rielle's children Dorothy Lee, Joan, and Ned. (Courtesy of SHS.)

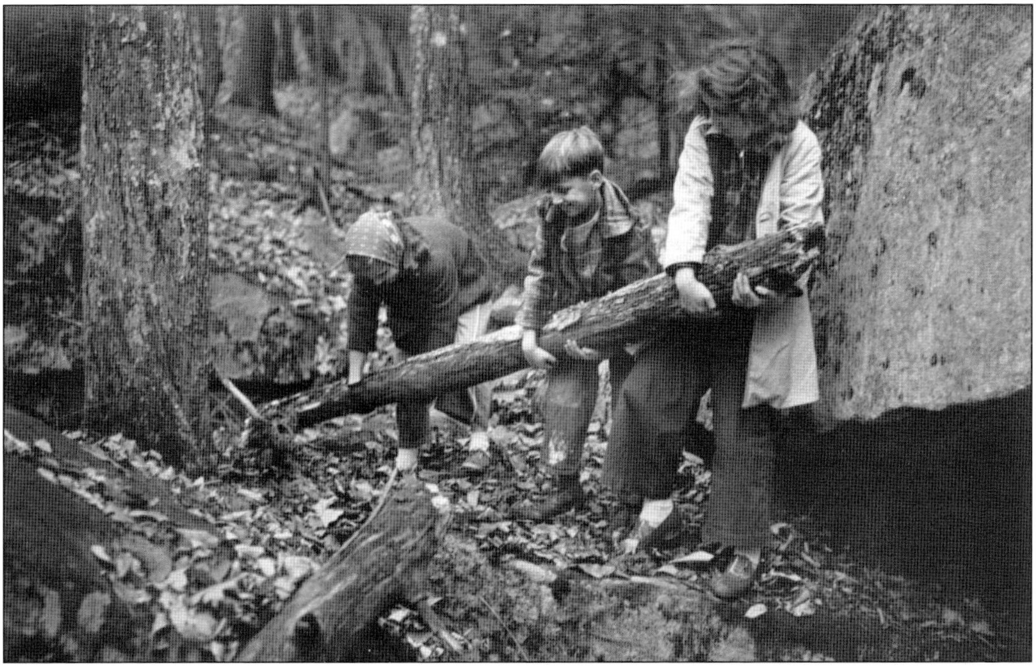

The Anderson family was like many families that become a part of the AT community—the entire clan became devoted to the trail. In 1940, three of Alice Rielle's children (Ned Anderson's grandchildren), from left to right, Dorothy Lee, Robert, and Joan, cleared a blowdown from the trail. The photograph was taken by Frederick S. Best of Berkeley Heights, New Jersey. (Courtesy of SHS.)

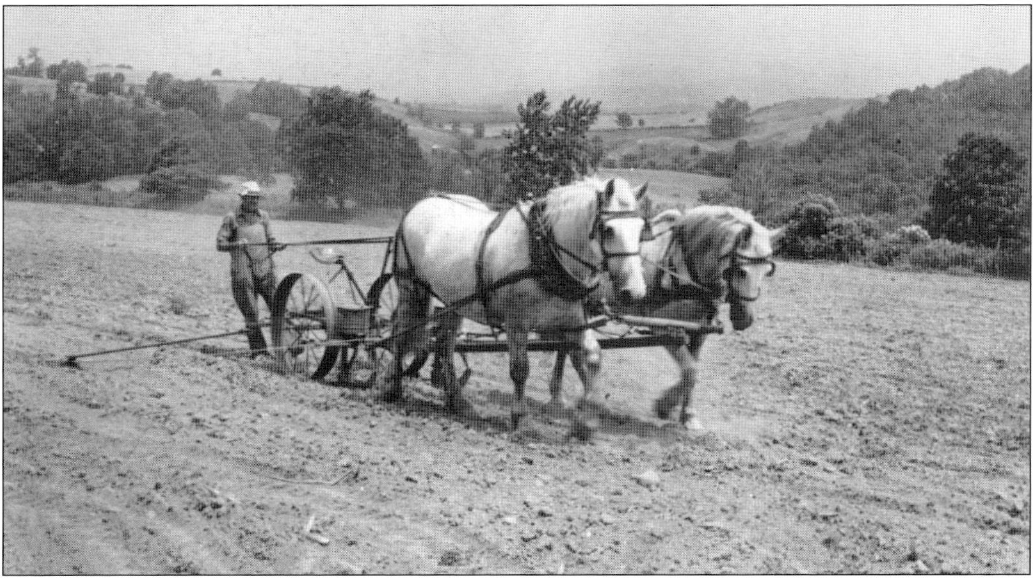

The AT parallels the Housatonic River and passes through the Housatonic Valley for much of the way through Connecticut. In addition to being an active trail volunteer, Boy Scout master, and even school bus driver, Ned Anderson was a farmer, the primary occupation of many valley residents. Here, in 1942, Anderson plows his fields at Brae Burn, the farm his father purchased in 1906. (Courtesy of SHS.)

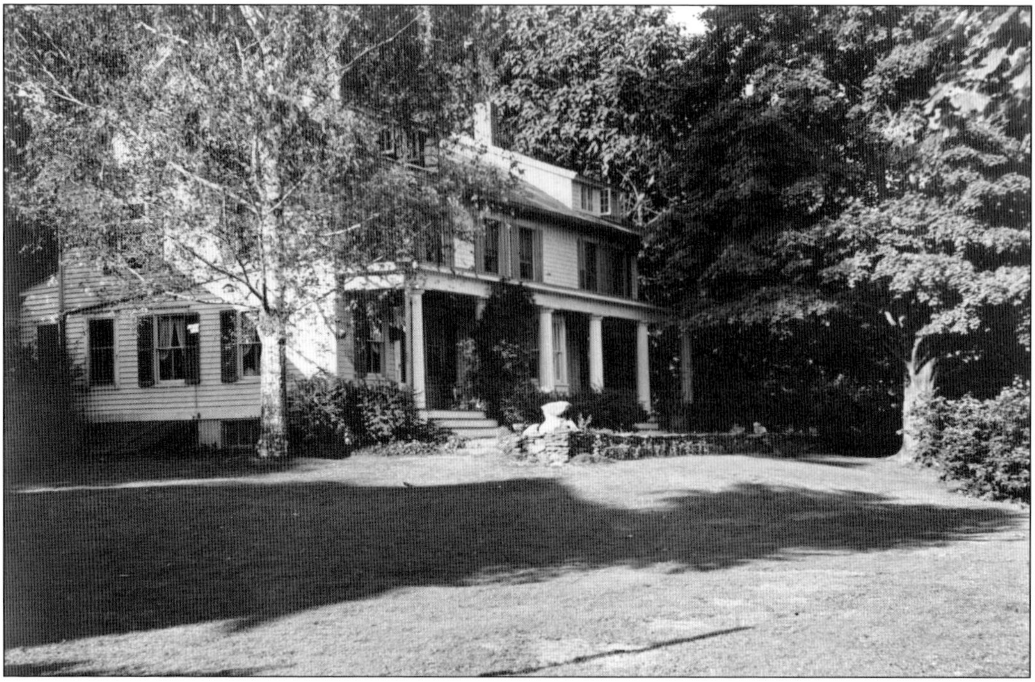

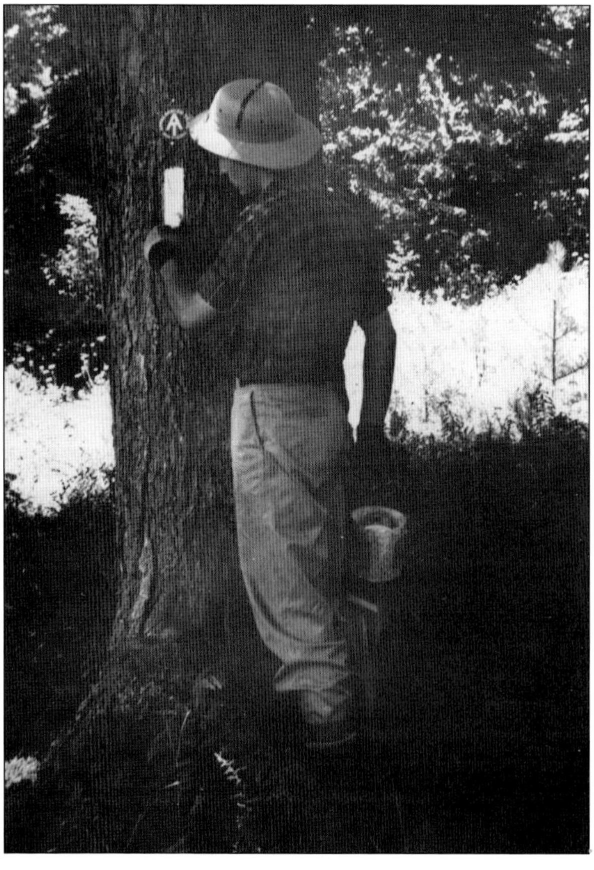

Brae Burn was not only the family home, but it also became the center of activity for Ned and Edna Anderson's dealings with the Housatonic Trail Club and the Boy Scouts. It also became a workshop and store for the jewelry and baked goods Edna handcrafted and the works of other local artists. In addition, the Andersons offered farm vacations, a forerunner of today's rural bed-and-breakfasts. (Courtesy of ATC.)

Wearing a pith helmet like Earl Shaffer wore during the AT's first thru-hike in 1948, George Helmke, a Housatonic Trail Club member, blazes a tree in 1940. The AT in Connecticut was marked with blue blazes, while some of the trail in New York was blazed with yellow. It was not until the 1940s, after acrimonious discussions among trail supporters, that the white blaze became standard from Georgia to Maine. (Courtesy of SHS.)

Paul Osborn, who as a child rode on Ned Anderson's school bus, uses an axe to clear trail in 1941. Most trail clubs did not own chain saws, as they were almost prohibitively expensive at the time. Even today, maintainers are not permitted to use mechanized equipment when working in federally designated wilderness areas. (Photograph by Frederick S. Best; courtesy of SHS.)

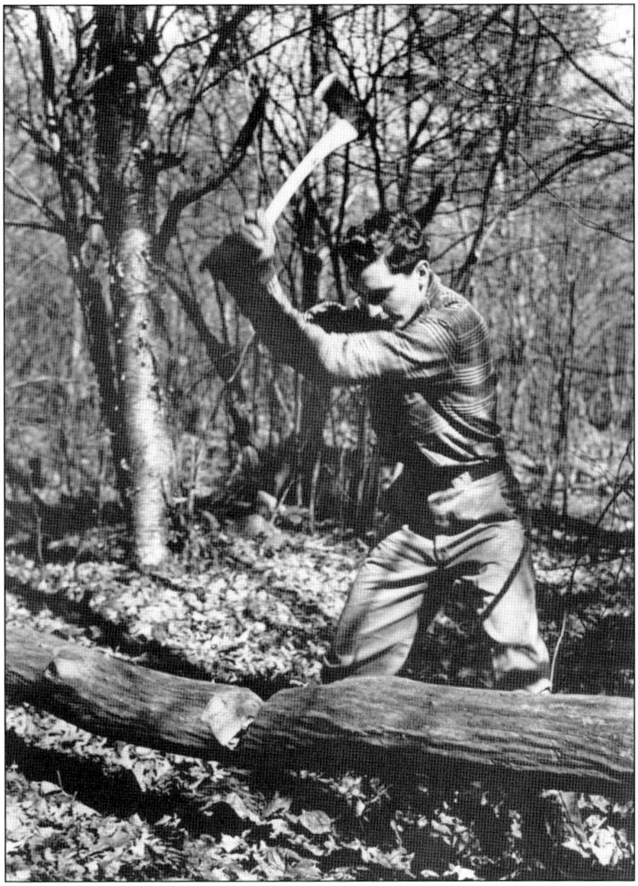

The same relocation that took the AT across the Ned Anderson Memorial Bridge also brought the trail close to Bulls Bridge, south of Kent. There has been a bridge at this location since the mid-1700s, and the current structure, shown on this early-1900s postcard, was constructed in 1842. It has been repaired a number of times since then but never replaced. (Courtesy of the Collotype Company.)

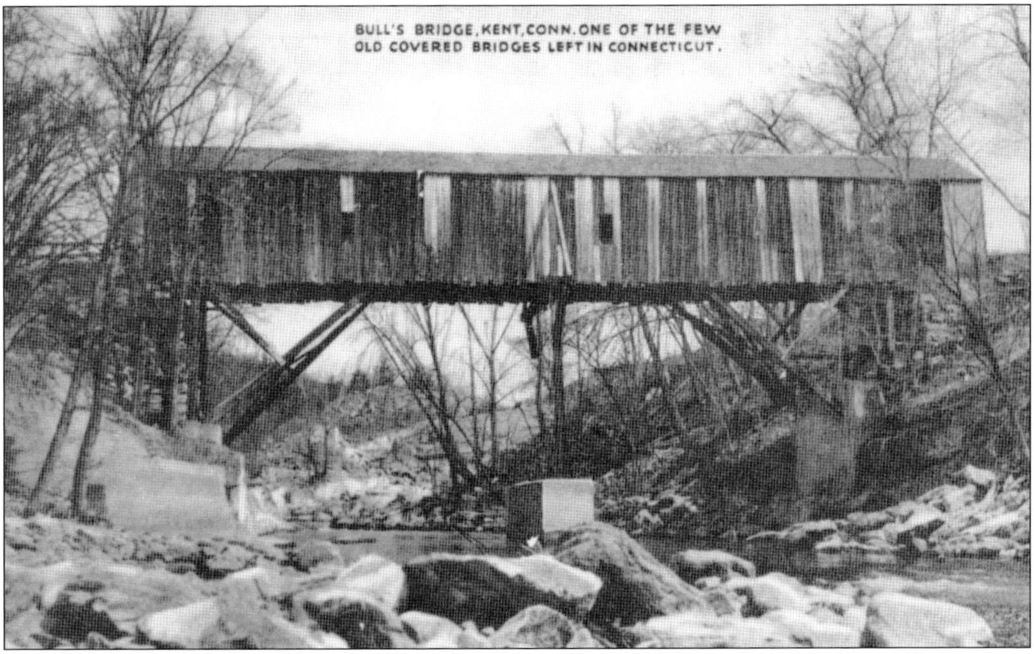

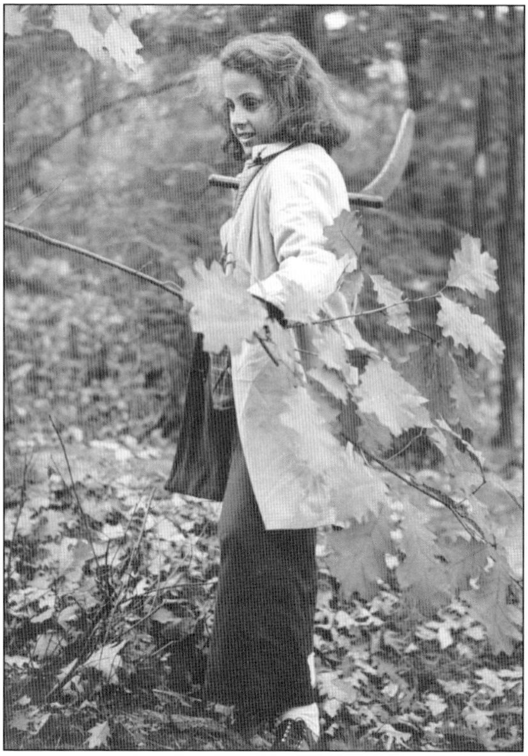

Alice Mildred Anderson was the first of the four children of Ned Anderson and his first wife, Lena "Lee" May Clark, who passed away during the 1919 flu epidemic. Alice returned to live at Brae Burn Farm after ending her marriage to Robert Rielle, and her children often joined Ned Anderson for farm chores and outings on the AT. In 1941, Dorothy Lee (left) was provided with a corn knife to clear small limbs and low-growing brush from the trail. Joan (below), two years younger than Dorothy Lee, was given the job of painting blazes on trees, which, given her small stature at the time, meant the blazes were closer to the ground than those painted by adults. (Both, courtesy of SHS.)

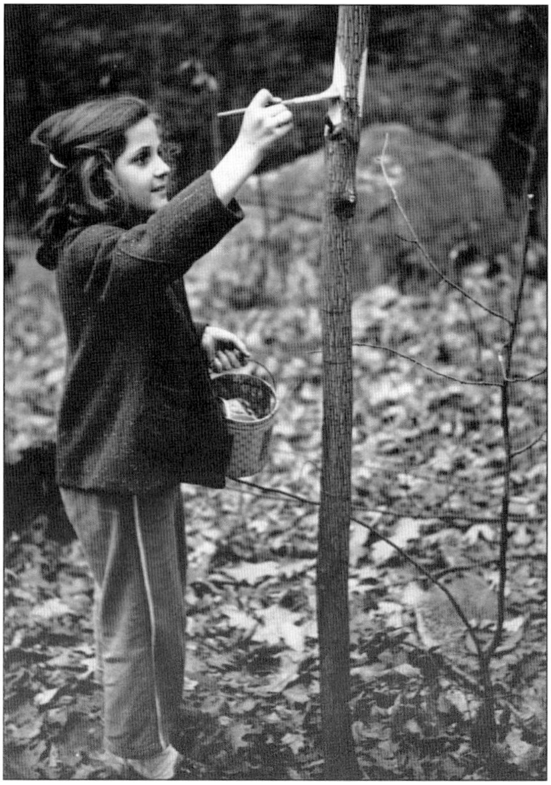

Benton MacKaye, the "father" of the AT, was born in Stamford, Connecticut, in 1879 and always had an interest in adventure and the outdoors. Moving to Massachusetts at the age of nine, he soon began keeping a journal of a number of his ramblings about the rural landscape. A bicycling and hiking trip in the wilds of New Hampshire introduced him to "a second world—and promise!" (Courtesy of ATC.)

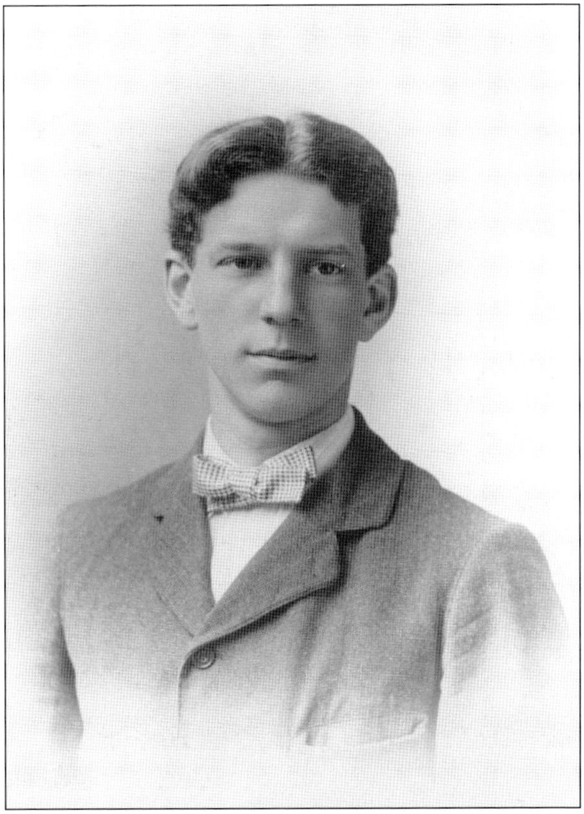

Benton MacKaye's parents wrote and presented plays after they moved to Shirley, Massachusetts, and their home was visited by actors and musicians. This is what may have prompted MacKaye (right) to pick up a banjo to accompany and sing along with guitar player Howard Davenport (left). (Courtesy of ATC.)

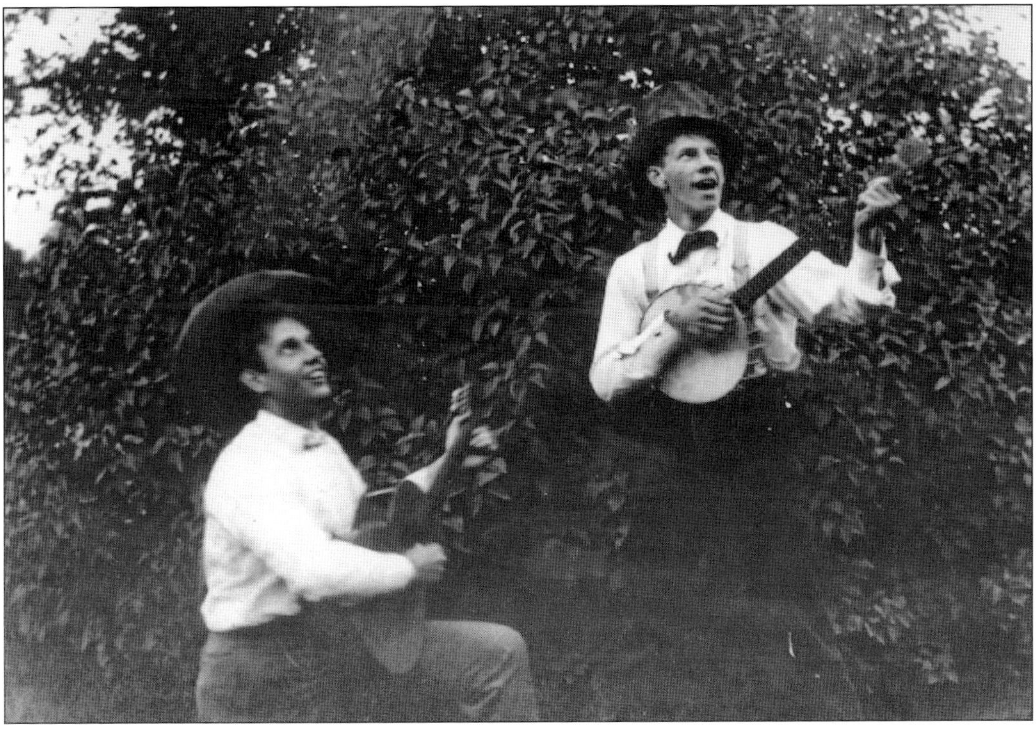

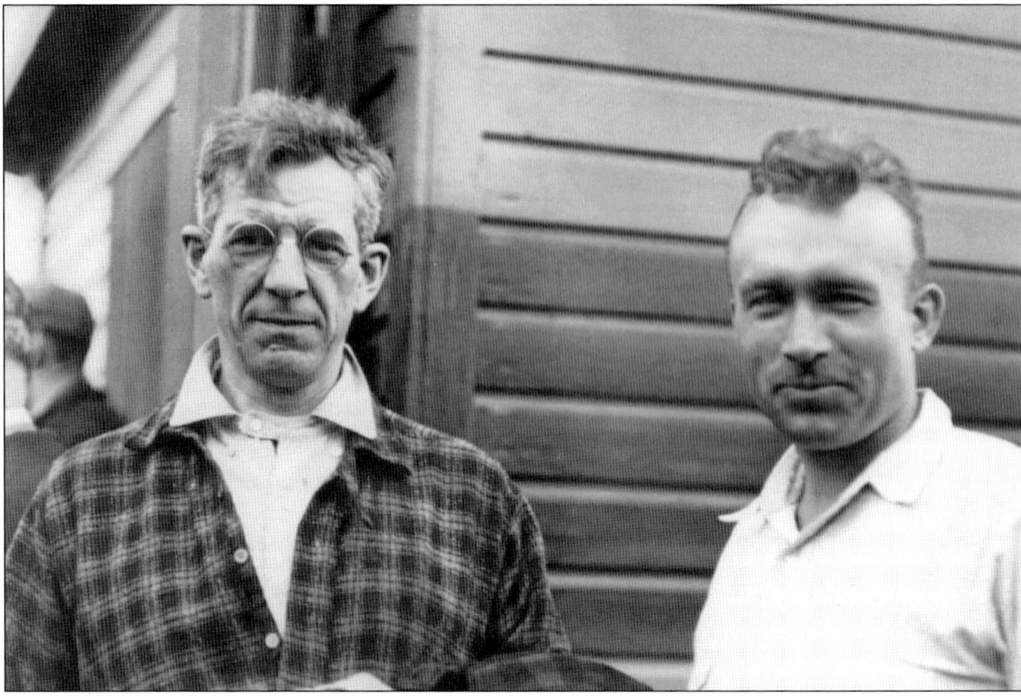

Benton MacKaye's and Myron Avery's visions for the trail differed so greatly that they had a tumultuous relationship, and by time the AT was completed in 1937, they were no longer speaking with each other. This rare photograph of the two together was taken on October 12, 1931, when they met to celebrate the dedication of a new section of trail. (Courtesy of ATC.)

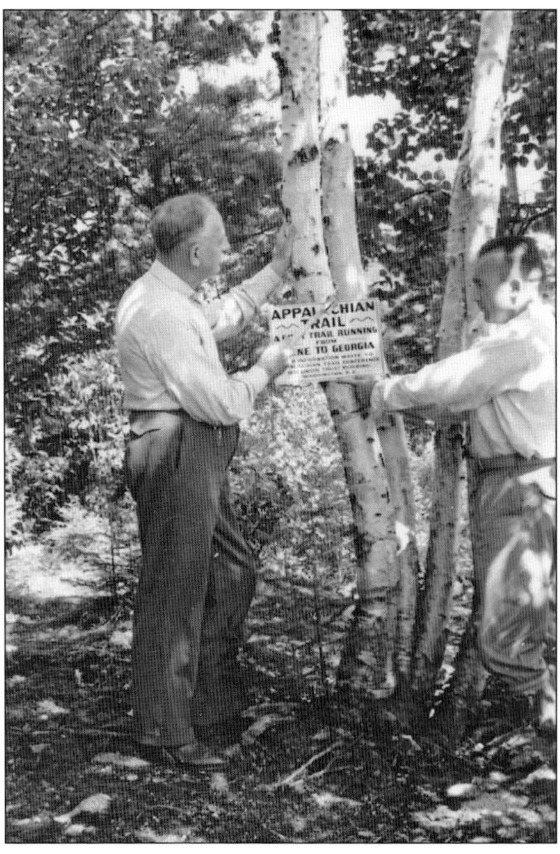

Robert C. Fechner (left), director of the Civilian Conservation Corps (CCC) from 1933 to 1939, accompanied Myron Avery on a trip to the AT, not only to work on it, but also to generate publicity for the role the CCC was taking in helping to complete the trail. (Courtesy of ATC.)

In 1964, Benton MacKaye presented this signed photograph "To Edna and Andy." At ATC's first meeting in 1925, MacKaye said the AT's ultimate purpose "is to conserve, use and enjoy the mountain hinterland which penetrates the populous portion of America from north to south." In 1971, he stated that its ultimate purpose was "to walk, to see and to see what you see." (Courtesy of ATC.)

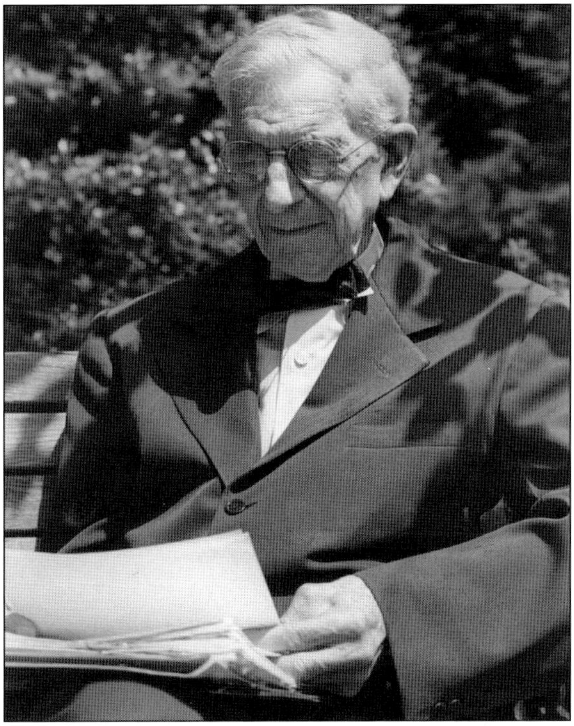

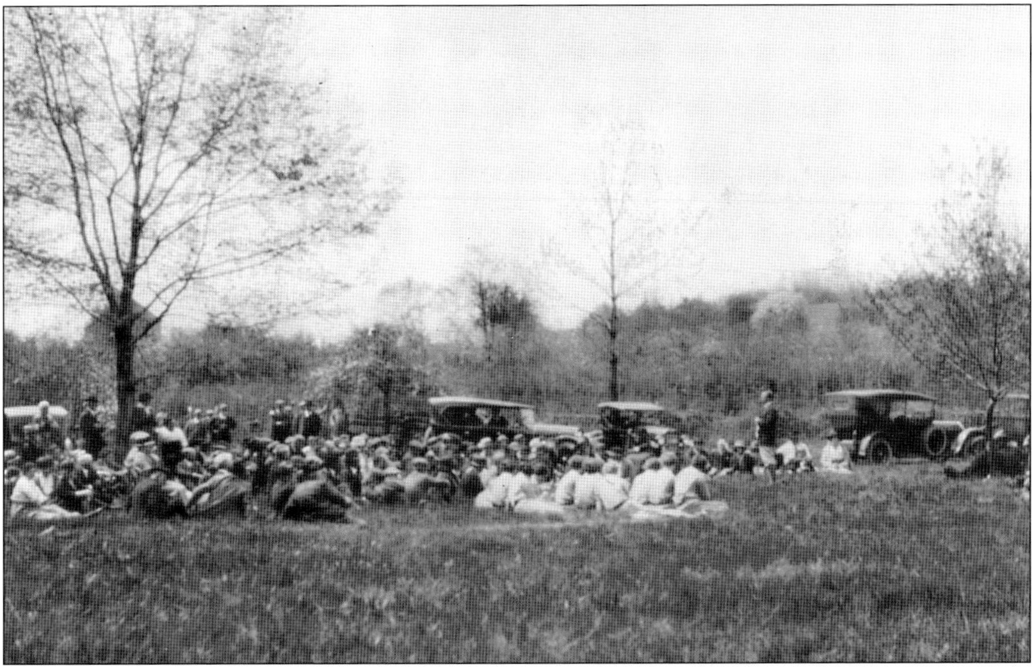

The Connecticut Forest and Park Association (CFPA) was established in 1895, nearly two decades before Benton MacKaye proposed the AT. On May 23, 1907, it held this event on an estate near Middlebury. The photograph was taken by Walter Filley, who later became active in the CCC. In 1929, the CFPA began working on a system of trails throughout Connecticut. (Courtesy of CSL.)

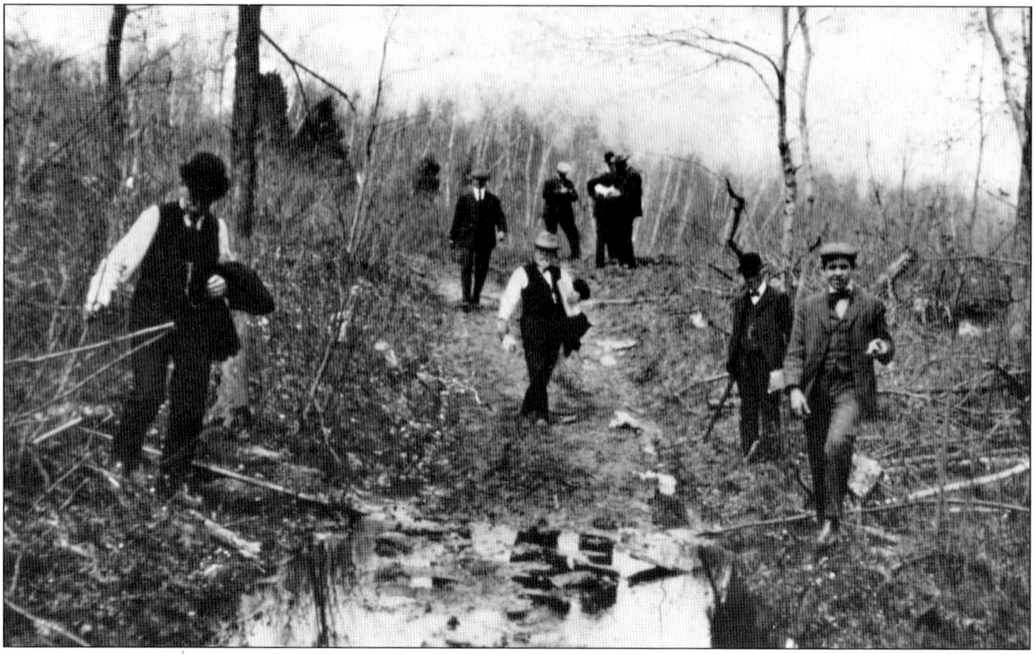

Also in May 1907, the CFPA had its first field meeting in Meshomasic State Forest, the first state forest established in New England. The CFPA worked closely with ATC to establish the AT in Connecticut. Its efforts also resulted in the statewide Blue Trail System and the publication of the *Connecticut Walk Book*. The organization still oversees trails and publishes updated editions of the book. (Courtesy of CSL.)

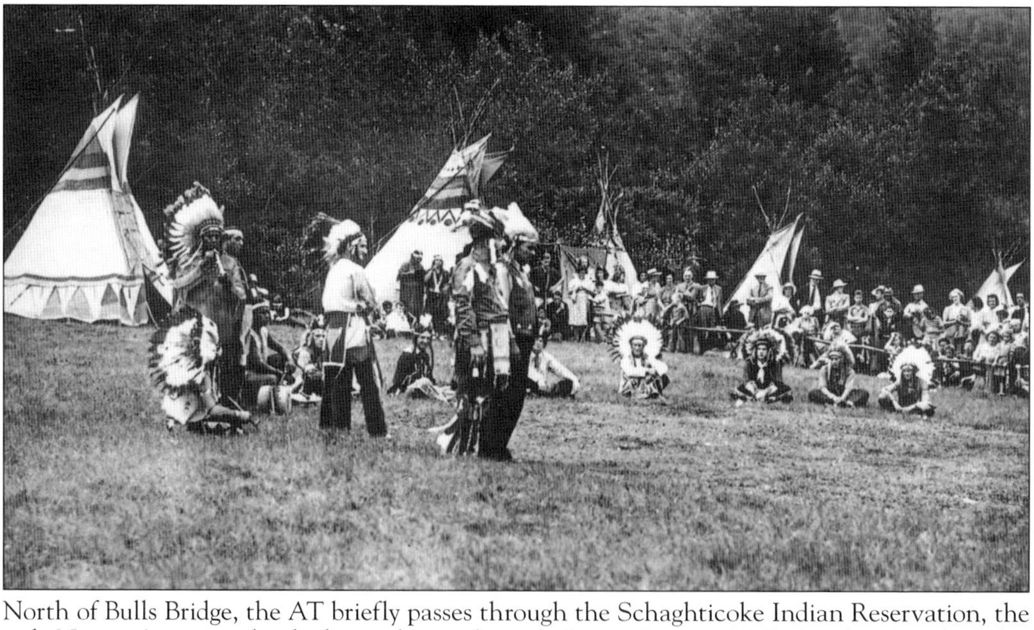

North of Bulls Bridge, the AT briefly passes through the Schaghticoke Indian Reservation, the only Native American lands the trail goes through. Lewis Sprague Mills Sr. photographed this event in the 1930s, which was staged to fit the tourists' Hollywood image of Indians. Teepees and feather headdresses were used by tribes in the Great Plains, not in eastern America. (Courtesy of CSL.)

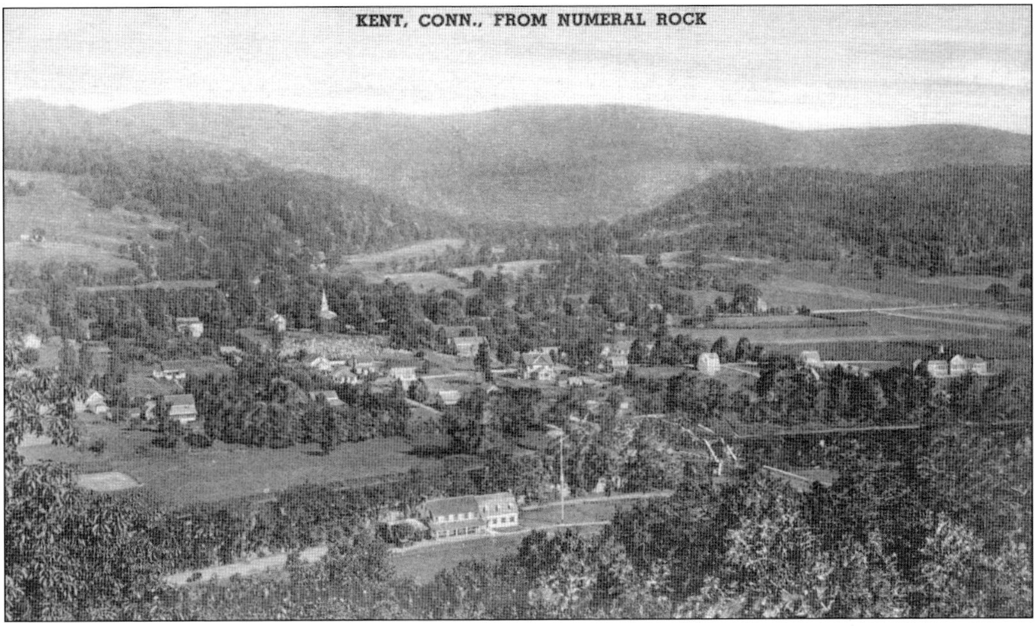

On its earliest route, the AT took a miles-long loop around Macedonia Brook and went by Numeral Rock. The early-1900s collotype postcard above captured the view of the nearby town of Kent. Numeral Rock receives its name from the ever-changing number that is painted on it by each year's graduating class from the nearby Kent School. The rock is now reached by a short side trail that is designated as a bypass route when Macedonia Brook becomes too dangerous to ford due to high water. The photograph below, taken in July 1941, concentrated on the Housatonic Valley's bucolic scenery. (Above, courtesy of the Collotype Company; below, courtesy of SHS.)

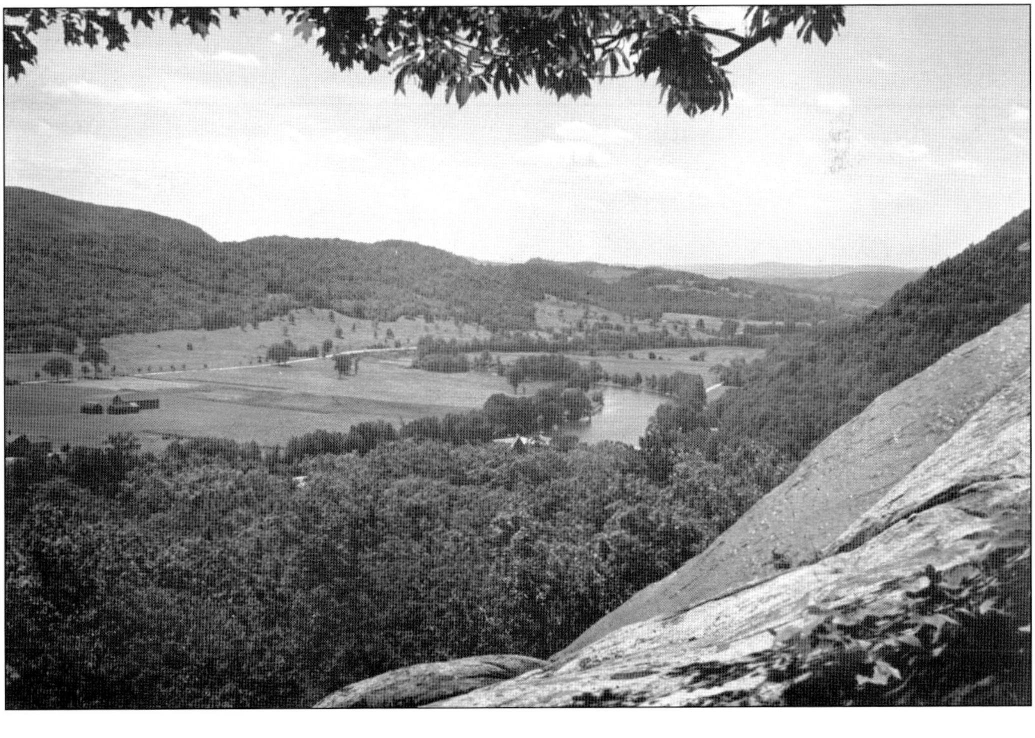

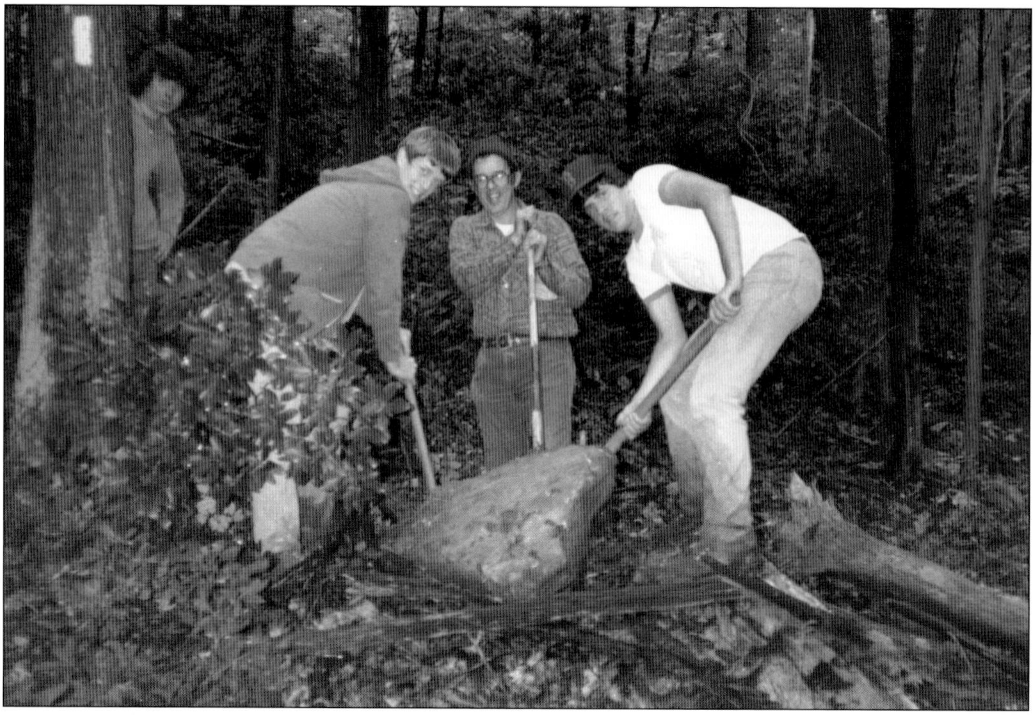

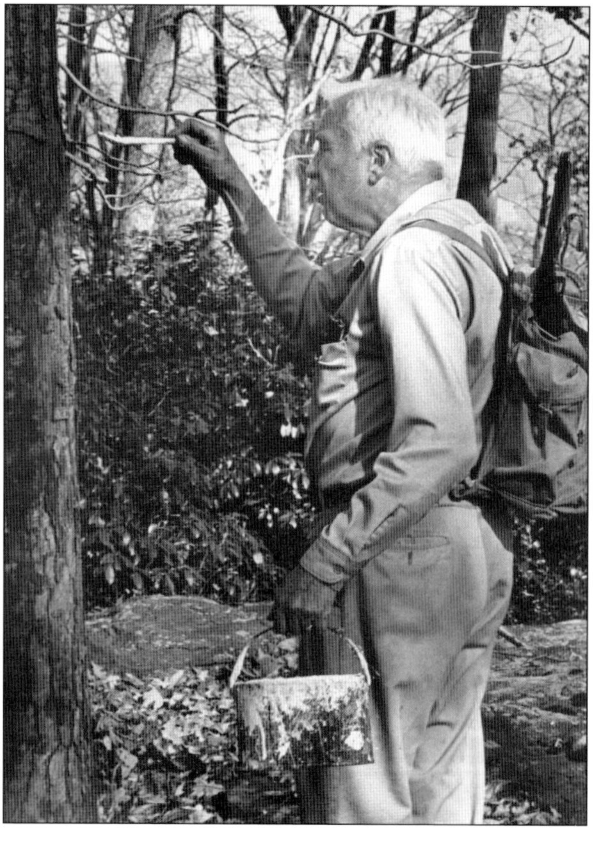

Above, three members of CT-AMC attend a trail skills workshop in Macedonia State Park on September 15, 1984. The chapter was formed in 1921 as an affiliate of the Appalachian Mountain Club, America's oldest nonprofit conservation and outdoors recreation organization. In 1949, the trails committee of the chapter assumed responsibility from Ned Anderson for maintaining 33 miles of the trail west of the Housatonic River. Seymour Smith of Watertown (left), who went on to become chairman of the chapter in 1952, took on the responsibility for all 23 miles of the trail that were on the east side of the waterway at that time. Among other duties he assumed, Smith also acted as the map editor for the *Guide to the Appalachian Trail in Massachusetts and Connecticut.* (Both, courtesy of ATC.)

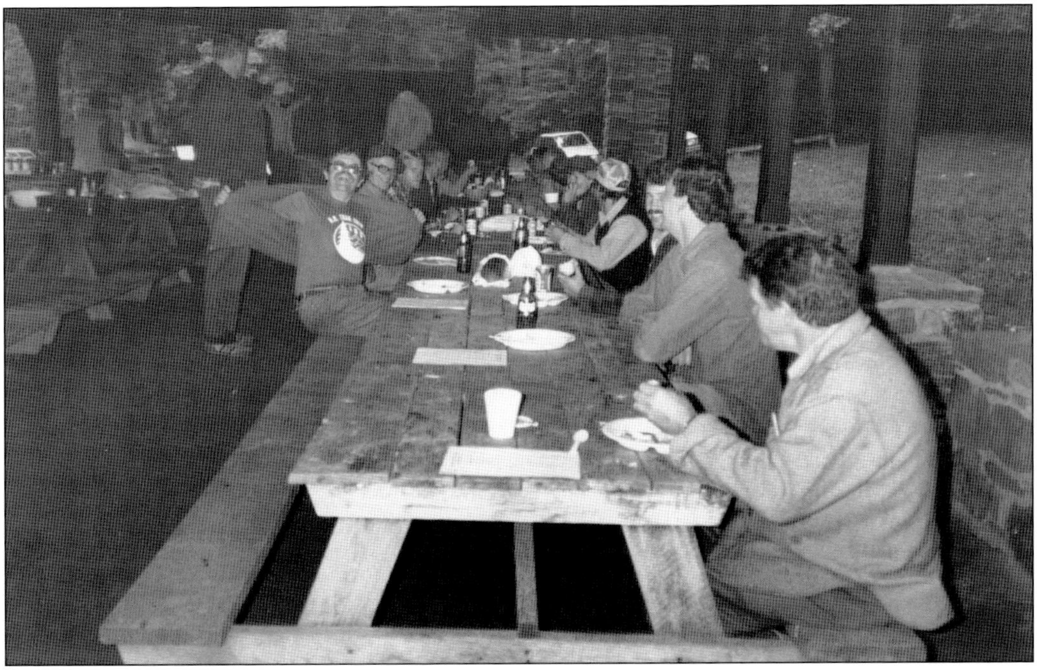

The CT-AMC attendees of the trail skills workshop on September 15, 1984, enjoyed the camaraderie of the trail by sharing food, drink, and conversation in a pavilion in Macedonia Brook State Park. John Hicks, seated on the left, showed off a trail crew T-shirt. Volunteers are awarded different items, often a T-shirt, for devoting varying amounts of time to working on the AT. (Courtesy of ATC.)

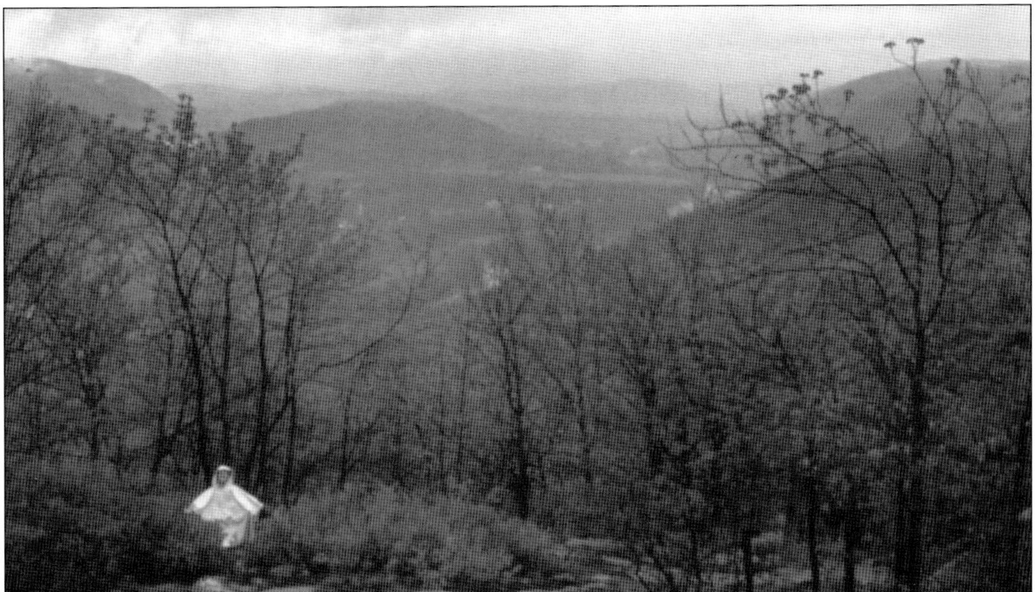

On the wet and dreary day of May 20, 1972, Matthew Donahue photographed the view that was visible from Caleb's Peak. This illustrates a phrase often repeated to northbound thru-hikers: "Those who do not hike in the rain are those who do not make it to Maine." The summit is named for Caleb Barton, who farmed nearby in the 1700s. (Courtesy of SHS.)

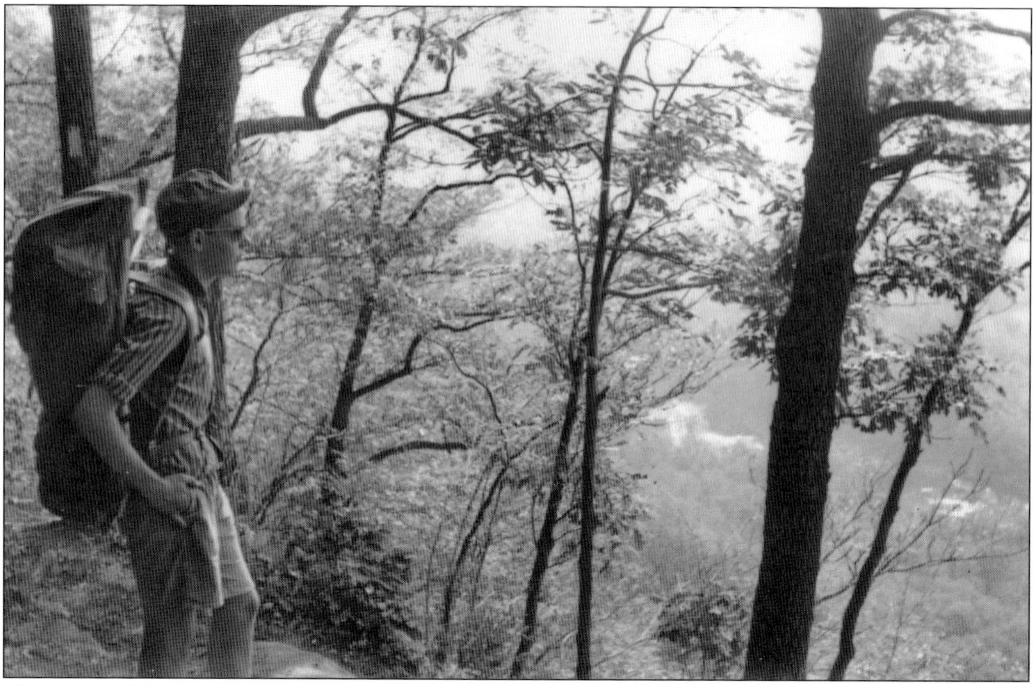

The view of the Housatonic River from the top of St. John's Ledges, photographed in 1964, has always been a part of the AT. The descent has always been memorable, too; it was described in the 1968 AT guidebook as "steep, extremely rough . . . *use caution*." Later on, the downhill became notable for the superb set of rock steps constructed by a crew from AMC. (Courtesy of CSL.)

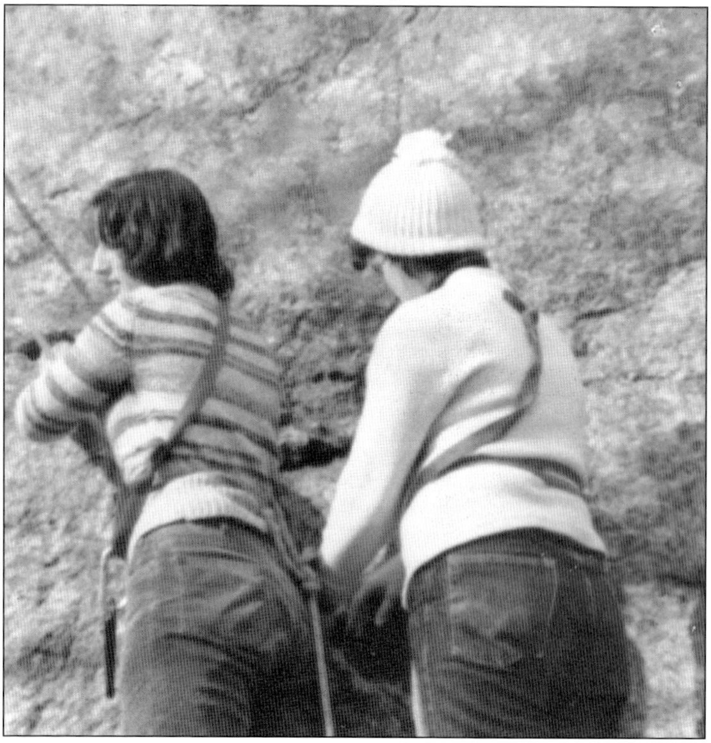

The AT is used for many things other than hiking. Some people come to the trail to bird watch, while others walk the pathway slowly to study the multitude of wildflowers, trees, lichens, and mushrooms. Some arrive for more active pursuits, such as trail running or bouldering. In 1977, CT-AMC sponsored a beginner's course in rock climbing at St. Johns Ledges. (Courtesy of CT-AMC.)

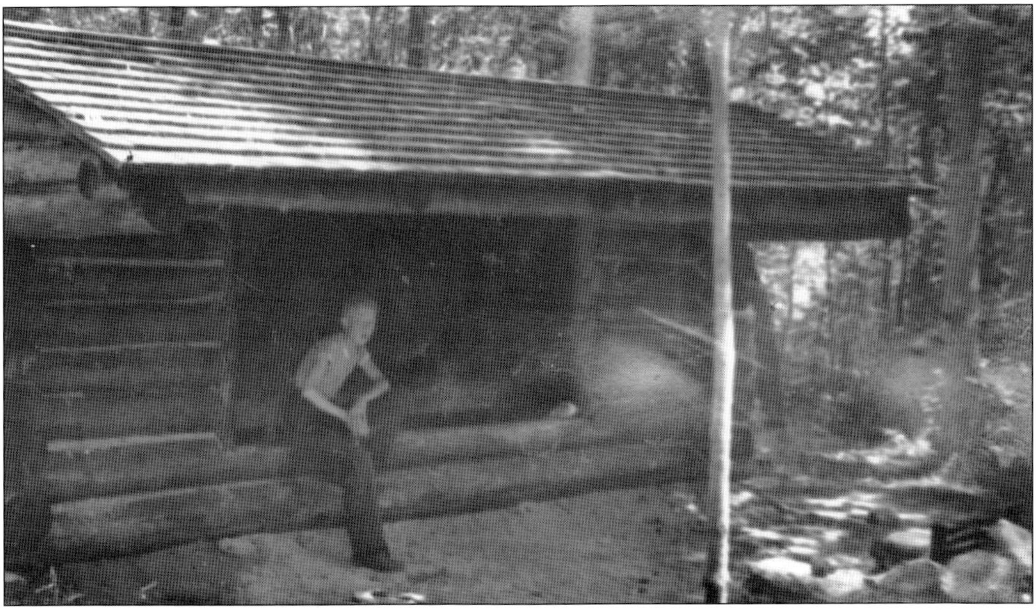

The Mountain Brook Lean-To was photographed by C.E. Dornbusch in 1941, one year after it was built by the CCC. Like many shelters of the day, it accommodated six people with bunks made of wire fencing, which would squeak with movement and eventually break to puncture sleeping pads. The lean-to was replaced by the Stewart Hollow Brook Lean-To, built a short distance north in the 1980s. (Courtesy of ATC.)

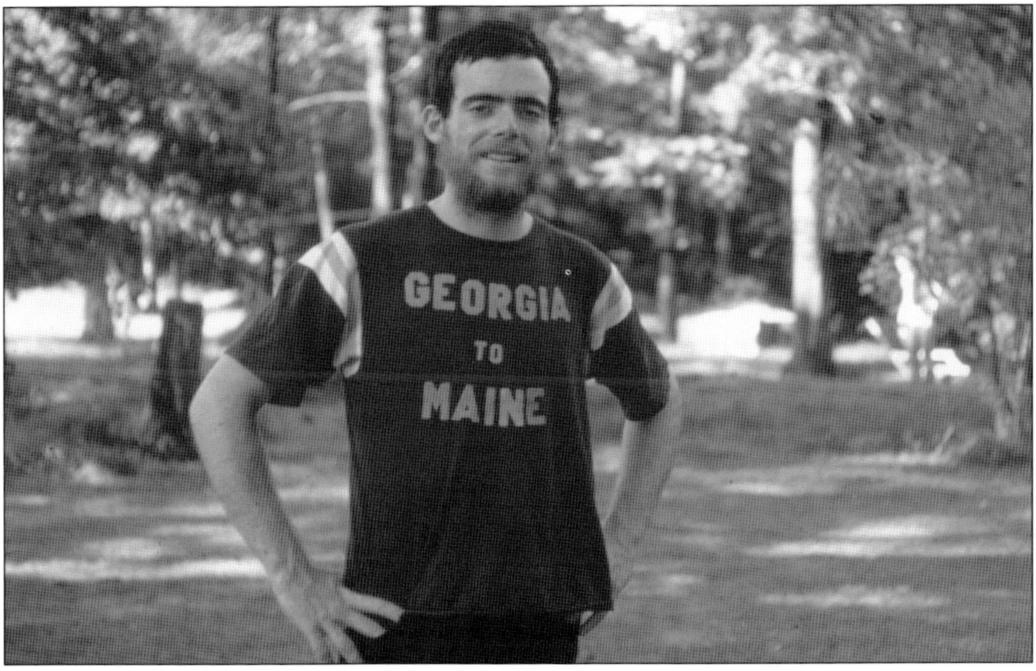

Born and raised in Connecticut, Warren Doyle set the personal goal of walking the AT in the fastest time. In 1973, at the age of 23, he completed the trail in 66 and one-third days, a record at the time. He was photographed on August 4 in Woodbridge by his fiancée, Naydine Simonds, the day after he finished the hike. (Courtesy of Warren Doyle.)

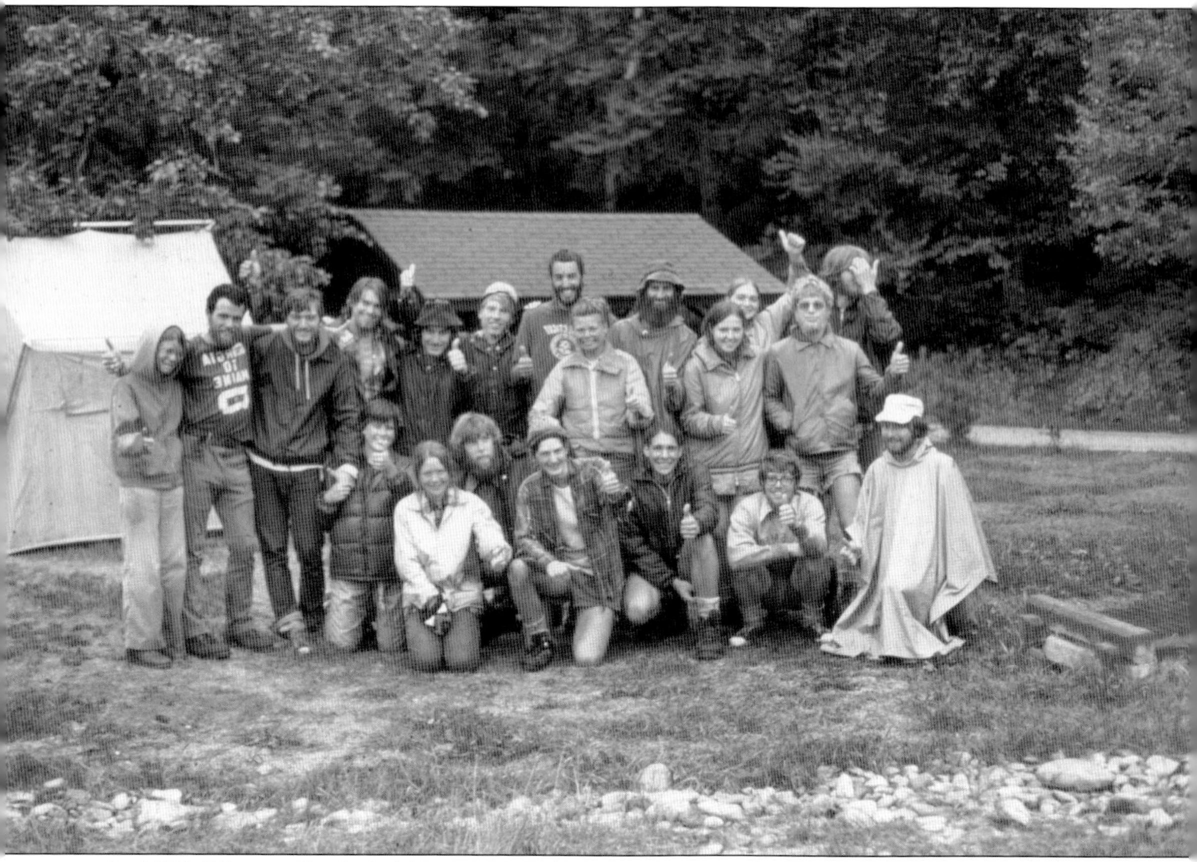

In 1975, Warren Doyle led University of Connecticut students on the first of his AT Circle Expeditions. Members pledged support to each other, with the result that all of them finished the trail that year, a remarkable feat. From left to right are (kneeling) Leslie Scott; Ginger Bowes; David Hall, an expedition member but not a university student, who later founded the company PC Connections; Kirk Sinclair, who later organized the first group hikes of the Pacific Crest and Continental Divide Trails; David Eveleth; Kenneth Bell; and Jeff Peterson; (standing) Naydine Simonds; Warren Doyle; Steve Messier, a member of Sinclair's Continental Divide Trail group; Randy Eis, not a university student nor an expedition member; Steve Markiewicz; Gary Ardel; George Puglisi; Katie Brown; Marty Marcus; Barb Dyer; Rachael Cohen (partially hidden), who was the support van driver; Don Pelletier; and David Beffa-Negrini, a member of Sinclair's Pacific Crest Trail group. (Courtesy of Warren Doyle.)

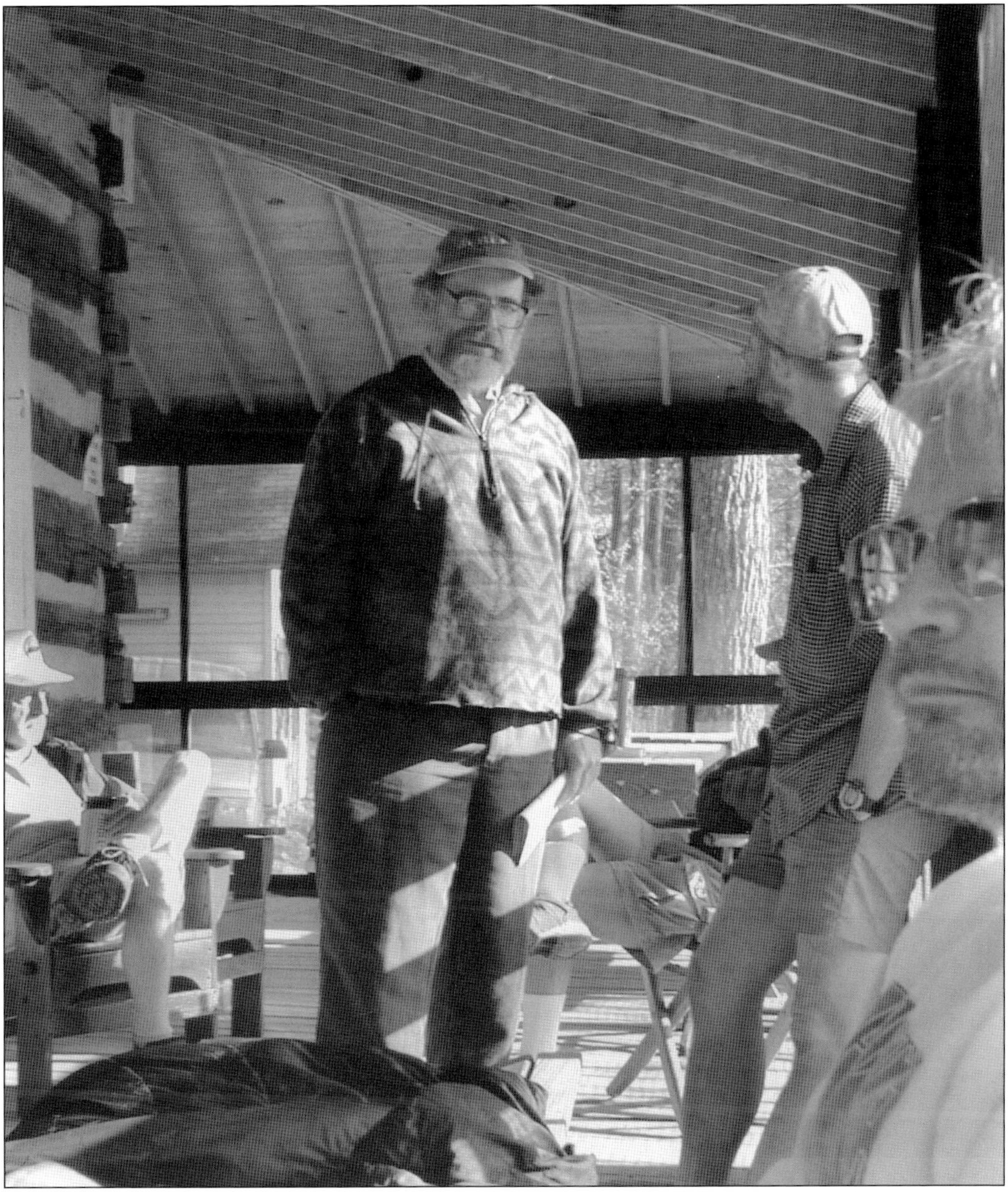

As of the publication of this book, Dr. Warren Doyle has walked the entire AT 16 times and led a total of eight AT Circle Expeditions (another is planned), seven of which had a 100-percent completion rate. He is the founder of the Appalachian Long Distance Hikers Association and its "Gathering," attended by hundreds of 2,000-milers and 2,000-mile dreamers annually. He also created and directs the Appalachian Trail Institute, which has prepared hundreds of people to complete their thru-hikes; is a charter member of the Wilderness Education Association; and was named the Outdoors Person of the Year by *Blue Ridge Outdoors* magazine in 2009. Doyle also founded the Appalachian Folk School in Laurel Bloomery, Tennessee, a nonprofit organization dedicated to preserving the traditional dance and other arts of the Appalachian Mountains and helping them to thrive. Doyle is standing in the center of this photograph, taken in 2001. (Courtesy of ATC.)

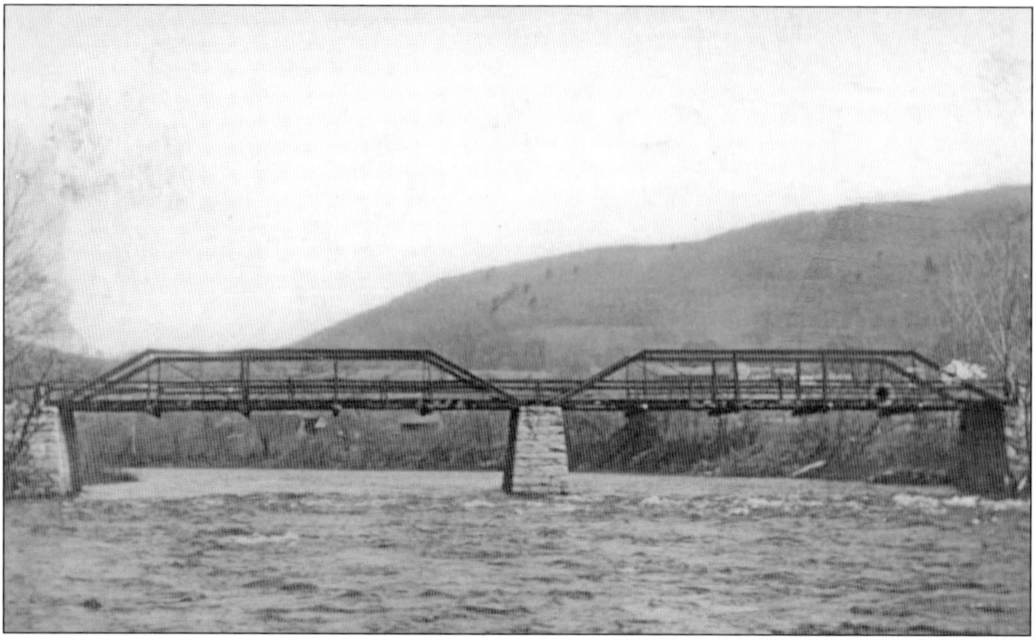

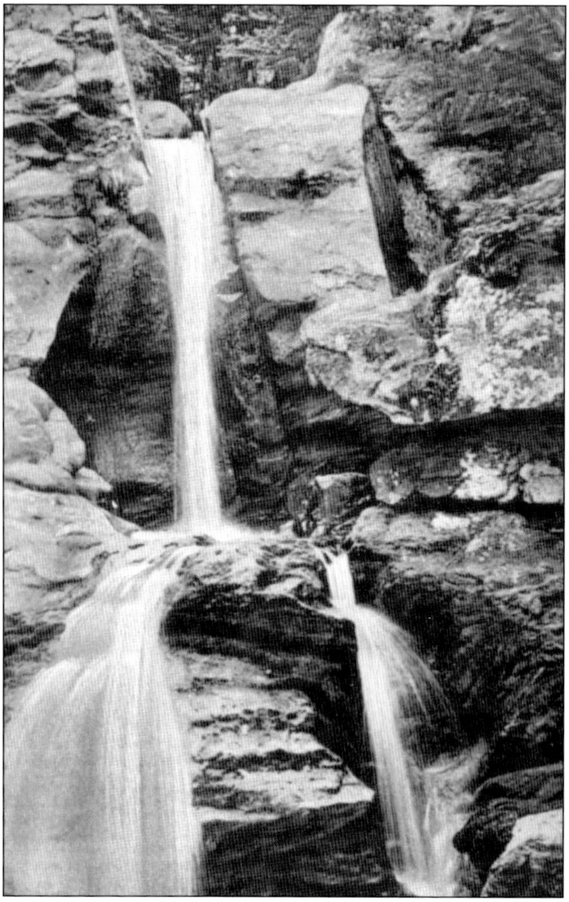

As originally constructed by Ned Anderson in the late 1920s and early 1930s, the AT crossed the Housatonic River on North Kent (also known as Flanders) Bridge and followed the stream's eastern bank for more than a mile. The bridge was destroyed by a major flood in 1936 that took out other bridges that had spanned the river. (Courtesy of Leonard M. Adkins; publisher unidentified.)

From the east bank of the Housatonic River, the original AT ascended beside Kent Falls, as seen in this postcard published by the Collotype Company of Elizabeth, New Jersey, and New York and mailed in January 1930. The falls drop approximately 250 feet in less than a quarter mile in Kent Falls State Park, a gift to the state in 1919 by the White Memorial Fund. (Courtesy of CSL.)

The AT's original route ascended to Mohawk Mountain and its metal fire tower. Local lore says the mountain received its name because the Native Americans who lived close by would light fires as a warning to others that the Mohawk Indians, who did not live in the area, were approaching for a raid. This photograph was taken in the 1940s by C.E. Dornbusch. (Courtesy of ATC.)

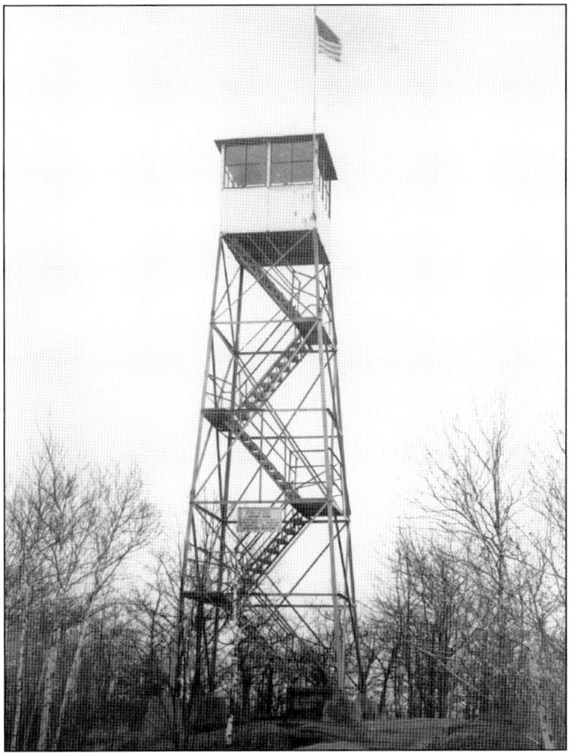

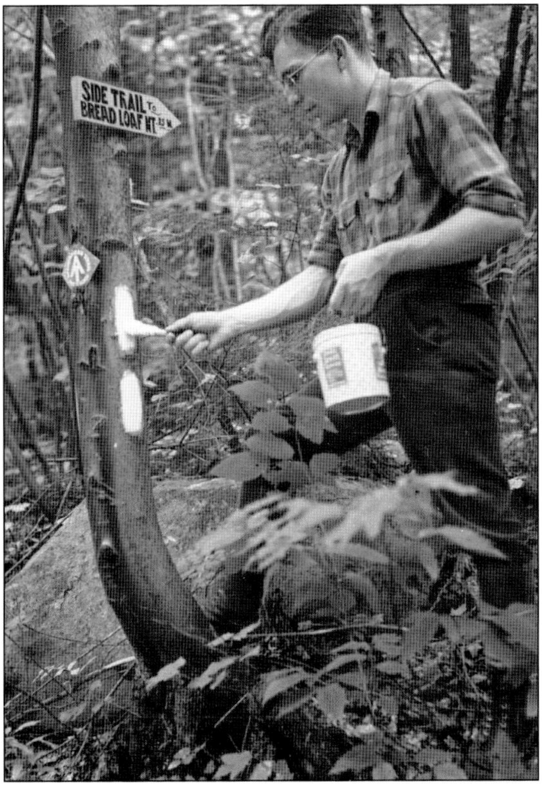

Ned Anderson relocated the AT onto the west side of the Housatonic River as far north as Cornwall Bridge after the destruction of the North Kent Bridge in 1936. In the 1940s, Frederick S. Best photographed Fred Heitcamp of New York City marking the side trail to Breadloaf Mountain, shortly after Heitcamp became a member of the Housatonic Trail Club. The summit's view includes the Housatonic River. (Courtesy of SHS.)

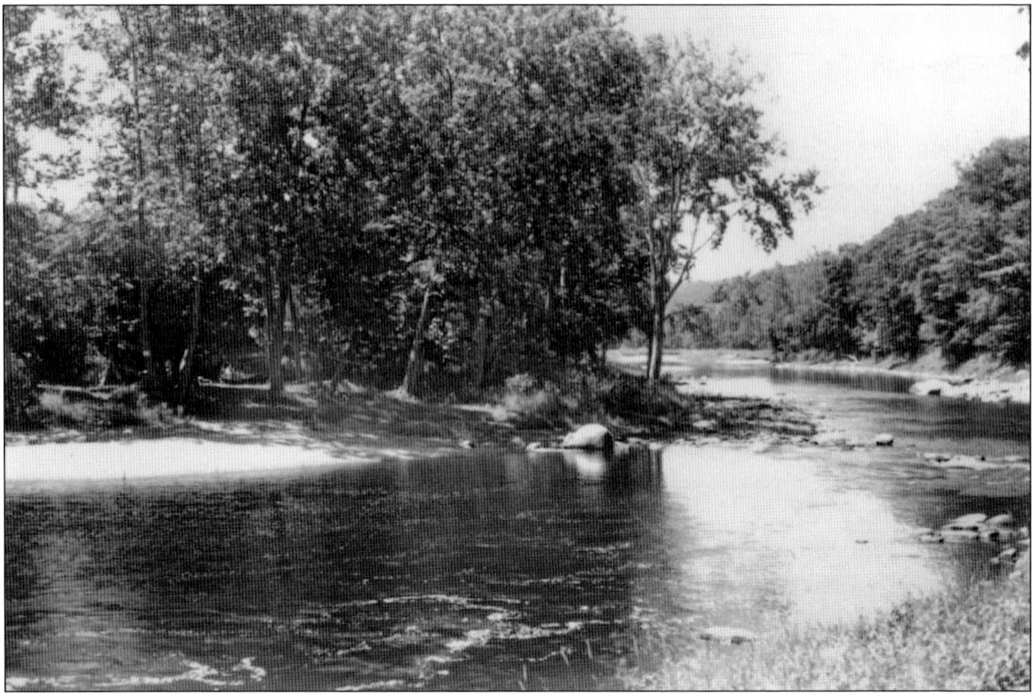

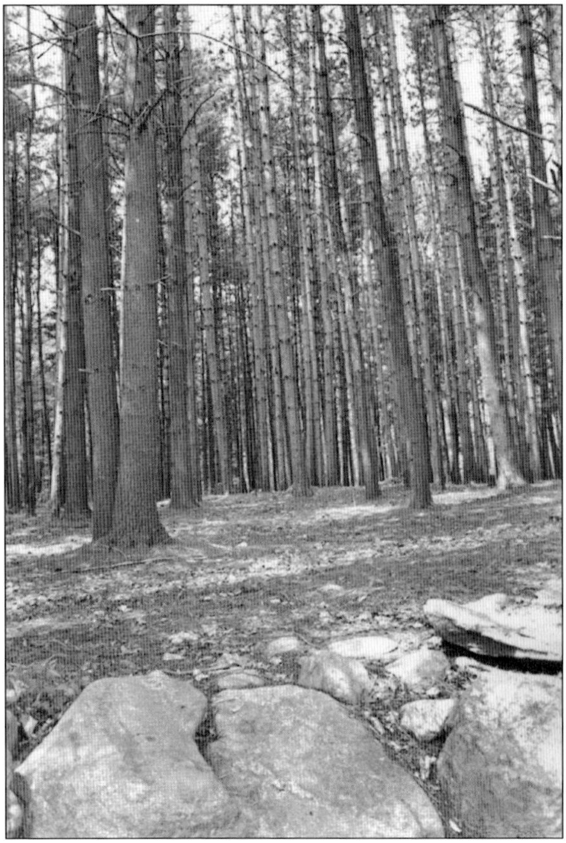

The AT section beside the Housatonic River is the trail's longest single stretch beside any stream, a distance of approximately five miles. Flowing southward, the river drains in western Massachusetts and Connecticut, is close to 340 miles long, and empties into Long Island Sound. From the early 1700s to the present, it has been harnessed to power machinery of one kind or another. (Courtesy of ATC.)

In 1910, the Stanley Works Company of New Britain purchased land along the Housatonic River to build a dam, a project that never came to fruition. The company permitted the AT to pass through the property when asked in the 1930s. In the 1980s, it sold the land, which included an impressive grove of towering evergreens, to the National Park Service. (Courtesy of ATC.)

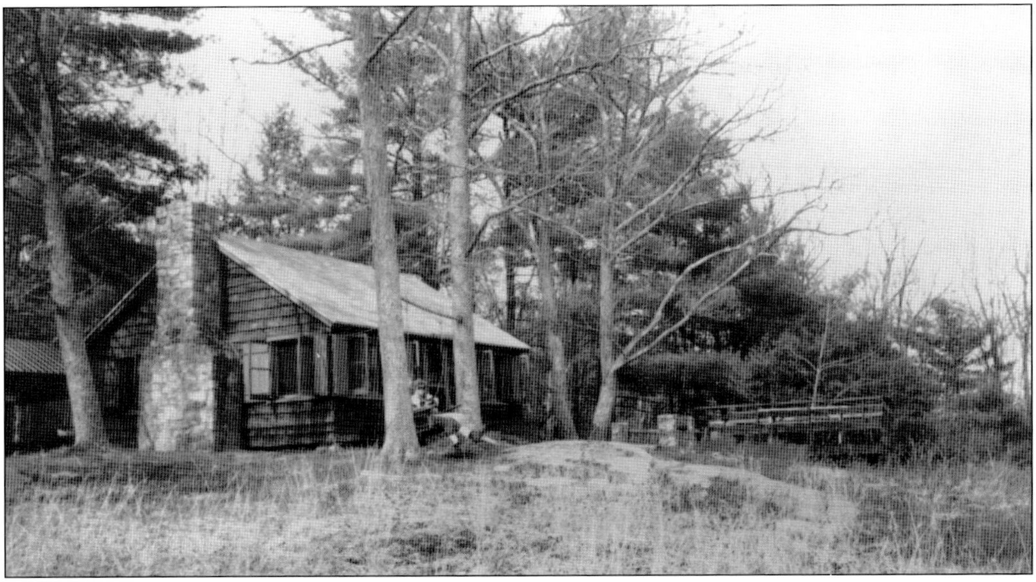

A small cabin was included on land that was purchased from the estate of Chelsea Everson to protect the trail in the late 1980s. Members of CT-AMC worked on bringing the cabin up to National Park Service codes, and it was opened to hikers in 1989 as Silver Hill Shelter. (Courtesy of CT-AMC.)

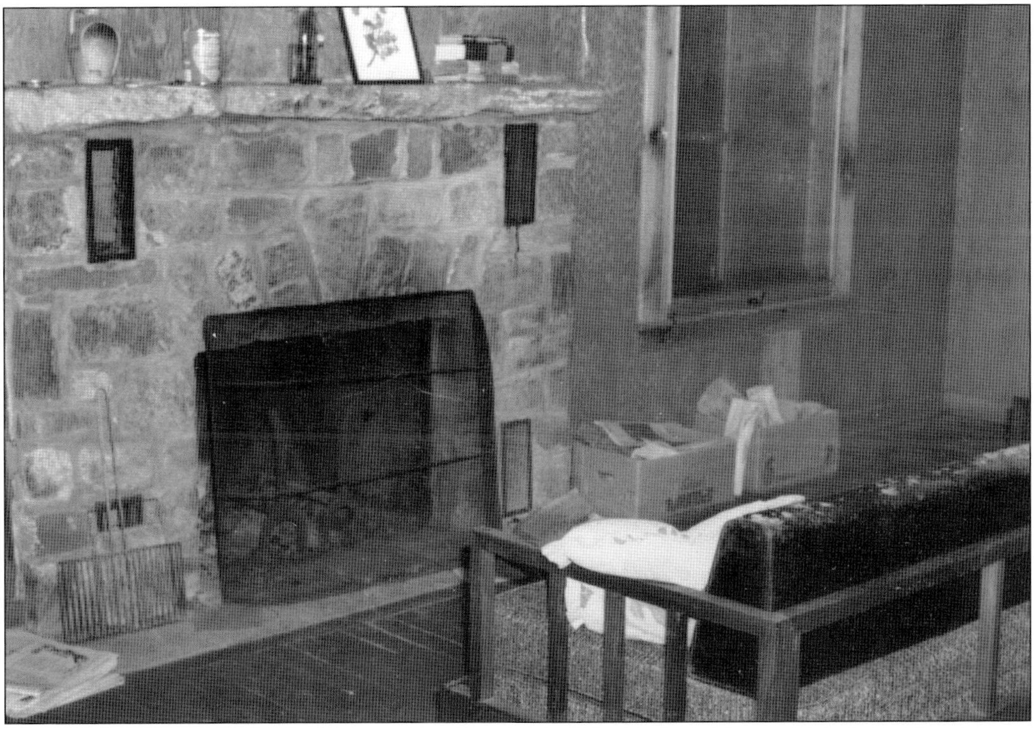

Silver Hill Shelter was one of the most deluxe accommodations available to hikers on the AT. On top of being enclosed by four walls, it had a fireplace, a complete kitchen, and, most deluxe of all, indoor plumbing. Built upon a low knoll, it and its outdoor swing overlooked the surrounding land above the Housatonic River. (Courtesy of CT-AMC.)

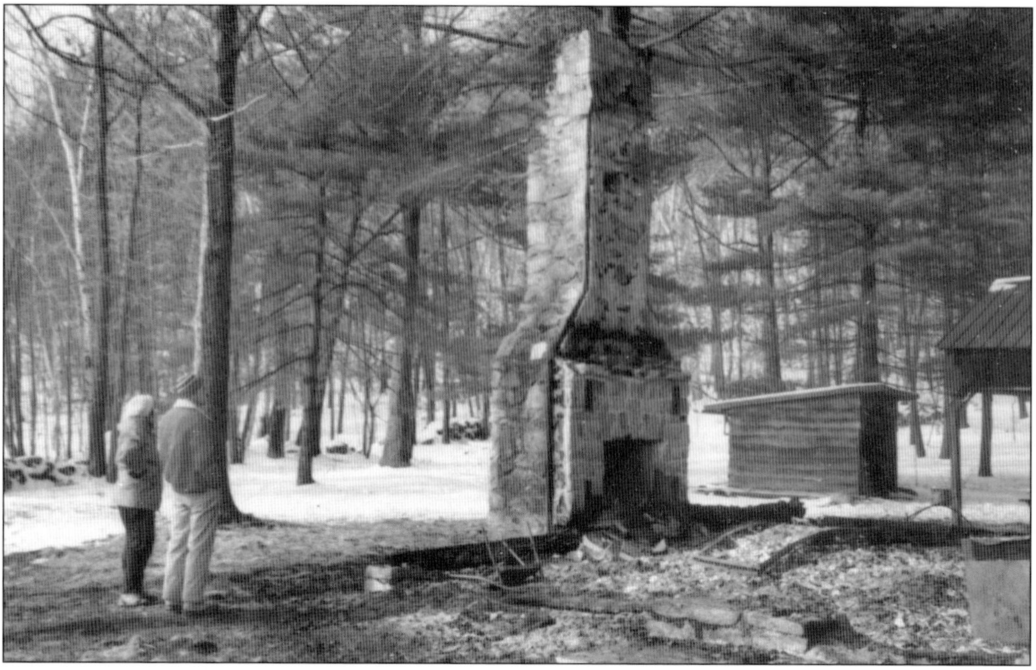

Through the years, a number of the local AT maintaining clubs have built or incorporated existing four-wall structures to be used as shelters. Unfortunately, many have met the same fate as Silver Hill Shelter, which burned to the ground in January 1991, when a group of college students lost control of a fire built in the fireplace. The area is now a campsite. (Courtesy of CT-AMC.)

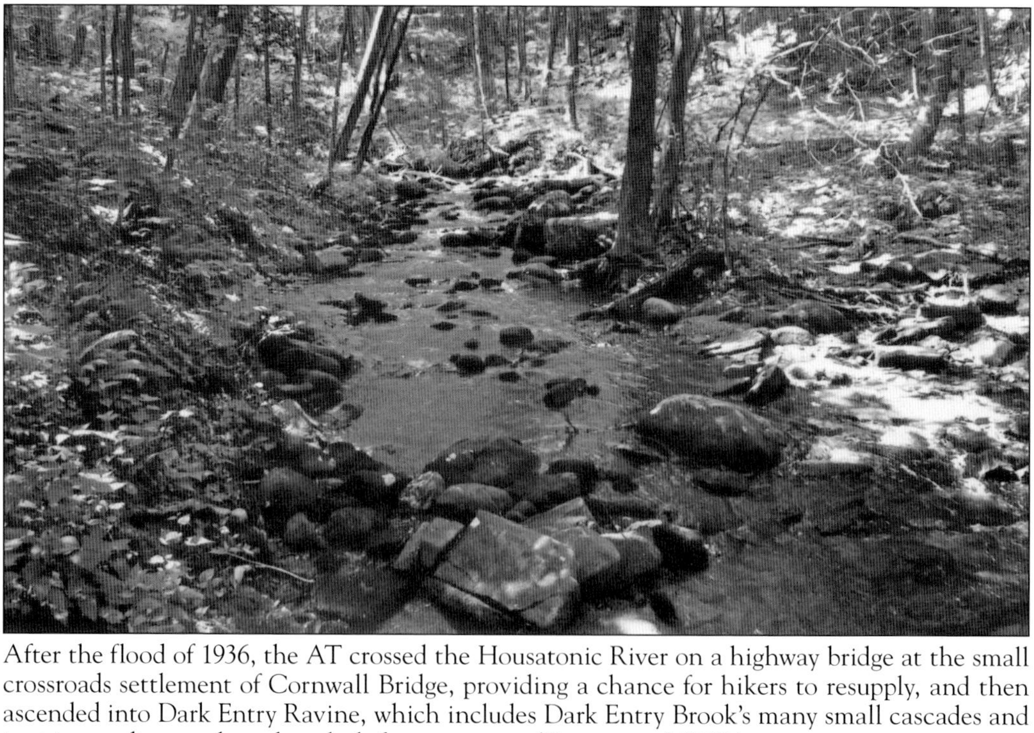

After the flood of 1936, the AT crossed the Housatonic River on a highway bridge at the small crossroads settlement of Cornwall Bridge, providing a chance for hikers to resupply, and then ascended into Dark Entry Ravine, which includes Dark Entry Brook's many small cascades and inviting wading pools under a lush forest canopy. (Courtesy of ATC.)

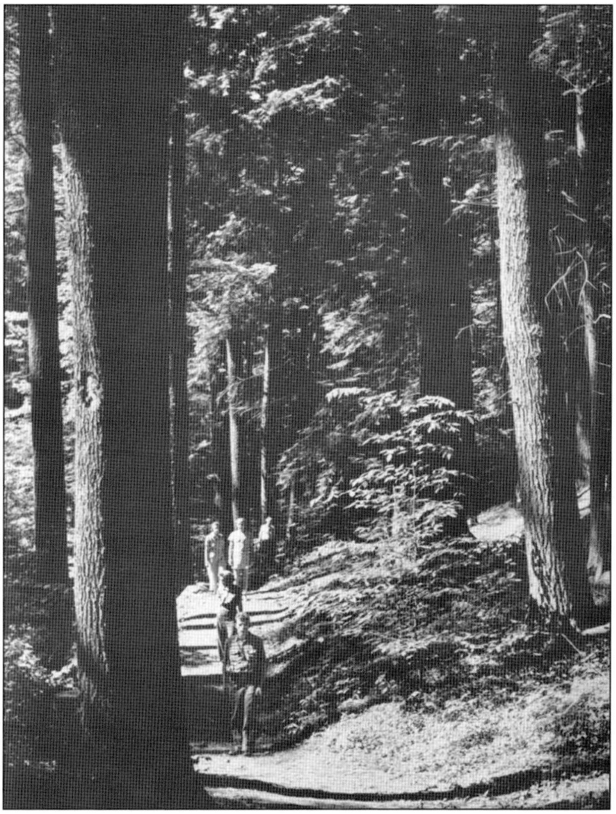

One of the most outstanding places along this route was a stand of evergreens that inspired visitors with such awe that it was named Cathedral Pines. Owned by the Nature Conservancy, it is still Connecticut's largest stand of old-growth white pine and hemlock trees, but, sadly, three powerful tornadoes blew through the area in July 1990, bringing down a very large percentage of them. (Courtesy of SHS.)

Now called the Mohawk Trail, a part of the CFPA's Blue Trail System, this reroute meets up with the original route as it continues northward and reconnects with the AT near Falls Village, making a 37-mile loop hike possible. Yet the Camping Zone Lean-To, located just one-tenth of a mile from Route 4, is so lightly used that vegetation was growing in its dirt floor in 2013. (Courtesy of Leonard M. Adkins.)

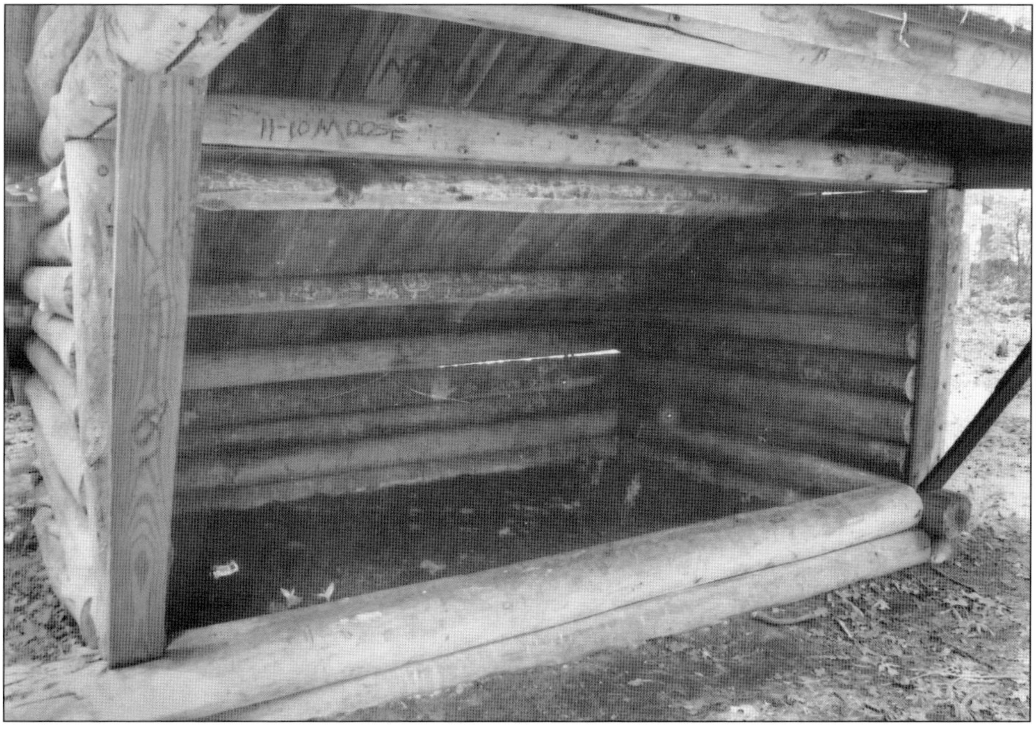

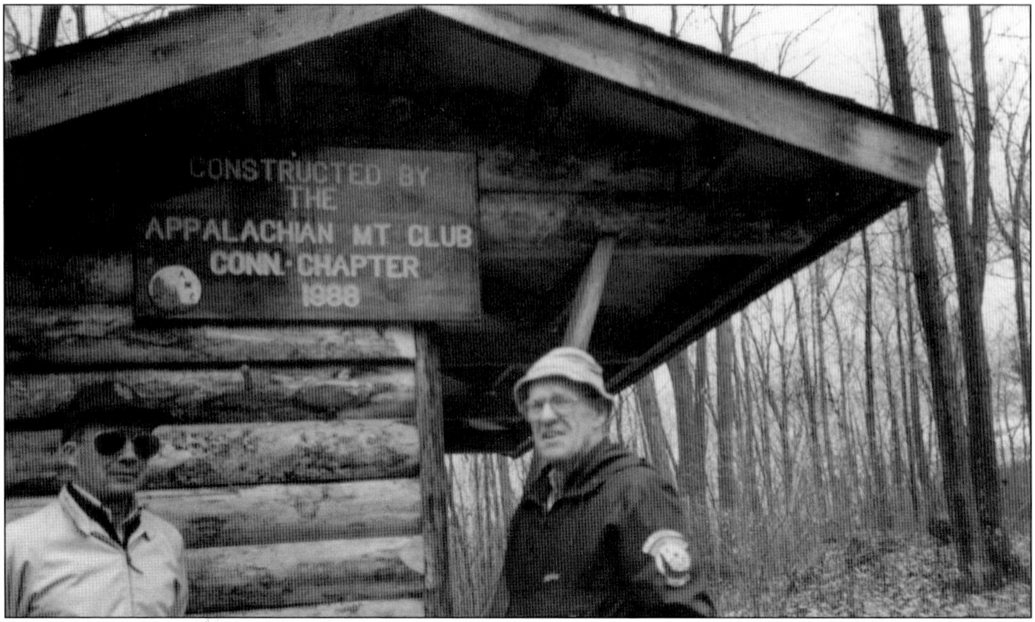

Although the Mohawk Trail is no longer part of the AT, members of CT-AMC continue to work on it. In 1988, Richard Blake (right) and an unidentified man inspect the newly constructed Pine Knoll Lean-To, which replaced the earlier CCC-constructed lean-to, which had wire bunks that accommodated six people. (Courtesy of CT-AMC.)

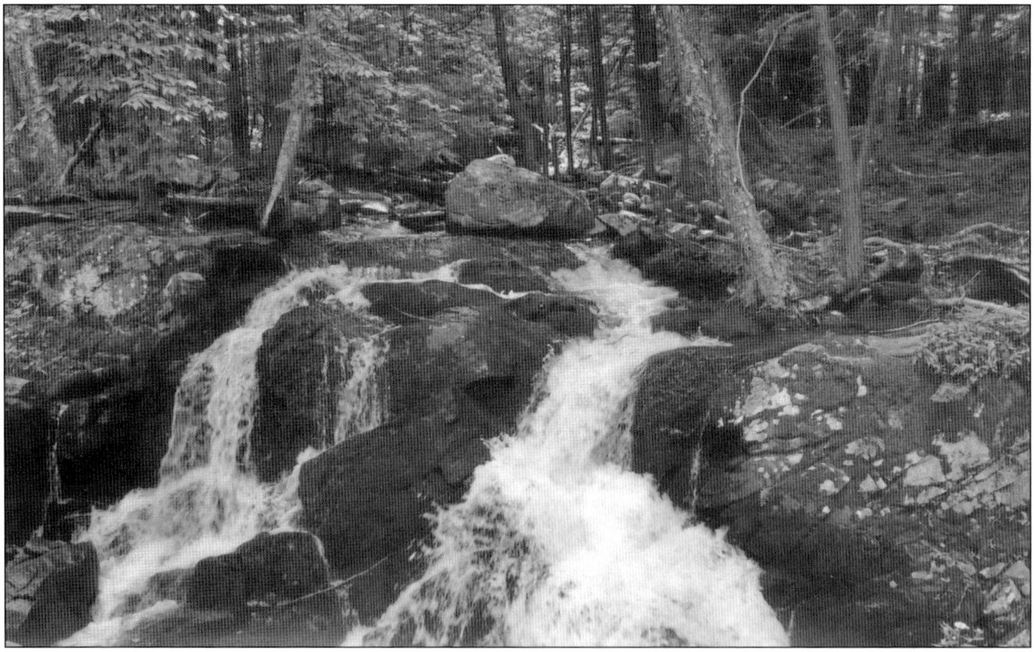

A waterfall at the head of Dean's Ravine, another particularly beautiful place that was along the original route of the AT and is now a part of the Mohawk Trail, is located beside Music Mountain Road. Music Mountain is America's oldest continuing chamber music series and is located a short distance from the ravine, enabling past thru-hikers to attend free Sunday afternoon concerts. (Courtesy of Leonard M. Adkins.)

Barrack Mountain was also an original part of the AT that is now part of the Mohawk Trail. The 1970 photograph of these two hikers on the steep, rough, and rocky ascent illustrates how, sometimes, the trail is not just an easy walk in the woods. (Courtesy of ATC.)

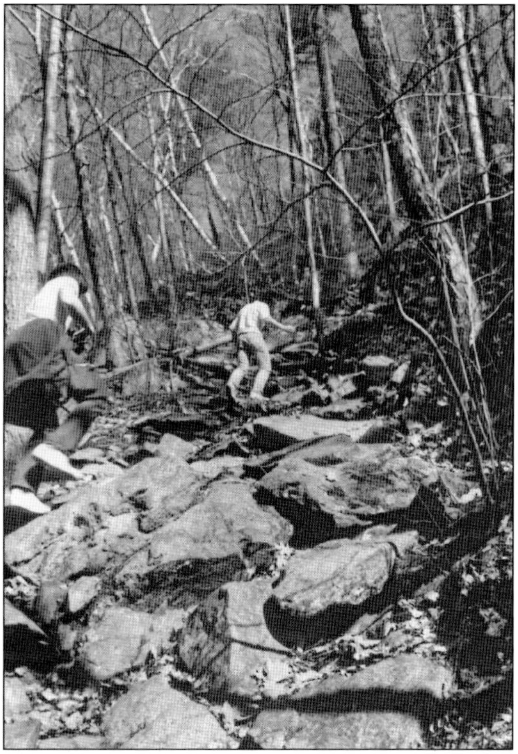

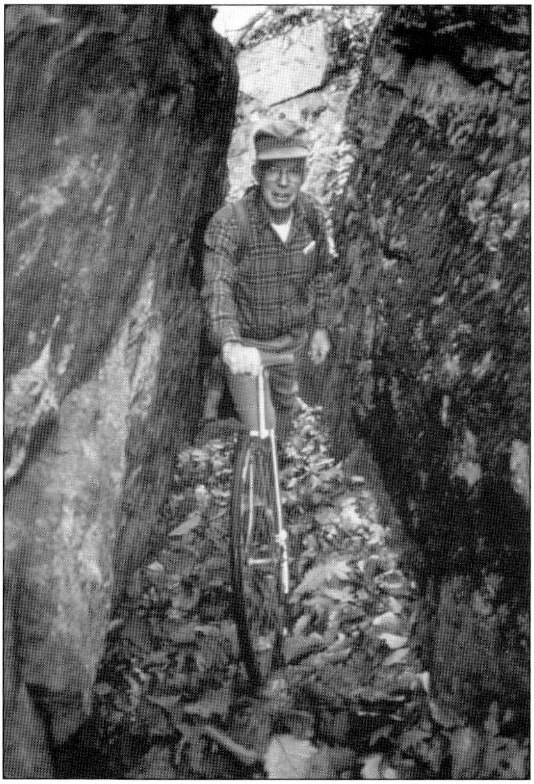

Seen measuring trail on Sharon Mountain in 1984, Norman Sills was named to the Honor Roll of Volunteers during ATC's 75th anniversary celebration in 2000. Among the many things he did on behalf of the AT, Sills was AMC's Connecticut AT coordinator from 1979 to 1984, the Connecticut AT guidebook editor, and the chairman of CT-AMC's trails committee. He hiked the entire trail in the mid-1980s. (Courtesy of CSL.)

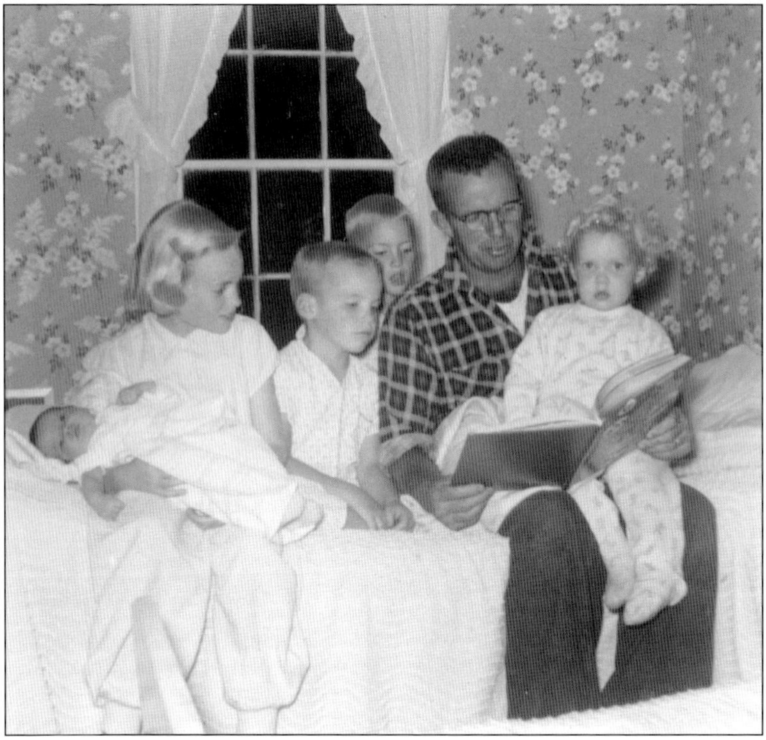

Norman Sills met Nancy Grupe in 1948 when he was a student at the University of Connecticut. Two years later, they married, during the time he was working for the State of Connecticut in Hartford. A number of years after that, he was photographed reading a bedtime story to their children (from left to right) Eugene, Margaret, Mark, Jeff, and Virginia. (Courtesy of Norman Sills.)

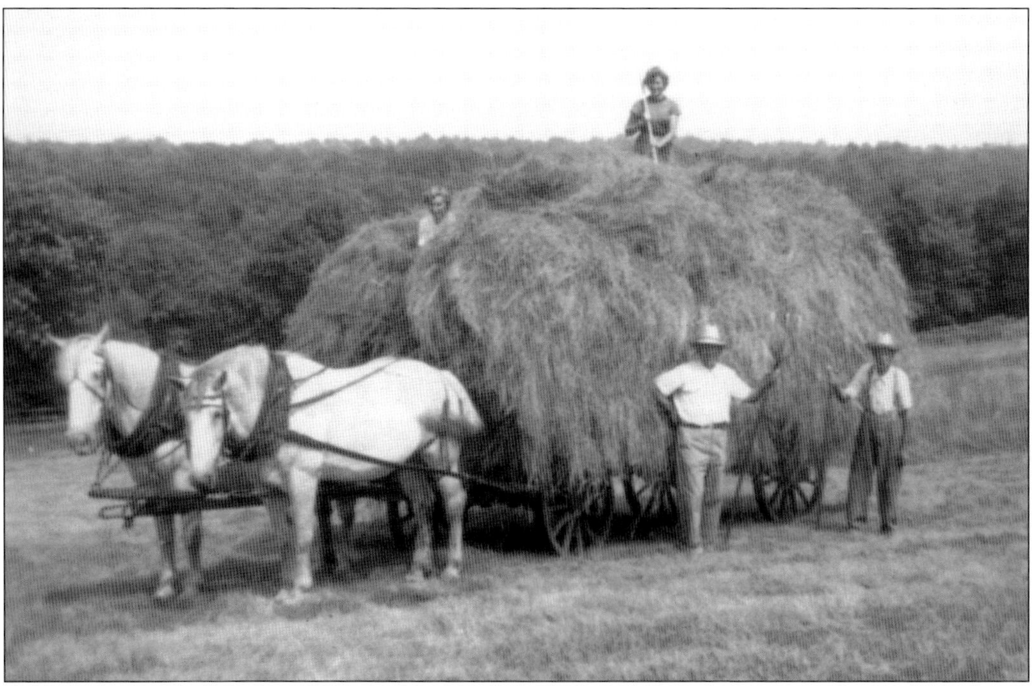

Nancy Grupe was raised on a farm in New Canaan, where she was photographed by her father, Howard Grupe, sitting on top of a wagonload of hay harvested in 1946 or 1947. Her sister Carol is almost hidden by the hay in the front of the wagon, William Valien is in the center of the photograph, and Howard Ogden is to the right. (Courtesy of Norman Sills.)

Although the AT is more than 2,000 miles long, Norman Sills, like many who hike and work on the trail, wanted to broaden his experiences, so he took a trip to neighboring New York to hike that state's highest point, Mount Marcy, on a snowy winter day. (Courtesy of Norman Sills.)

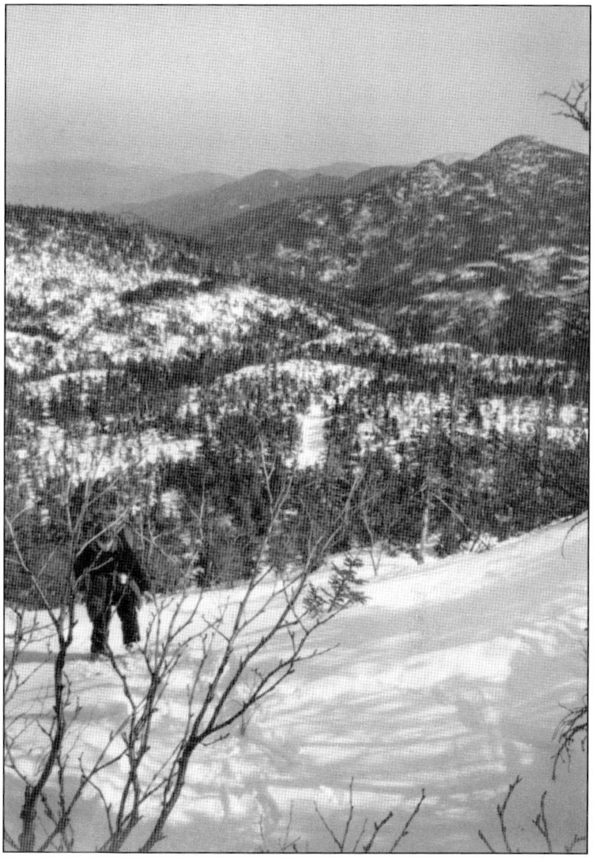

Norman and Nancy Sills were photographed later in life during a hike to Bear Mountain, where they could look down onto Twin Lakes, where they lived on a dairy farm in the early days of their marriage. The two had been married for 61 years when she passed away in 2012. (Courtesy of Norman Sills.)

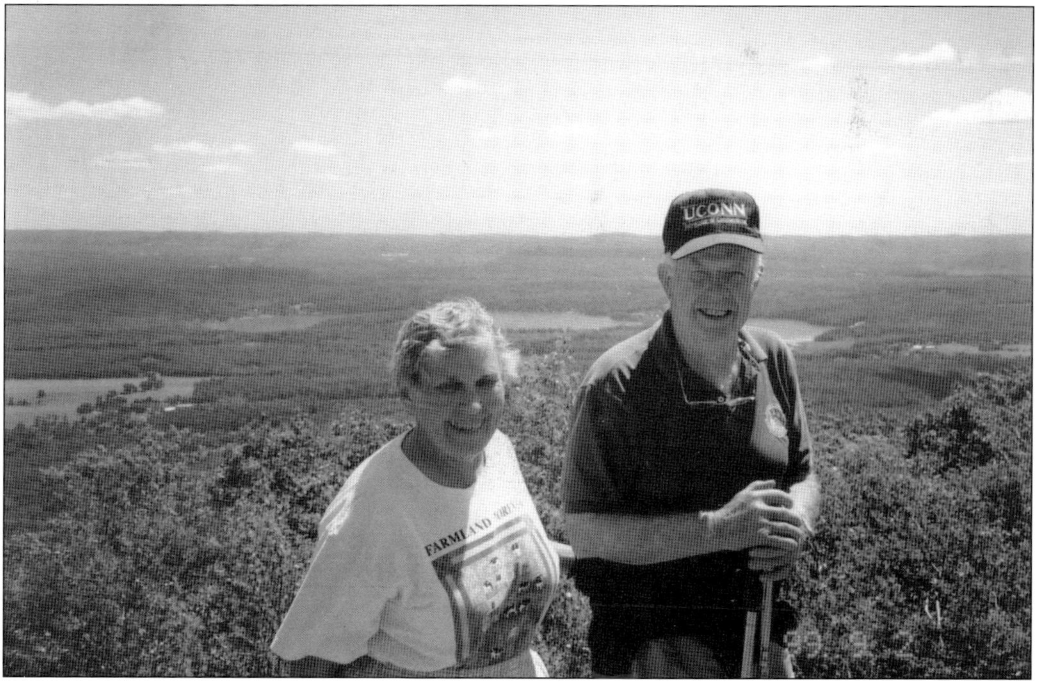

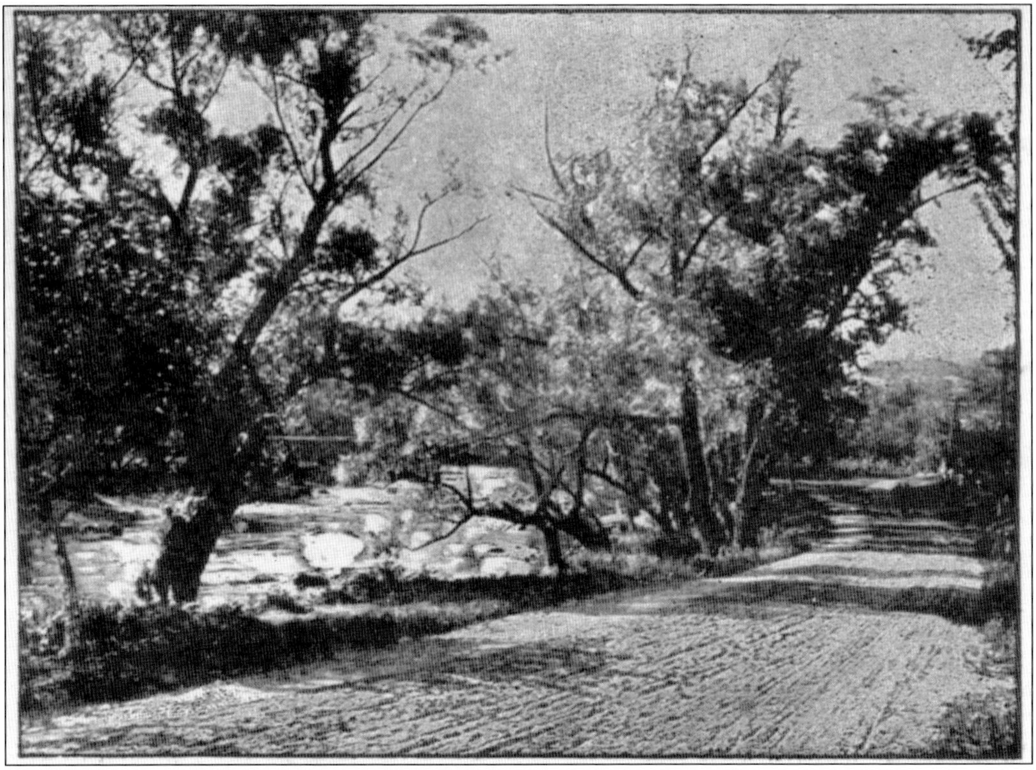

What was Water Street, seen in this postcard mailed from Falls Village on October 26, 1904, is now the approximate location of the AT near Falls Village. This is also near the first handicapped accessible portion of the AT, built around 2000 on the site of an abandoned horse racetrack at a cost of $40,000. (Courtesy of Leonard M. Adkins; publisher unidentified.)

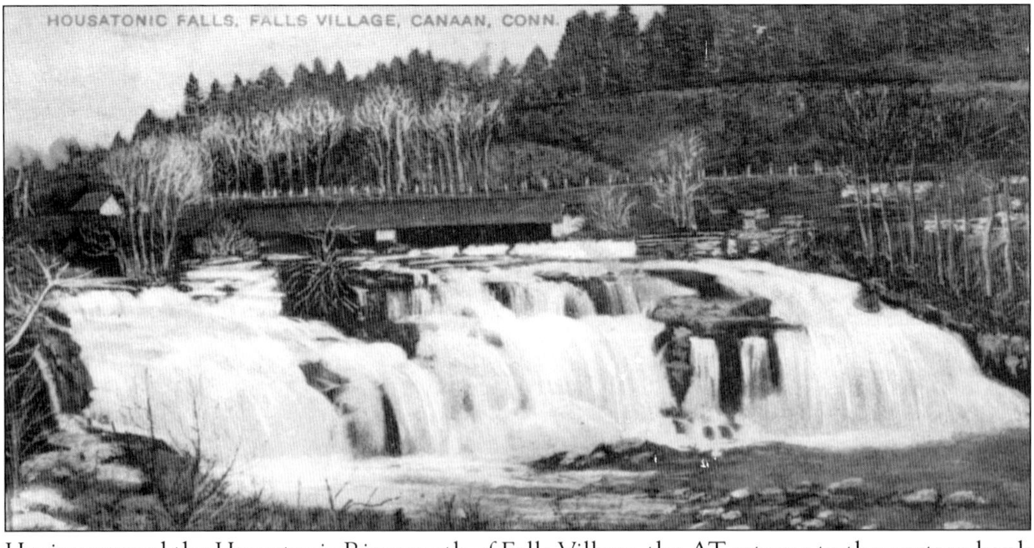

Having crossed the Housatonic River south of Falls Village, the AT returns to the western bank on an old highway iron bridge beside Great Housatonic Falls. This Canaan Printing Company postcard was mailed in 1909, three years before a diversionary canal was built above the falls for a hydroelectric plant. The falls are now only "great" after heavy rains. (Courtesy of CSL.)

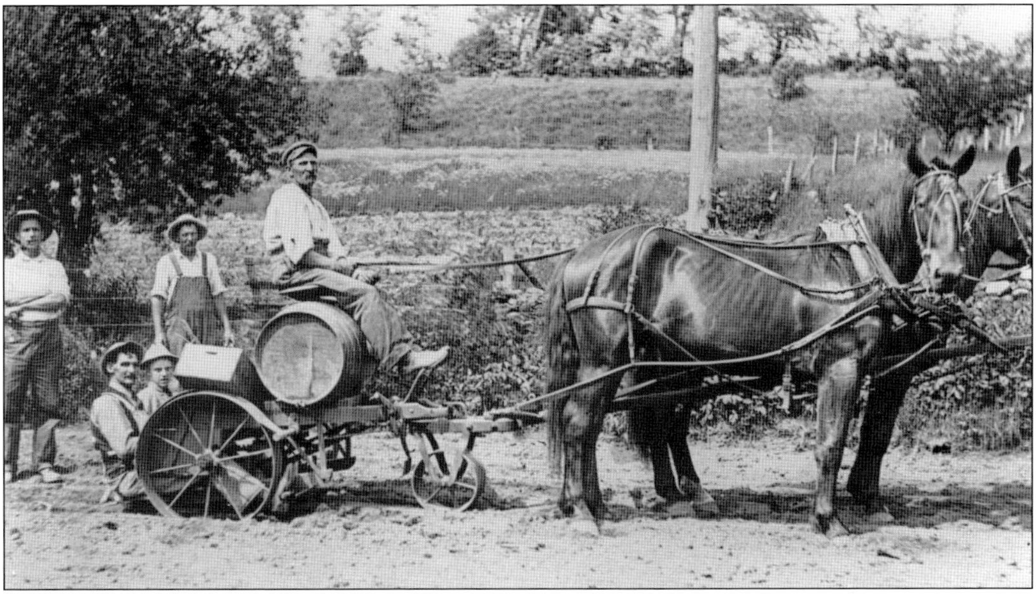

Wrapper tobacco, used to produce cigars, was a major crop in the Housatonic Valley at the time the AT was being established in the 1920s and 1930s. Around 1925, workers used an ingenuous mechanism to plant the tobacco: a small wheel made a furrow, two men planted shoots, and a chain on the barrel was pulled to water the shoots. (Courtesy of SHS.)

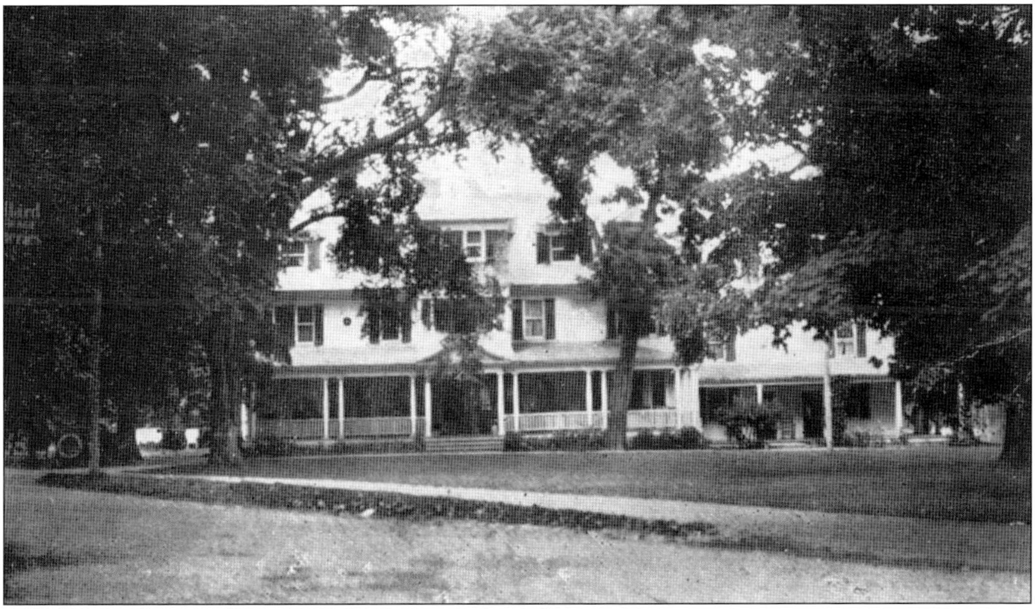

The White Hart Inn, in Salisbury, seen in this postcard mailed on July 14, 1924, is located at the intersection of Routes 44 and 41, both of which the AT crosses. It opened as an inn and tavern in 1803. Many thru-hikers stayed here on rainy days, but it was for sale as this book went to press. (Courtesy of A.M. Simon, New York.)

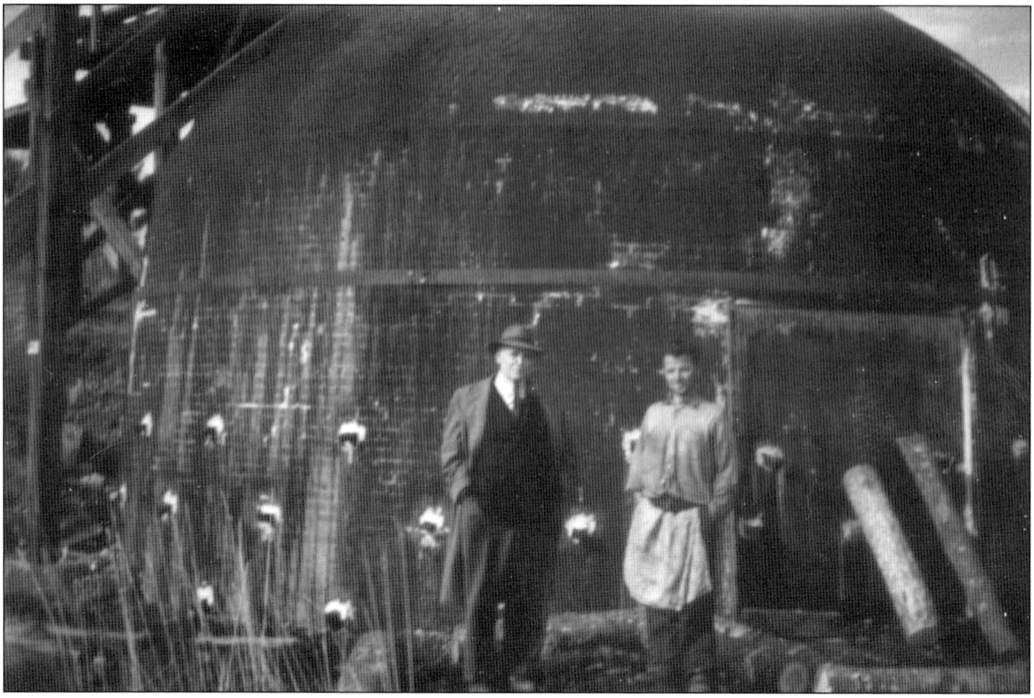

From the late 1700s to the early 1900s, iron production was a major industry in many of the areas that the AT passes through in the Mid-Atlantic and New England states. Photographed in western Connecticut in the early 1900s, this kiln produced charcoal needed to fuel nearby iron furnaces. Much of the AT on the Taconic Mountain Range follows old charcoal roads. (Courtesy of CSL.)

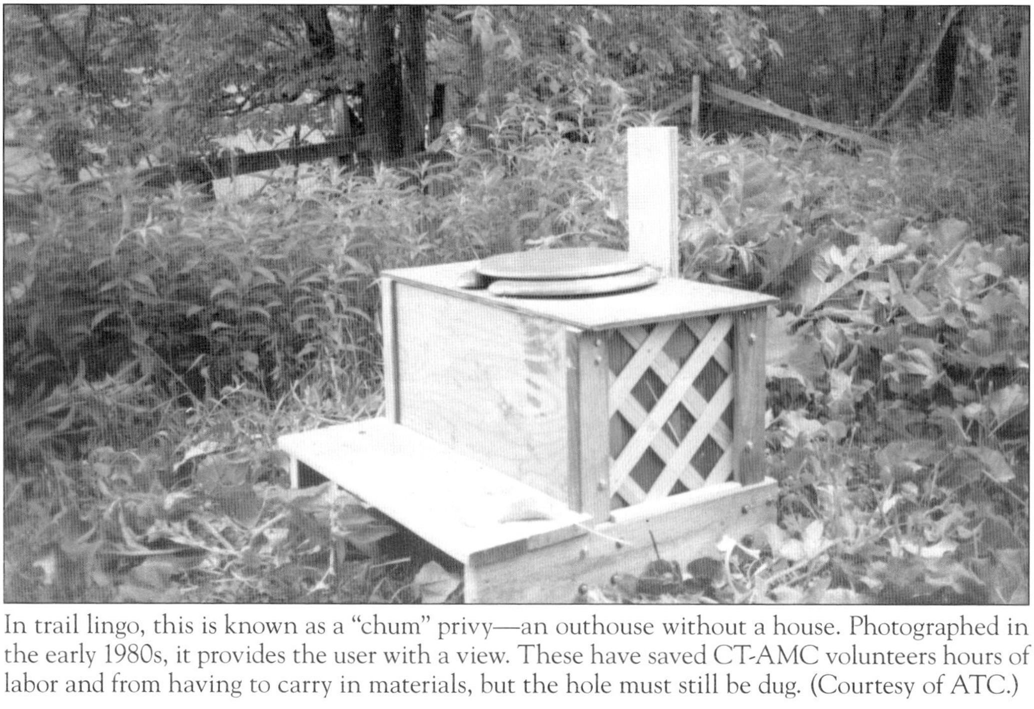

In trail lingo, this is known as a "chum" privy—an outhouse without a house. Photographed in the early 1980s, it provides the user with a view. These have saved CT-AMC volunteers hours of labor and from having to carry in materials, but the hole must still be dug. (Courtesy of ATC.)

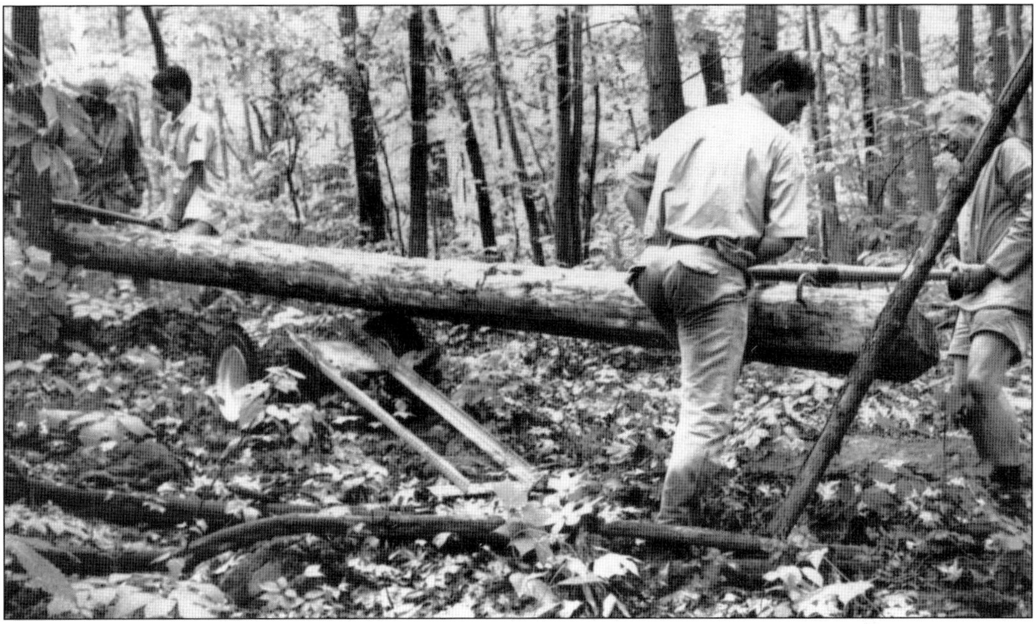

Some of the trees that died in the red pine plantation farther south on the AT along the Housatonic River were harvested and used to build the Riga Lean-To in 1990. After the trees were cut and planed, they were loaded onto a log truck that transported them on the main highway to a spot on the Mount Riga Road, where volunteers put them on Robert Toleski's small trailer, which was then pulled by a tractor as far as possible into the woods. The volunteers then lifted the logs by hand (above) onto a two-wheeled trailer that was hand-pulled (below) to the lean-to building site. (Both, courtesy of CT-AMC.)

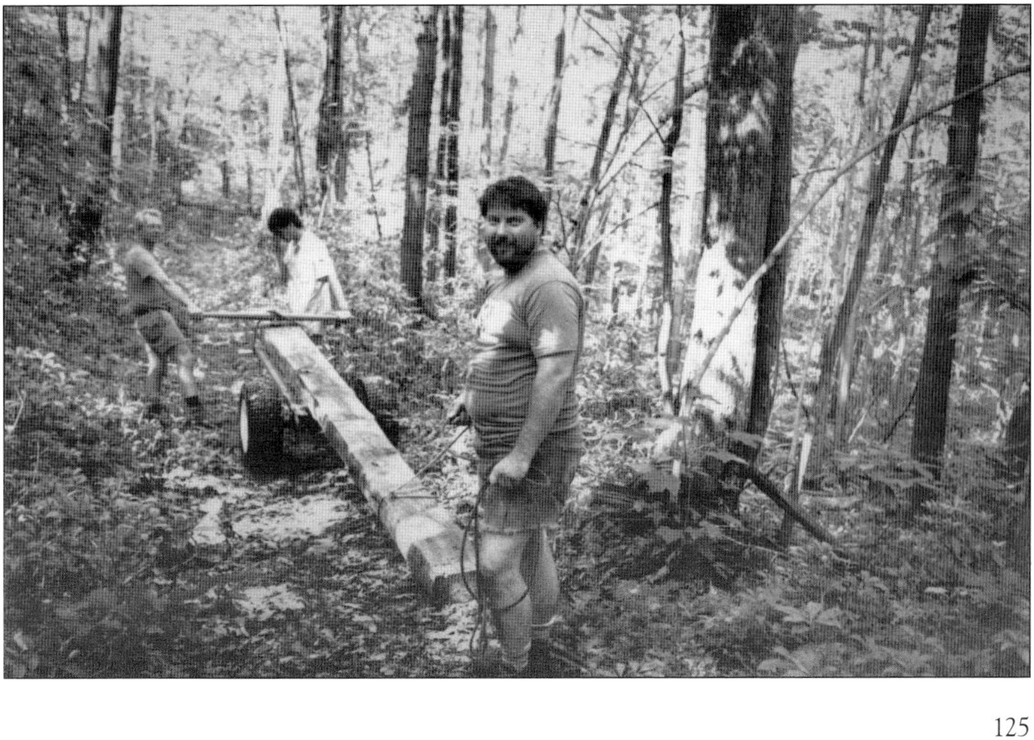

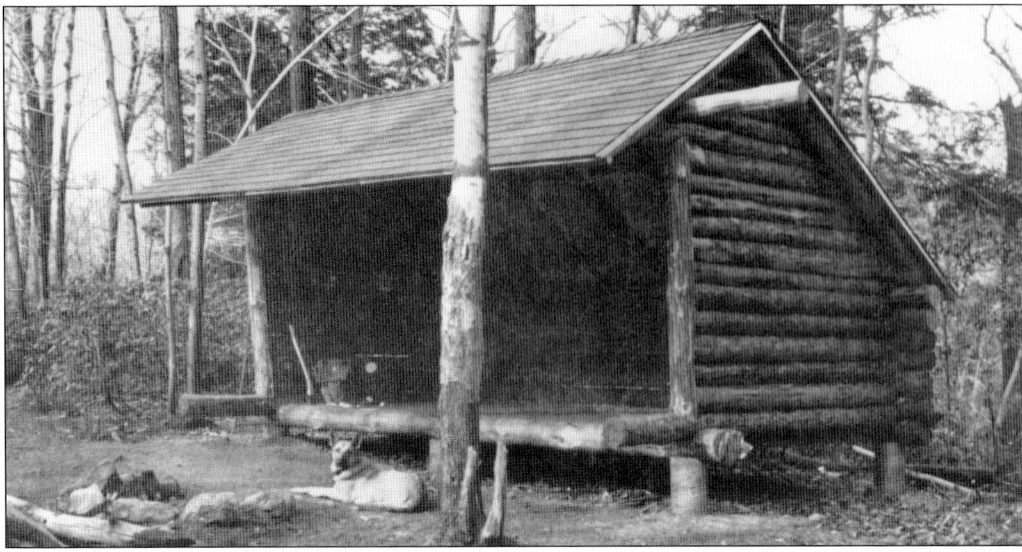

Norman Sills helped volunteers put the roof on Brassie Brook Lean-To, whose construction was completed in 1980. It had originally been named for Keith Bond, who represented Salisbury on the Connecticut Appalachian Trail Management Committee. The committee formed in 1978 to help determine the preferred route of the AT through the state; it disbanded in 1980 after the route had been identified. (Courtesy of ATC.)

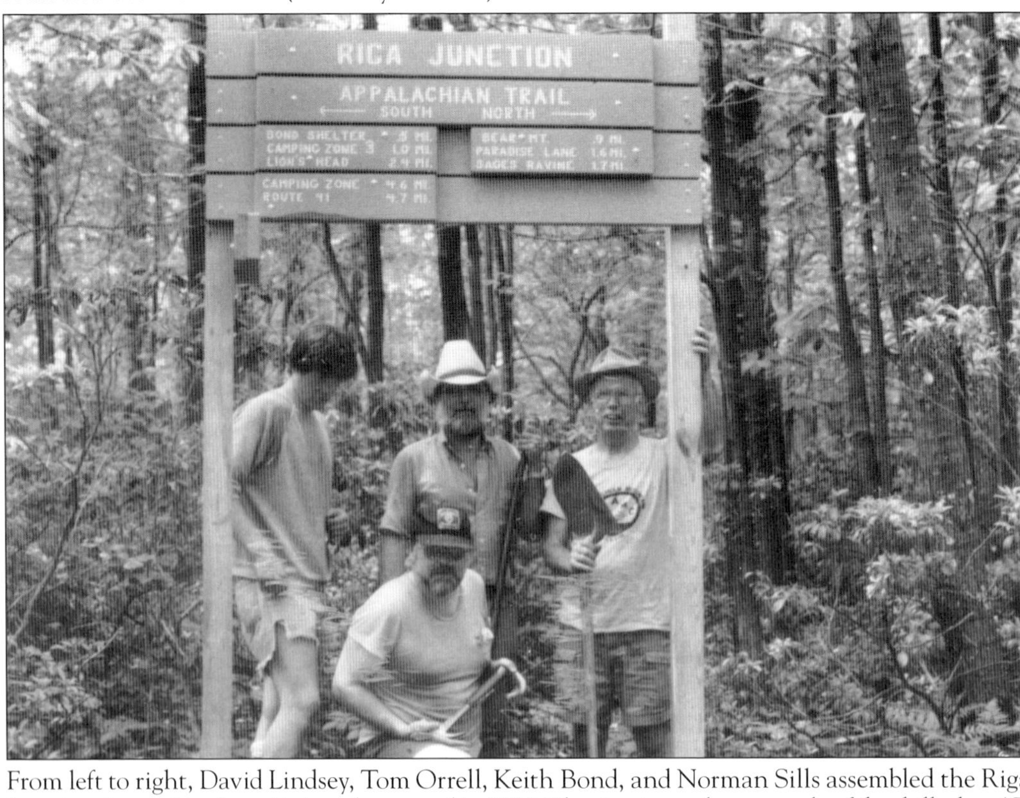

From left to right, David Lindsey, Tom Orrell, Keith Bond, and Norman Sills assembled the Riga Junction sign and anchored it into the ground in 1980. The sign is another example of the skills that AT volunteers possess—it was made by CT-AMC member Jack Rogers. (Courtesy of CT-AMC.)

The Bear Mountain monument tower is seen at right around 1900, a little more than a decade after it was built in 1885. The construction of the 20-foot-square, 22.5-foot-tall tower was financed by Robbins Battell of Norfolk, who wanted to celebrate what was thought to be the highest point in Connecticut. It is now known that the highest point is on the side of Mount Frissel, on the Connecticut-Massachusetts border. Although the tower's stones were not mortared, it stood for 80 years before it started to crumble due to use and vandalism. It has been repaired twice, once with the aid of a helicopter. By the time of the 1979 photograph below, it was only one-third as high as it once was. The AT enters Massachusetts about one mile north of Bear Mountain as it descends into Sages Ravine. (Right, courtesy of CT-AMC; below, courtesy of ATC.)

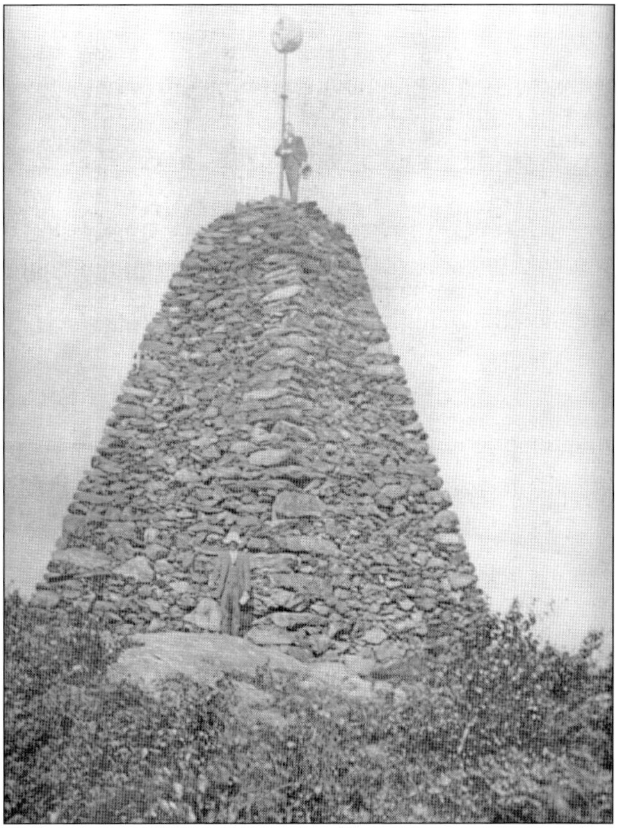

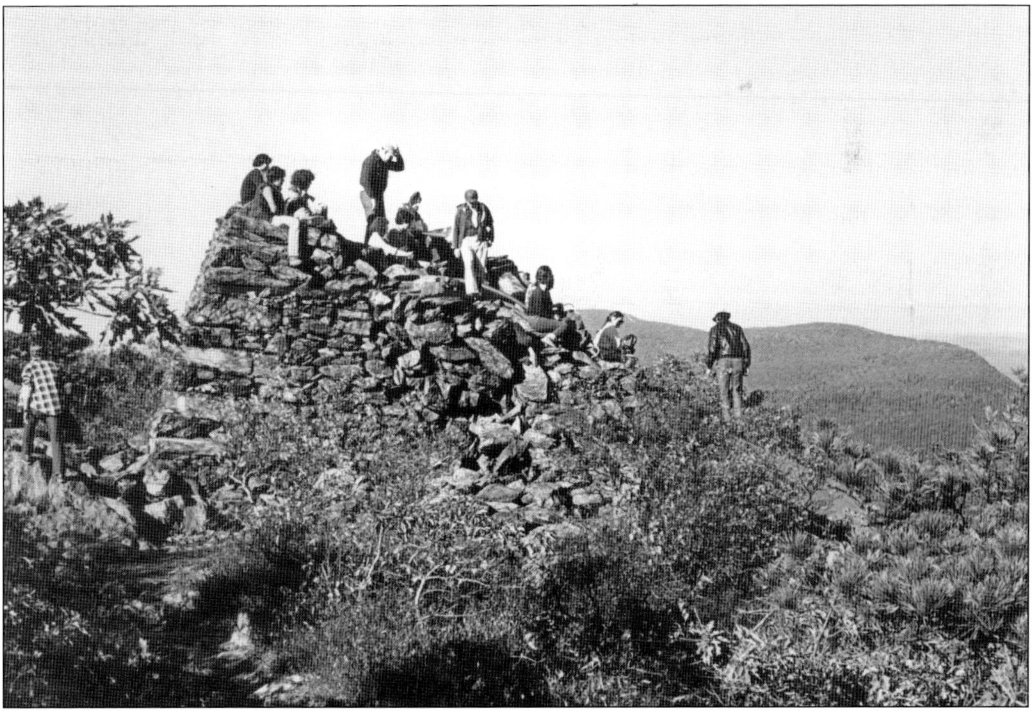